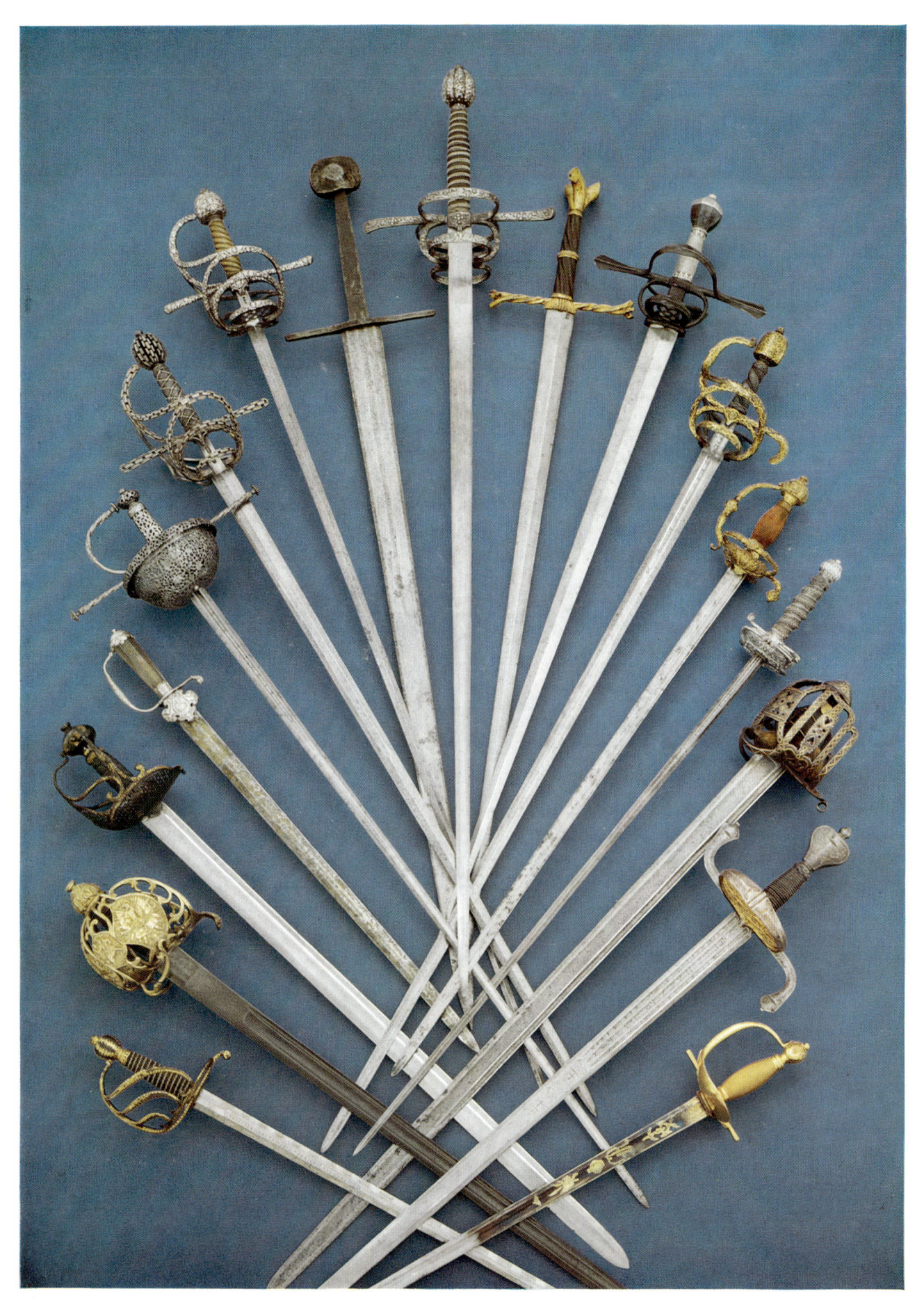

Frontispiece: A group of swords ranging in date from the fifteenth to the early nineteenth centuries. (The swords are described from left to right under the following Plate numbers: 43*d*, 69*b*, 46, 58*c*, 32*a*, 27*d*, 26*d*, 4*d*, 14*b*, 5*c*, 21*b*, 27*b*, 31*a*, 63*b*, 54*c*, 38, 76*b*.)

A

DEPARTMENT OF THE ENVIRONMENT

EUROPEAN SWORDS AND DAGGERS
IN THE TOWER OF LONDON

ARTHUR RICHARD DUFTY

Master of the Armouries

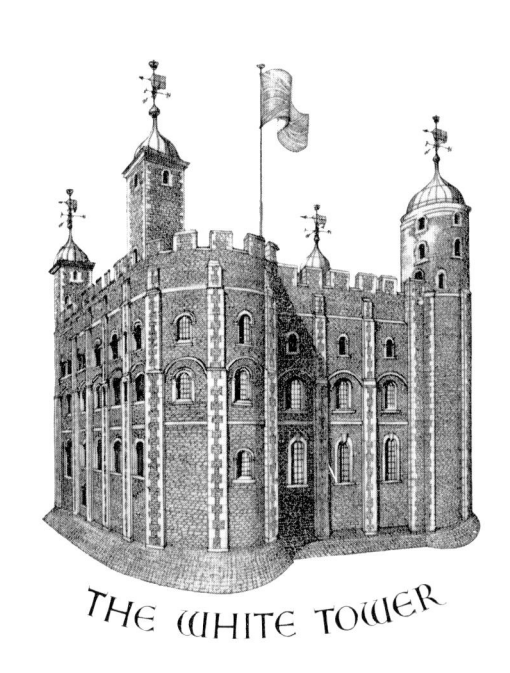

THE WHITE TOWER

LONDON: HER MAJESTY'S STATIONERY OFFICE: 1974

© *Crown copyright 1974*

ISBN 0 11 670572 8*

EUROPEAN SWORDS AND DAGGERS
IN THE TOWER OF LONDON

CORRECTIONS

Page 21, under 33*a*: for Pl. 30*a* read Pl. 32*a*.

Plate 17: for (b) early 17th century read (b) mid 16th century

Plate 85: for (a) read (a,b); for (b) read (c).

Department of the Environment
July 1975
LONDON: HER MAJESTY'S STATIONERY OFFICE: 1975

NTENTS

page 5

page 7

page 14

page 37

TABLE of Inventory and plate numbers with dimensions of the pieces illustrated   *after plate*

PREFACE

European Swords and Daggers in the Tower of London is the second publication in the series of picture books devoted to the collections in the Armouries of Her Majesty's Tower of London. The first volume, *European Armour in the Tower of London*, was published in 1968.

Little has been written on the collections as a whole since C. J. ffoulkes published his *Inventory and Survey of the Armouries* in two volumes in 1916, which was sparsely illustrated. These picture books will thus not only provide supplementary visual records of the national possessions in the Tower in all their richness and variety, but also serve in some measure as up-to-date guides to them until such time as full catalogues are produced. Cataloguing so large and miscellaneous an assemblage of objects in detail is a huge undertaking; but it is envisaged, and has indeed been begun.

This volume will be found, on the one hand, to reaffirm that swords were often creations of the highest skills in craftsmanship and distinguished by elegance of form and beauty of applied decoration and, on the other, to show that the Armouries contain many treasures of such a kind for the enlightenment of historians of art and the delectation of connoisseurs of fine things as well as for the instruction of technicians and students of war.

Swords have attracted a legendary lore of heroic ownerships or fairy origins so voluminous as to suggest that every collection must contain one or more of these fantastic weapons, but unfortunately nothing so remarkable as the sword of Mars owned by Attila, who hoped thereby to conquer the world, or the sword of Constantine the Great owned by Athelstan or even such run of the mill productions as the swords forged by the goblin smith Wayland survives in the Armouries. Neither Galahad's sword drawn from a floating stone nor Arthur's 'Excalibur' wrenched from within an anvil has come down to us. More is the pity, for such swords often had the gift of prophecy, though the message was not always easy of interpretation. At his birth, said Simon Frazer, Lord Lovat, all the swords in the house leaped out of their scabbards: still surviving in the Tower are the block and axe used at his beheading in 1747.

Nor, in the less colourful realm of reality, do the Armouries contain examples of weapons of tenure, non-fictional indeed, such as the thirteenth-century Sockburn falchion now preserved in the Treasury of Durham Cathedral; or if they do, identification is no longer possible, for the inadequacy of record-keeping in the Tower in times past has been such that the associations of many of the historic weapons therein have been lost, though the present members of the Armouries' staff have by their careful researches in recent years been remarkably successful in rehabilitating some of the pieces.

The production of *Swords and Daggers in the Tower of London* has in one way and another involved most of the members of the Armouries' staff. Dr. Alan Borg wrote the Introduction and selected the swords for illustration, and throughout he was helped and advised by both Mr. Russell Robinson and Mr. Howard Blackmore.

Mr. Jeremy Hall took most of the photographs for the half-tone illustrations and deserves a special word of commendation.

The subject of the next picture book in the series will, it is hoped, be the firearms in the Tower Armouries.

Finally, I should like to record my indebtedness to my colleagues in the Armouries for their industry, devotion and unfailing good humour in the preparation of these picture books. The work is additional to the other multifarious duties devolving upon a small staff engaged in running a great national museum. I am glad of this opportunity to express my sincere gratitude to them.

24th January, 1974   A. R. DUFTY

INTRODUCTION

SWORDS, as fighting weapons, have had an important and sometimes decisive influence on the course of human history. For centuries the sword was both the most common and the most revered of weapons, and, despite the rapidly growing importance of the gun from the sixteenth century onwards, it remained a standard item of military equipment up to the early part of the twentieth century. In the course of time, swords have come to stand as symbols of power, majesty, justice and honour. They have also long been items of fashionable dress and of ceremonial apparel and as such were worn more for the display of rich materials and skilled craftsmanship than for purposes of self-defence. Today the Armouries of the Tower of London contain a collection covering the whole range and development of the European sword, from the early middle ages to the present century. As befits a collection housed in the nation's most important fortress, the majority of these weapons are fighting swords, and many of them undoubtedly saw service on the battlefields of Europe. The collection also includes fine civilian and dress swords, richly decorated and beautifully wrought, ceremonial swords, processional swords, presentation swords, and execution swords.

Examples of mediaeval defensive armour are now a rarity, but a comparatively large number of mediaeval swords and daggers survive. Moreover, the sword continued in use long after the abandonment of body armour, and thus the student has an unparalleled opportunity to trace the prolonged development of the weapon. Yet swords are far more than simply objects for typological analysis. Almost all the swords in the Tower were worn, and perhaps used, and it is sometimes possible to trace the detailed history of a particular weapon. It is only in rare instances that a weapon is associated with a known individual or a known event, and even then investigation may reveal that such association depends upon tradition alone; nevertheless such tradition is often a reminder of a weapon's historical setting. One such concerns the sword, complete with scars on the blade said to have been made by musket balls, reputed to have been used by Cromwell when he led the third and final assault on Drogheda in 1649 (Pl. 46). This story has no historical pedigree and the chances are that it is an invention, but there is little doubt that Cromwell wielded a weapon of this type during his Irish campaign. Sometimes the association is more certain. This is the case with the daggers which are said to have been carried by Colonel Blood during his attempt to steal the Crown Jewels, and which have a respectable pedigree going back to at least the early eighteenth century (Pl. 103). Swords presented as gifts or made for special occasions can also be identified, such as that which George III gave to Colonel Prince in gratitude for his skill in choosing horses (Pl. 76*b*), or the great two-hand sword carried in procession before the Beer Brewers' Guild of Cologne in the mid seventeenth century (Pl. 10*b*).

Despite the fact that the great majority of swords and daggers preserve the anonymity of their owners, it is often possible to discover something of their makers. From earliest times swordsmiths adopted the habit of signing their blades, either with their name or with their mark, and numerous individuals, families, and workshops have been identified. The position is somewhat complicated by the fact that certain marks were in use with little or no change for several centuries. Smiths in different areas might independently adopt the same or similar marks, and famous makes of blade were copied by smiths who had little compunction about placing false marks on their own products: it is perhaps no accident that the two English meanings of the verb 'forge' have the same etymology. The best known example is that of Andrea dei Ferrari, an Italian smith of the second half of the sixteenth century, whose name, in the form Andrea Ferrara, became a symbol of quality in Scotland in the seventeenth and eighteenth centuries. Another example is provided by the numerous 'Toledo' blades made in Germany, and it is probable that many other instances of misleading signatures still await detection. A further difficulty arises from the fact that the bladesmith did not normally make the hilt, and swords of a particular type may have blades produced in a number of different places. A report on the sword-making industry in the Italian town of Brescia, drawn up in 1610, indicates that at least ten people were involved in the manufacture of each weapon, and such a division of labour may probably be taken as normal. From the seventeenth century onwards signed hilts occasionally occur, but they are much less common than signed blades. Parts of a sword might have to be renewed more than once in the course of its working life, grips and scabbards being especially likely to wear out. By no means the least complexity may arise from the work of restoration carried out by dealers and collectors, especially in the nineteenth century. Since a sword can usually be taken apart, it is all too easy to make up a fine specimen from two or three individually damaged ones. Indeed, this sort of association of diverse elements was sometimes done within the period the sword was in use, which can make it extraordinarily difficult to distinguish between the genuine and the spurious weapon. In short, it is always unwise to take a particular sword at its face value. Information given by signatures or marks will probably not apply to the complete sword, and such information may be totally misleading. Equally, a sword of unusual appearance, seeming to combine a variety of different elements, need not necessarily be considered a fake in the ordinary sense of the term.

In the absence of any information about the maker or the user it is still usually possible to fit a sword into a known category or type, such as a broadsword, small sword, etc. An approximate date can also be assigned to it. The more recent the sword, the more precise the typology, until, in the second half of the eighteenth century, the developing regulation military sword can generally be identified as to type, pattern, and date on the basis of extant military dress regulations. However, much research still needs to be done before all regulation patterns can be identified with certainty. For the earlier periods the uncertainties are greater, and reliance has to be placed upon three main sources of evidence: first, upon weapons for which a 'documentary' date can be provided, either in the form of an unambiguous date on the sword itself or a written document referring to a specific weapon; secondly, upon representations of swords in dated or datable examples of the visual arts, and thirdly upon an established typology. Ideally this last should derive from the two other sources, but in fact much sword typology has been based upon a sort of historical Darwinism and on the dangerous concept of 'development'. The problems do not end here, for even when a sword is dated, the date is usually on the blade and the hilt may be considerably later. By the same token, a sword shown in a dated picture may have been old when the artist painted it. Nevertheless, cumulative evidence in all its variety shows the general trends in the evolution of both swords and daggers. As more work is done, the picture will gain increasing definition.

Obviously the present Picture Book is not intended to be a textbook or a guidebook to European edged weapons although, such is the scope of the Tower collection, it could serve as one. It is primarily a pictorial survey of some of the best and most representative swords and daggers in the Tower Armouries, and for this reason something should be said about the growth of the collection.

Certainly there have always been swords in the Tower, even though we have no specific information about them. When John de Hermesthorpe took over as Keeper of the Privy Wardrobe in 1381 eighty-two swords *(gladii)* are recorded in the inventory, and these weapons recur in subsequent lists of the Tower Wardrobe. In the absence of any descriptive details, it must be assumed that they were most probably infantry weapons rather than valuable and decorated knightly swords. In other surviving mediaeval inventories it is normal to find the ordinary swords grouped together as *gladii* or *espees*, whereas the richer weapons are singled out and briefly described, as having silver hilts and velvet scabbards for example. The first such specific Tower references seem to be to certain items which were removed from the armouries in 1455 and which included *'viii swerds and a long blade of a swerde made in wafters some gretter and some smaller for to lerne the king to play in his tendre age'*. The king was Henry VI, who had come to the throne in 1422 when he was less than one year old; like all well educated boys of the time, he must have been trained to use the sword. The swords referred to in 1455 were clearly training weapons, and a wafter was a sword with the blade set at right angles to the grip, so that a blow would be struck with the flat rather than with the edge. In the same 1455 list is *'a scottysh swerde hylte and pomell covered with sylver and a small corone aboute the pomell which was stolen oute of the kings chambr and the blade broken and caste into tempse*[Thames]*'*. At this date a Scottish sword probably referred to a cross-hilted weapon with down-sloping quillons, that is, the type of hilt now familiar from surviving claymores of the sixteenth century (Pl. 9a).

In 1547, after the death of King Henry VIII, an inventory of his possessions was drawn up, and in this a large number of swords are listed. They include 302 *'armynge swordes of flaunders makynge'*, which must again represent a group of ordinary swords for military use. In addition, a number of weapons are listed more precisely because they are obviously special: *'One sworde the hilte and pommell guilte the hande bounde about with wier with a skaberde of black vellet embroidered with venyce golde'*. Yet even such descriptions are too brief to allow identification of any of the swords listed in 1547 with ones still in the collection, partly because the most distinctive elements described are often the scabbards, which have not survived. Thus, though the Tower houses several of the armours identifiably made for Henry VIII, none of his swords is identifiable with any one still in the collection. It has been suggested that a combined estoc and gun could be the *'longe Tocke with Gonnes'* mentioned in the inventory, but even here the description does not really fit. The most that can be done is to identify certain classes of swords from the 1547 list, such as the *'grete slaghe swordes'*, which must have been two handers, or *'a shorte hanger the hafte of bone'*, which provides an early reference to this well known type of hunting sword.

Tower inventories become relatively common in the later sixteenth and seventeenth centuries, and the swords listed fall into the same sort of categories, with the addition (from 1561) of rebated swords for use in foot combats. Some further information can be gleaned from the seventeenth-century national inventories, such as the *'Generall state of all the Ordnance, Carriage, Shott, Powder, and all other amunicion, stores, and habiliments of War'* drawn up in 1691 and consisting in large part of Tower stores. Here grouped together are the swords which would now be termed broadswords; they are subdivided into Ordinary, Basket-hilted, and Extraordinary. There are two additional types included, hangers and 'tucks or rapiers'. The value of these various weapons is also listed: ordinary and basket hilted broadswords are quoted at 4s 6d, but extraordinary ones at 6s 6d, with hangers at 5s 4d and rapiers at 4s 6d. Blades for broadswords are valued at 1s 4d, but for hangers at only 10d. This emphasises the fact that the expensive part of the sword was the hilt, valued at 3s 2d for an ordinary broadsword as against 1s 4d for the blade.

From the 1680s, when the 'Line of Kings' was set up in the Armouries, the Tower became a museum of ancient arms and armour as well as being the headquarters of the Board of Ordnance. Several visitors to the Tower recorded their impressions of the Armouries, but their comments are for the most part confined to the Line of Kings, and weapons are only mentioned in a most general fashion. However, the earliest Tower guidebooks, which date from the mid eighteenth century, do mention *'a wilderness of arms'* in the Small Armoury and, in particular, a trophy arranged in the form of the rising sun incorporating *'marine hangers, of peculiar make, having brass handles, and the form of a dog's head on their pommels'*. Several of these distinctive hangers are still preserved in the Tower, and they can perhaps be further identified with the brass-hilted hangers which the Board of Ordnance ordered from the London Cutlers' Company in 1692, and which were described as for 'matrosses' (gunners' assistants).

The description of the Armouries in the early guidebooks is the basis of the various descriptions which are to be found in several books on London published in the late eighteenth and early nineteenth centuries. One such book, Skinner's *History and Description of the Cities of London and Westminster* (1796), quotes the 1783 guide verbatim (and without acknowledgement), but adds a print showing some of the weapons and instruments of torture to be seen in the Armouries. Among these are two swords which are described in the text as *'the sword of Justice (having a sharp point) and the sword of Mercy (having a blunt point) carried before the Old Pretender when proclaimed in Scotland in 1715'*. These are still in the collection (Pl. 9c), and since this description occurs in the earliest guides the historical association is probably correct even though the swords themselves date from the seventeenth century.

During the nineteenth century the Tower collection was greatly expanded. There was a proliferation of military swords, and samples of the various patterns (and some of the pattern weapons themselves) remain at the Tower. Indeed, if a particular pattern proved to be wholly unsuitable for military needs the Tower might be left with a large batch of the rejects; this would seem to have been so with the brass-hilted sword designed for the Household Cavalry in 1805, a large number of which are still in the Armouries (Pl. 79b). Swords were also coming into the collection as the fruits of conquest and of growth of empire. In 1815 the Allies split up among themselves much of the contents of the Musée de l'Artillerie in Paris, and as a result a large collection of guns and edged weapons came to England and eventually to the Tower. Many of the European military swords of the eighteenth and early nineteenth centuries came into the collection from this source, just as they had come to Paris in the first place as Napoleon's spoils of war. As always, it is difficult to identify specific weapons from the brief inventory descriptions drawn up in 1815, but occasionally a particular sword can be picked out. For example, among the several two-hand swords listed, one is said to be of the date 1573; it is thus almost certainly the Brunswick sword in the collection which is dated 1573 on the blade (Pl. 8b). Further acquisitions were made in 1826, when a quantity of arms and armour came to the Tower from the old armoury of the Knights of Malta; among the swords, a group of swept-hilt Italian rapiers stamped with a Maltese cross on the ricasso may be identified as part of this consignment.

In 1841 occurred the great fire at the Tower. The Grand Storehouse, including the Small Armoury, was burnt out, and since much of the sword collection seems to have been kept here the losses must have been considerable. However, since no proper inventory was kept the extent of the damage cannot be assessed, but at least one item is known to have been saved from the flames through the bravery of a certain Captain Delmé Davis. When the fire broke out, he rushed into the building and grabbed the sword and sash of the Duke of York, severely cutting his hands when he smashed the glass case containing them. These are not perhaps the first things a modern student would choose to save, but Captain Davis' action has ensured that these trophies, which came to the Tower in 1827, are still preserved (Pl. 94a). After the fire many damaged items were sold off as souvenirs, so depleting the collection still further.

The disaster of 1841 must be set alongside the continuous growth of the collection in the nineteenth century. Apart from the bulk acquisitions from Paris and Malta, the Armouries, under the guidance of Robert Porrett and John Hewitt, began to buy fine weapons and fine armour from private individuals and from dealers, and this practice has continued to the present day. Generous gifts have provided another major source of new acquisitions. An important group of Royal swords, from the time of George II onwards, was deposited by King George VI in 1937, and a decade later Sir Bernard Eckstein bequeathed the Collingwood sword to the Tower (Pl. 65). But it would be invidious to single out individual gifts, for many fine weapons have come into the collection in this way. Thus, the collection is by no means static, and, as it grows, so the wealth of material for study increases. It is a source of regret, not least to those in charge of the Armouries, that less than 10 per cent of the weapon collection is at present on display; but a Study Collection for the use of students is planned. Meanwhile, it is hoped that the present Picture Book will help to extend the knowledge of this great collection. Herein, almost for the first time, is a series of pictures of representative swords and daggers in the Tower, together with brief notes on every sword shown. It is not intended to be a substitute for an inclusive catalogue (indeed, it cannot be, for to keep within comparatively limited bounds the choice of arms pictured must be highly selective), but it will perhaps give some idea of the richness and variety of this particular collection in the Tower Armouries.

The illustrations in this book are divided into two sections. The first and main section is devoted to swords, the second to daggers. The collection of daggers is neither as large nor as inclusive as that of swords, although there are some fine individual pieces.

ALAN BORG

SWORDS

NOTES ON THE PLATES

SWORDS

Frontispiece: A group of swords ranging in date from the fifteenth to the early nineteenth centuries. (The swords are described from left to right under the following Plate numbers: 43*d*, 69*b*, 46, 58*c*, 32*a*, 27*d*, 26*d*, 4*d*, 14*b*, 5*c*, 21*b*, 27*b*, 31*a*, 63*b*, 54*c*, 38, 76*b*.)

1

a. Sword of late Viking type, *c.* 950–1100. Such swords, with their comparatively short blades and rounded points, were essentially cutting weapons and of little use for thrusting. The quillons are short and straight, and the pommel is of the characteristic 'tea-cosy' form.

b. Sword of late Viking type. The blade is much corroded, but traces of an inlaid inscription are still visible, perhaps recording the name of the smith.

c. Sword of *c.* 1100. This clearly derives from the Viking swords, but the blade is slightly longer than *b*, so are the quillons. However, it remains primarily a cutting weapon and represents the classic sword type of the epoch of the First Crusade.

2

a. This sword was found in a peat bog near Newbury and may therefore be English. It has the disc pommel commonly found on mediaeval swords and straight quillons. The blade bears traces of an inlaid inscription. It probably dates from between 1150–1250.

b. Sword similar in form and date to *a*. It is covered with a hard black patination which suggests that it was a river find.

c. This sword, which probably dates from *c.* 1200, has an unusually broad blade and a so-called brazil-nut pommel. The wooden grip is a modern restoration. Mark, Pl. 106.

d. An unusual type of sword, perhaps dating from the second half of the thirteenth century. The blade is broad, the quillons turn down, and the pommel has matching horn-like projections. A similar sword is in the Archaeological Museum at Antwerp.

3

a. This sword differs from the preceding examples in that the blade has a sharp point, and so it could be used for thrusting as well as cutting. It probably dates from *c.* 1300, although the technique of using the point seems to have become common in Europe during the thirteenth century.

b. Sword of the thirteenth century, with a brazil-nut pommel and straight quillons. The blade is inlaid with the initial L and designs.

c. Fourteenth-century sword, which is unusual in having a single-edged blade. It was found on the site of Bankside House, Southwark, in 1951, and is perhaps of English manufacture.

d. Fourteenth-century sword, found on the site of the Houses of Parliament in 1838.

4

a. Fourteenth-century sword for cutting and thrusting, with down-curved quillons. The wooden grip is a restoration. Mark, Pl. 106.

b. Probably a boy's sword, rather than a dagger, since it reproduces on a small scale all the features of a full size sword of the fourteenth century. It was designed for a child aged about eight.

c. Fourteenth-century sword, with a long narrow blade, very much corroded. In the nineteenth century it was reputed to have come from 'a tomb of a Count of Treves' (Trier), but the corroded condition suggests rather that the weapon has been buried in the ground or immersed in water.

d. A fine fourteenth-century sword, bearing an arabic inscription on the blade which reads 'Inalienable property of the treasury of the march province of Alexandria, may it be protected.' Several such swords, taken as loot by the arabs and placed in their armouries, have survived. Mark, Pl. 106.

e. Another fourteenth-century weapon captured by the arabs. The arabic inscription states that it was taken in Cyprus by the Sultan El-Melik El-Ashr in 1424. The hilt provides an early example of the use of a finger ring; the forefinger was hooked over the quillons to give a firmer grip, the ring forming a protective guard. Mark, Pl. 106.

f. Late fourteenth-century sword found in Lake Constance. The long blade, of diamond section, is acutely pointed, making this a fine thrusting weapon.

5

a. Sword, dating from *c.* 1400, found in the Thames near London Bridge. The pommel is of elongated octagonal form.

b. Sword of similar type and date to *a*, although in this hilt the quillons are turned down at the ends. The wooden grip is restored.

c. German sword of the second half of the fifteenth century. The hilt is of gilt bronze, the grip of wood. The quillons and pommel are in the form of twisted branches.

6

a. German two-hand sword, *c.* 1560. The pommel and quillons are spirally fluted and the original grip is bound in cord. The blade bears a mark of Christoph Stantler of Munich (Pl. 106) who worked in the second half of the sixteenth century; a number of his blades survive (*cf.* Pl. 11).

b. German two-hand sword, dated 1529. The straight two-edged blade has a ricasso with two lugs shaped and engraved as animals' heads. Each face of the blade is inscribed with the words IOHANNES ME FECIT 1529: IN HOC SIGNO VINCES.

c. Two-hand sword of the type carried by Landsknecht mercenaries in the sixteenth century. The section (the ricasso) of the blade nearest the quillons is left unsharpened and covered with leather so that the blade could be gripped here with one hand, thus effectively shortening the sword during close combat. The blade itself is flamboyant (Mark, Pl. 106) and the grip retains its velvet cover and fringes, which were part of the modish fashion adopted by these troops. Examples of the short swords carried by Landsknechts are shown in Pls. 16–17.

7

a. German two-hand sword, *c.* 1600. The quillons and ring guards are engraved with flowers and foliage and the blade is flamboyant.

b. German two-hand sword, late sixteenth century. The hilt is of blackened iron and the ricasso covered in leather. The blade, which is flamboyant, bears an orb and cross mark.

c. German two-hand sword, late sixteenth century. The distinguishing feature of this sword is that the blade broadens towards the tip.

8

a, b. Two-hand sword for the State Guard of the Duke of Brunswick. A number of these swords survive, the majority still in the ducal collection now at Hanover. The form of the sword is related to the Landsknecht type (Pl. 6c), but it has developed into a purely ceremonial weapon. Every example is numbered and dated on the ricasso, the present one being No. 69, 1573. It was taken by the British from Paris in 1815. Mark, Pl. 106.

9

a. Scottish claymore of the mid sixteenth century. The name, often applied to the Scottish broadsword, originally denoted a two-hand weapon. This example has characteristic down-sloping quillons with quatrefoil terminals. Mark, Pl. 106.

b. Claymore of the so-called Lowland type, dating from the late sixteenth century. Mark, Pl. 106.

c. Claymore of the early seventeenth century, which differs from the previous examples in having oval shell guards (one missing). Traditionally this sword was carried before the Old Pretender when he was proclaimed king in 1715. Mark, Pl. 106.

10

a. Great sword, nearly 2·5 metres long, intended for processional use. A number of similar swords, of fifteenth-century date, are preserved, and the Tower collection includes a second identical sword and the reused blade of a third. The German blade of this example is inlaid with symbols in copper.

b, c. Processional sword for the guild of Beer Brewers of the city of Cologne. The blade is etched with the arms of the guild. Mid seventeenth century.

11

a–c. Processional sword for a doge of Venice, *c.* 1580. The blade is by Christoph Stantler of Munich (*cf.* Pl. 6a); it is etched on one side with the lion of St. Mark, on the other with a panel containing a doge and a bishop. The scabbard is made of wood covered with tooled leather. Mark, Pl. 107.

12

a–c. Executioner's sword, German, dated 1674. The blade is etched with four scenes of men's punishments: execution, impaling, hooked from a gibbet, and breaking on a wheel, accompanied by lines in German from a Lutheran hymn, which may be translated: 'I live and know not for how long; I die I know not when; I wander I know not whither; I wonder that I am so contented;' on the other side, 'Let everyone raise his eyes, look well, and see that it is evil to build with the powers of evil, for that raised by pride cannot last long. Punishment already hangs over the head of the evil thinker.'

d. Executioner's sword, German, second half of the seventeenth century. The German lines on this example may be translated: 'When I raise this sword I wish the sinner everlasting life; the Lords judge evil and I execute their judgment.' This message is reinforced by the etched representation of a gallows and a spiked wheel.

e. Executioner's sword, German, *c.* 1620. The blade bears the words ME FECIT SOLINGEN and the angel mark of Clemens Keuller. The Keuller family produced several generations of bladesmiths; Clemens, who occasionally signed himself *Von dem Engel*, worked in the first half of the seventeenth century. Mark, Pl. 107.

13

a. German hand-and-half sword, *c.* 1500. Swords of this type, also known as bastard swords, were carried by mounted knights. Marks, Pl. 107.

b. German hand-and-half sword, early sixteenth century. The wooden grip is fitted with a steel cap instead of the more usual form of pommel.

c. Hand-and-half sword, probably German, of the second half of the sixteenth century. The lower ring guards are fitted with pierced shells. The blade is not that originally fitted to the hilt. Mark, Pl. 107.

14

a. German hand-and-half sword, *c.* 1550. A fine example of the type, retaining its original leather-covered grip. The blade bears an unidentified maker's mark, Pl. 107.

b. German hand-and-half sword, *c.* 1600. This is of fine quality, with the guards and pommel chiselled and overlaid with incrustations of silver. Two very similar swords are preserved in the Schweizerischen Landesmuseum, Zurich, one of which is dated 1614.

c. Italian hand-and-half sword, perhaps Venetian, dating from the middle of the sixteenth century. The sheath is of wood covered with red velvet with steel mounts. Mark, Pl. 107.

15

a. An unusual short sword, with a single-edged blade and a guard with a knuckle bow. It has been suggested that it may be English since a similar sword was found on the site of the Battle of Wakefield (1460).

b. This sword, with its single-edged curved blade, seems to be a development of the type seen in the previous example. The notch at the base of the blade is for the forefinger. Early sixteenth century.

c. Short sword, of characteristic Italian form. The blade bears the mark of Biscotto, two other examples of whose work are in the Tower collections: a Landsknecht sword (Pl. 16*b*) and an Italian bill. Early sixteenth century.

16

a. Landsknecht sword, *c.* 1520. In addition to a two-hand sword (Pl. 6*c*), the Landsknechts carried short swords of this type. The S-shaped quillons are characteristic. This example preserves its original leather scabbard and a set of four implements: one knife, one stiletto, and two sharp bodkins.

b. Italian Landsknecht sword, with a cap pommel. This sword has the same blade mark as Pl. 15*c* and is inscribed ME FECIT BISCOTTO. The Biscotto family were armourers in Villa Basilica, near Lucca. Early sixteenth century. Mark. Pl. 107.

17

a. Another typical Landsknecht sword, German, mid sixteenth century. The hilt has a knuckle bow and a side bar, with a single counter guard; the quillons have developed into a closed S figure.

b. Landsknecht sword, German, mid sixteenth century. In this, the hilt has evolved into an elementary basket guard. Mark, Pl. 107.

18

a. Estoc or thrusting sword, German *c.* 1500. The wooden grip is modern, and the blade is not that originally designed for the hilt.

b–c. Richly decorated Landsknecht sword, of Italian type, *c.* 1500. The blade is etched with figures of St. Barbara and the Virgin on one side and foliage patterns on the other. On the quillons and blade are etched sardonic inscriptions, in a Swabian/Swiss dialect, which may be translated: 'A new saint is called ruffian: it is he who everyone now wants to celebrate. Look around and watch out for he who will harm you; infidelity is now. Beware, have a care of me, if I catch you I'll mince you.' Doubt has been expressed about the authenticity of this sword, but it is known to have been in Dr. Samuel Meyrick's collection in the 1820s, before the forgery of such weapons became common.

d. Italian sword, *c.* 1540. This fine quality weapon has an iron hilt chiselled with cherubs' heads and foliage designs.

19

a. Italian broadsword, with a wide blade which is closely related to the Cinquedea type (see *b*). At the base of the blade is a notch for the forefinger. The hilt is of black iron, with its original leather-covered grip, and the blade is etched with a figure standing beneath an arch. Mid sixteenth century. Mark, Pl. 107.

b. Typical and well preserved example of the Cinquedea, a civilian sword developed in Italy in the second half of the fifteenth century. The blade is etched on both faces with scenes from the legend of Mucius Scaevola. The hilt is also of typical form, and the grip retains its original velvet covering into which are set two Roman coins, one of Trajan and one of Nero. The scabbard is of parchment covered with tooled leather, with a chape and locket of pierced steel. Early sixteenth century, north Italian. Mark, Pl. 107.

c. Cinquedea of similar type and date to *b*. The blade is etched with classical scenes and inscribed FORTES TIMET FORTUNA VIROS (Fortune fears the brave) and ESTOTE FORTIS (*sic*) IN BELLO (Be brave in war). The blade bears a mark which is found on other cinquedea blades (Pl. 107), and on other Italian weapons of the period, but which has yet to be identified. The hilt is modern.

20

a. Blade detail of Pl. 19*b*.

b. Blade detail of Pl. 19*c*.

21

a. Estoc, German, mid sixteenth century. A thrusting sword, with a triangular-sectioned hollow-ground blade and a complex guard. The wooden grip is modern.

b. Saxon sword-rapier of the late sixteenth century. The pommel and grip are decorated in silver, and the blade is of flattened diamond section.

c. Saxon estoc, *c.* 1580, probably from the Armoury of the Dukes of Saxony at Dresden. The hilt is of blued steel, and the blade has a characteristic triangular section. There is a metal locket at the base of the blade which would have fitted over the mouth of the scabbard. Mark, Pl. 107.

d. German rapier, *c.* 1560–70. The steel hilt is similar to those found on contemporary estocs. The grip, bound in steel wire, is original, and the blade is inscribed MAILLANT. Mark, Pl. 107.

22

a. Hilt of Pl. 21*b*.

23

a. Three mediaeval sword pommels, probably of the fourteenth century, of rock crystal, bronze, and chalcedony respectively. Rich swords frequently had pommels of rare materials, and sometimes relics were inserted or attached to them.

b. An Italian pommel and sword hanger mounts of the second half of the sixteenth century. The ovoidal pommel, damascened in silver and gold, is from a rapier of *c.* 1590. The mounts for sword hangers are also damascened in gold. They originally held straps and belts for attaching the scabbard.

24

a. Typical military rapier of the late sixteenth century, probably Italian. The complex guard consists of two small shells surmounted by four rings, recurved quillons, and a knuckle bow. The long two-edged blade is inscribed with the letter M four times in the fuller. Mark, Pl. 107.

b. Similar to the previous example, except that the number of rings is increased to seven. Mark, Pl. 107.

c. Steel swept-hilt rapier, late sixteenth century, Italian. A simple version of the classic rapier hilt.

d. Steel swept-hilt rapier, devoid of all decoration; another example of the standard type of rapier for military use. Probably Italian, late sixteenth century.

e. A slightly more elaborate rapier than *d*, in which the shells are pierced with the heads of *putti* and the bars are filed to resemble beading. The blade is inscribed with the letters DNRS, which are repeated several times in various combinations. Mark, Pl. 107.

25
a. German rapier of *c.* 1610, shown with its accompanying left-hand dagger. The plain swept hilt is of blued steel, and the blade is inscribed IHS with a design of crescents and dots at the forte.

b, c. German rapier, *c.* 1610, fitted with an extending blade; the lower portion fits over the upper like a sleeve, allowing the guard to be slipped away from the grip, increasing the length by 22 cms. The blade locks in position when extended. The weapon is shown here with the blade in both positions.

26
a. German swept-hilt rapier, *c.* 1610. The steel hilt is gilt and chiselled to represent chains, including medallions with figures. The blade is inscribed HEINRICH BRABENDER ME FECIT, SALINGEN. Several members of this family bore the name Heinrich, but this blade must be the work of the eldest, whose other signed blades date from around 1600. Mark, Pl. 107.

b. German swept-hilt rapier, early seventeenth century. Hilt of bright steel somewhat coarsely chiselled to represent medallions containing classical figures and foliage. There is an unidentified maker's mark on the ricasso of the blade, Pl. 107.

c. Sword-rapier, probably German, *c.* 1600. The elements of the hilt are chiselled with a basket-work pattern. The blade is signed BATISTA FACIEBAT, perhaps identifiable with a Giovanni Battista who is recorded as having a forge at Belluno (Italy) in the late sixteenth century.

d. German rapier of *c.* 1600. The fine quality hilt is of russet iron encrusted with silver. The blade is stamped CAINO.

27
a. Italian swept-hilt rapier, *c.* 1610, decorated in gold and silver against a blued ground which was originally covered with silver foil. The blade is inscribed FRANCESCO VALESQUEZ.

b. Swept-hilt rapier, the hilt of blued steel inlaid with gold, the grip bound in silver wire. The blade is stamped with the letters GAHX in various combinations. Italian, early seventeenth century.

c. Rapier, probably Italian, early seventeenth century. The guard of looped bars forms a pierced cup, which is decorated with figures of the Virtues in medallions. The knuckle bow and quillons have medallions at their terminals enclosing classical heads. The pommel is modern.

d. Swept-hilt rapier, Italian, *c.* 1600. The elements of the hilt are pierced and chiselled to represent chains, and the grip is bound in silver wire. The pommel is restored. The blade section changes from octagonal at the base to hexagonal and then to diamond at the tip.

28
a. English rapier, *c.* 1620. The hilt, of typical English form, is of russet steel encrusted with silver. The blade, stamped with an orb and cross (Pl. 107), is very slightly curved.

b. English rapier, *c.* 1625, with a hilt of blued steel bordered with silver *pointillé* bands, between which foliage patterns are inlaid in gold. The wooden grip is bound in silver wire. The associated blade is inscribed VERVNN DOMINI, presumably for Verbum Domini.

c. English rapier, *c.* 1635. The iron hilt has pierced shell guards, and the grip is covered in fish skin. The blade is signed IOHANNES KINNDT, a German smith who worked at the Hounslow factory near London.

d. English rapier, *c.* 1630. The chiselled steel hilt is decorated with portrait busts of Charles I and Queen Henrietta Maria. It was originally gilded. Decoration of this type is well known from the hilts of so-called 'Mortuary' swords (*cf.* Pls. 46–48). The blade bears the name VINCENCIO GIMAN, who may perhaps be identified with Vincencio Gihami, a sword furbisher in Gromo, northern Italy.

29

a. English rapier, the blade dated 1634. The hilt is steel, with the pommel and quillon terminals each in the form of a woman's head. The cup guard is chiselled with foliage patterns and cherubs. The blade, which is not that originally fitted to the hilt, is inscribed IOHAN KINNDT HOUNSLOE 1634. (*cf.* Pl. 28*c*).

b. English rapier, *c.* 1630, the blade German. The steel hilt is chiselled with fleurs-de-lys and Prince of Wales feathers. The blade is inscribed HANS MOVM ME FECIT SOLINGEN. Hans was the best known member of another Solingen dynasty of bladesmiths, and a number of his signed blades survive.

c. English rapier, *c.* 1640, the blade Spanish. The hilt of blued steel is chiselled with heads of Charles I and with classical figures. The blade is signed DE FRANCISCO RUIS EN TOLEDO. There were two smiths of this name, father and son. The date of the hilt suggests that this blade is by the father.

d. Rapier, probably Dutch, *c.* 1630. The hilt is of silver, chiselled with scenes from the Odyssey. The blade is flamboyant.

30

a. English rapier, *c.* 1650. The hilt is of gilt iron with a complex guard related in construction to the 'Mortuary' hilts (*cf.* Pls. 46–48). The bowl is fretted and chiselled with foliage patterns and classical figures. The flamboyant blade is inscribed SAHAGOM.

b. English rapier, *c.* 1640, the blade German. The hilt is of chiselled steel. The blade is signed by Hermann Keisser, a member of a Solingen family of smiths which continued in the trade up to the nineteenth century. Several rapier blades by Hermann are known.

31

a. Sword rapier, possibly English, *c.* 1630. The steel hilt is decorated with medallions containing the heads of Roman emperors, and the grip is covered in red velvet. The single-edged blade is inscribed ANDRIA FARARA 1441; the signature is spurious and the numbers are probably not intended to represent a date but may be of some numerological significance.

b. Spanish sword rapier, *c.* 1650. The hilt is of steel, pierced and chiselled with foliage patterns. The associated blade is from an eighteenth-century small sword.

c. Sword hilt of steel, chiselled in a style which is associated with the Italian town of Brescia, dating from the mid seventeenth-century. Both the bone grip and the blade are associated. Marks, Pl. 107.

d. Sword hilt, another example of Brescian work, *c.* 1680. The grip is associated. The blade is oval-sectioned and pierced and grooved at the forte.

32

a. Spanish cup-hilt rapier of the mid seventeenth century. This is a fine example of this well known type of sword, with the hilt of pierced and chiselled steel. The blade is signed MARIA DE HORTVNO DE IESUS AVILE EN TOLEDO. Marks, Pl. 107.

b. Rapier, similar in type and date to the previous example. The blade is signed DE HORTVNO DE AGVIRE EN TOLEDO. A very similar rapier with the same blade signature and date 1604 is in the Real Armeria, Madrid, but the hilts of both must be some forty years later than the blades. Mark, Pl. 107.

c. Spanish cup-hilt rapier of the mid seventeenth century. The blade is inscribed DE PEDRO DE VELMONTE EN TOLEDO. Mark, Pl. 108.

d. Spanish cup-hilt rapier, *c.* 1700. This has a solid cup, japanned black and painted with gold foliage scrolls. The blade is German and marked IN SOLINGEN.

33

a. Another view of Pl. 30*a*, showing the *guardapolvo*.

b. Spanish cup-hilt rapier of the mid seventeenth century, the cup pierced and engraved with hunting scenes.

c. German cup-hilt rapier of the mid seventeenth century. The cup is pierced and chiselled with hunting scenes, and the blade is signed by a member of another prolific Solingen family of smiths, Hans Ollich. This is one of a small group of German rapiers with similar hilt decoration, another of which is in the Wallace Collection. Mark, Pl. 108.

34

a. Cup-hilt rapier, Spanish or Italian, *c.* 1680. The blade is inscribed IHS.

b. Cup-hilt rapier, probably Spanish, of the last quarter of the seventeenth century. The cup is pierced and chiselled with foliage patterns and beasts of the chase. The blade is inscribed ME FECIT VALENCIA. Mark, Pl. 108.

c. Spanish cup-hilt rapier, late seventeenth century, the blade German. The shallow, solid cup is of bright steel. The blade is inscribed IHN SOLINGEN.

d. Spanish cup-hilt rapier, late seventeenth century, the cup partly pierced and chiselled with foliage patterns. The ricasso of the blade is covered in black leather.

35

a. Sabre, probably Italian, *c.* 1500. The hilt has a curved wooden grip and a long front quillon bent back to form a knuckle guard. The long curved blade is crudely etched at the forte with figures of St. Catherine and St. Barbara. The quillons are etched with foliage patterns and with a Tudor rose on the central block. Marks, Pl. 108.

b. Characteristic Swiss sabre of the late sixteenth century. These bastard swords form a clearly defined group and are usually attributed to Switzerland. The blade of this sword bears the mark of Christoph Stantler of Munich (*cf.* Pls. 6*a* and 108).

c. Swiss sabre of the mid seventeenth century. The pommel, which is in the form of a monster's head, is joined to the forward quillon by a chain, a common device in sabres of this type and period. The blade is lightly etched with Latin slogans: PRO CHRISTO ET PATREA (*sic*), VINCERE AUT MORI. Mark, Pl. 108.

d. German sabre of the late sixteenth century. The hilt, with its single shell guard, is similar to those of German broadswords of the period. The curved single-edged blade is lightly etched with the sun and moon and an arm holding a sword.

36

a. German sabre, *c.* 1600. The hilt is of steel, with the pommel in the form of a truncated pyramid.

21

b. Sword of falchion type, dating from the second half of the sixteenth century. The single-edged blade is broad and heavy, with the back sharpened for 23 cms. from the point.

c. German sabre, *c.* 1600. This type of sword is known in modern usage as a Sinclair sabre; in the nineteenth century they were thought to have been carried by Sinclair's mercenary troops on an expedition to Scandinavia.

d. Another example of a Sinclair sabre. German, *c.* 1600.

37

Sixteenth-century sword pommels. This selection, all in steel, illustrates the variety of forms used. Many such detached pommels have been found, often reused as weights.

38

a–c. Broadsword, with a German blade, mid seventeenth century. The brass hilt has a single shell which is decorated in relief with the figure of a horseman; it has been suggested that this represents Gustavus Adolphus of Sweden. However, the blade is engraved with lines in Latin from the Office for Good Friday and from St. Luke's Gospel, and it seems unlikely that the image of the Protestant leader in the Thirty Years War would occur on a sword which has a clearly Catholic inscription on the blade. Swords of this general type are found in Sweden, but also in the Low Countries, and the mounted figure may represent one of the leaders of the Catholic forces. Marks, Pl. 108.

39

a. German tournament sword, dated 1650. This is one of a group of swords made for the court of the Elector of Saxony, for use in foot combat. The blade has rebated cutting edges and a rounded tip to prevent lethal wounds. The guard is of large open basket form. Mark, Pl. 108.

b. Broadsword, probably German, *c.* 1660–70. The hilt is of steel, with the grip bound in silver wire. The blade is stamped with a running wolf mark and the spurious signature ANDRIA FERARA.

c. German broadsword, *c.* 1660. The hilt is of steel and the blade is signed CLEMENS WEILMS ME FECIT SOLINGEN.

40

a–b. German broadsword, the blade dated 1641. The hilt consists of a lobed and pierced shell guard, recurved quillons, knuckle bow, and pommel, all engraved with foliage patterns. The blade is dated and signed by Peter Munich of Solingen and etched with German tags, which may be translated: 'Who can stand alone in misfortune? The blessing of God is all that matters. What God bestows remains undeserved.' Mark, Pl. 108.

c–d. German broadsword of the mid seventeenth century. The steel hilt is chiselled with animal forms. The blade is etched and gilt with trophies and a cartouche showing a figure above the words CAROLVS REX. The blade has the initials and mark of Peter Munich of Solingen, Pl. 108.

41

a. German broadsword of the late sixteenth century, with a large scalloped shell guard. The blade bears the letters I.O.P.R.A. Mark, Pl. 108.

b. German broadsword of the late sixteenth century. The broad blade is twice inscribed IOHANN. Mark, Pl. 108.

c. Broadsword, an example of the type which is known, for obvious reasons, as crab-hilted. It dates from the mid seventeenth-century and is probably German, although the associated blade is from a rapier.

d. Mid seventeenth-century broadsword, probably Italian. The quillons again have the crab form, but there is in addition a triangular knuckle guard, which is lightly engraved with foliage patterns.

42

a. Spanish broadsword of the late seventeenth century, of the type known as a Bilbo. This form is related to that of the cup-hilt rapier, with two solid curved shells replacing the cup.

b. Spanish sword of Bilbo type, with embossed and pierced shells. The blade is signed YOSEPH MARTI EN BARCELONA. Marti's name first appears in the Barcelona guild of sword cutlers in 1716, and he died in 1762 after a successful career. Mark, Pl. 108.

c. Sword of the mid seventeenth century, probably Italian. The steel hilt is pierced and chiselled with classical heads. The blade is associated.

d. Spanish or South American broadsword, *c.* 1700. The shells are chiselled with birds and animals. The German blade is etched with a crown surmounting a crowned eagle displayed.

43

a. Swiss broadsword of *c.* 1700, of the type known as a Berne cavalry sword. The brass hilt has an open basket guard and a lion's head pommel, There are two small shells, each of which is embossed with a bear. The blade is inscribed ME FECIT SOLINGEN.

b. French broadsword of *c.* 1720, the blade German. It has an expanding steel hilt, in which the back hand guard is hinged and can be closed to form one with the knuckle bow. The blade is etched with figures and foliage and with the common inscription NE ME TIREZ PAS SANS RAISON, NE ME REMETTEZ POINT SANS HONNEUR (Do not draw me without cause, never sheath me without honour).

c. French sword, *c.* 1720, the blade German. The brass hilt is cast with trophies of arms. The blade is engraved with figures of Prince James Edward Stuart, the Old Pretender, and inscribed VIVAT JACOBUS TERTIUS MAGNAE BRITANNIAE REX and WITH THIS GOOD SWORD THY CAUSE I WILL MAINTAIN/ AND FOR THY SAKE O JAMES WILL BREATHE (*sic*) EACH VEIN. This is one of a group of swords bearing similar Jacobite inscriptions.

d. Sword with a German blade, dated 1697, and an Indian hilt made for the English market *c.* 1770. The hilt is of russet steel encrusted with foliage in gold. The dated blade, which is filed to give a chequered appearance, is inscribed FRIED ERNERT UNFRIED BERBERTT/AN GOTTES SEGNEN IST ALLES GELEGEN (Peace nourishes, strife devours; God's blessing is all that matters).

44

a. Italian (Venetian) broadsword, of the type known as a Schiavona. The hilt is of typical oval basket form, with a 'cat's head' pommel. These swords derive their name from the Slavonic mercenaries employed by the Republic of Venice. This example dates from *c.* 1700. The stamp of the Lion of St. Mark can be seen on the pommel and on the basket, Pl. 108.

45

a. Venetian Schiavona. The characteristic hilt is of russet steel with small rosettes applied in white metal. The blade, which is associated, is engraved with the Imperial eagle and the date 1734.

b. Venetian Schiavona. The typical hilt is incised on one bar of the guard with the initials M.G. and the date 1781. The blade is inscribed NOSO EN TOLEDO. Marks, Pl. 108.

46

a–b. English sword of the mid seventeenth century. The hilt follows the form of the so-called 'Mortuary' type (*see* Pls. 47–48), but it is pierced and japanned and gilded with foliage patterns.

The grip is covered in fish skin and bound with copper wire. The blade is single edged. This is reputed to be the sword used by Cromwell when he led the final assault on Drogheda in 1649.

47

a. English broadsword, of the type commonly known as a 'Mortuary' sword. The hilt is chiselled with the heads of King Charles I and Queen Henrietta Maria and a figure of Charles on horseback. The grip is covered in fish skin and bound with copper wire. The short two-edged blade is German and stamped with a running wolf mark and the numbers 1553. Mid seventeenth century.

b. 'Mortuary' sword, mid seventeenth century. The hilt is of gilded iron, fretted and chiselled with the figure of an armoured pikeman and with heads of Charles I and Henrietta Maria. The wooden grip is a restoration, and the two-edged blade is German. Marks, Pl. 108.

c. 'Mortuary' sword, mid seventeenth century. The shell is embossed with profile heads of Charles I and with trophies of arms. The grip is covered in fish skin and bound with copper wire. The broad two-edged blade is inscribed ANDRIA FARARA.

d. 'Mortuary' sword, mid seventeenth century. The hilt, of gilded steel, is chiselled with a coat of arms which has yet to be firmly identified. The single-edged blade is stamped with a crescent moon mark.

48

a. 'Mortuary' sword, mid seventeenth century. The hilt bears the heads of Charles I and Britannia, and the blade is inscribed IHN SOLINGEN.

b. Backsword, with plain iron hilt of 'Mortuary' type. Mid seventeenth century.

49

a. English broadsword, first half of the seventeenth century, with a black iron hilt. The blade is inscribed FOR THE TOWER. Several similar swords are preserved in the collection, but this is the only one so inscribed. Mark, Pl. 108.

b. English broadsword of *c.* 1680, probably for an officer in the London City Train Band. The brass hilt bears the arms of the royal house of Stuart and of the city of London on the pommel and shells. The blade is inscribed ANDREA FERARA.

c. English military broadsword, of the second half of the seventeenth century. The steel hilt has two pierced shell guards and a barrel-shaped pommel. The blade is German and bears a running wolf mark, Pl. 108.

50

a. English broadsword, *c.* 1690. The hilt is of steel, and the blade, which is stamped with a running wolf mark, is inscribed GOD SAVE KING WILLIAM AND QUEEN MARY.

b. English broadsword, *c.* 1680. The hilt is of brass and is decorated on the shells and pommel with figures. The grip is bound in brass wire. The very heavy two-edged blade is unmarked.

c. English backsword, late seventeenth century. The steel hilt is japanned black and decorated with foliage patterns in gold (*cf.* Pl. 46). The grip is covered in fish skin.

51

a. English basket-hilted sword of the early seventeenth century. The basket is made up of flat ribbon-like bars and inlaid with foliage patterns in silver. The broad two-edged blade is stamped with a mark (Pl. 108) and inscribed ANDREA FERARA.

b. English basket-hilted sword, the blade dated 1648 and stamped with a running wolf mark, Pl. 108.

c. Similar to *b* but bearing the date 1681 on the blade. Mark, Pl. 108.

d. Scottish basket-hilted sword. The basket guard, with irregular piercings, long recurved quillons and fish-skin covered grip, dates from the early seventeenth century. The blade and pommel are nineteenth century.

52

a. English basket-hilted sword, *c.* 1620. The iron hilt is inlaid with foliage patterns in silver, and the exceptionally broad blade is stamped with the mark of Peter Paeter of Solingen.

b–c. Scottish basket-hilted sword of the early seventeenth century. The basket is formed of steel ribbon bands, coarsely finished, in the style known as West Highland. The broad, slightly curved blade is German and inscribed EDWARDVZ PRINZ ANGLIE, probably meaning the Black Prince. The sword is one of a group of seventeenth-century weapons bearing such antiquarian inscriptions.

53

a. Scottish basket-hilted sword, of the first half of the eighteenth century. The hilt, of characteristic type, bears the letter A under the quillon (Pl. 108), probably for John Allan (Sr.) of Stirling. The guard retains its tassel of wool under the pommel, sword knot of leather, and stout leather pad. The grip is covered in fish skin, and the single-edged blade bears a maker's mark, Pl. 108.

b. Scottish basket-hilted sword, *c.* 1760, with a German blade. The pierced steel guard is stamped W (?A) for Walter Allan (?) of Stirling. The grip is covered in fish skin, and the blade is inscribed ANDREA FARARA.

c. Scottish basket-hilted sword, *c.* 1770. The pierced steel basket relates in style to hilts by Walter Allan of Stirling. The associated Spanish blade is inscribed EN TOLEDO.

d. British military 'Claymore', dated 1857. The hilt is of traditional Scottish form, but the blade is stamped ENFIELD at the forte. Marks, Pl. 108.

54

a. Scottish basket-hilted sword, *c.* 1740, stamped with the initials of John Simpson of Glasgow (Pl. 108). On the front of the guard is a monogram containing the letters I I W, presumably the owner's initials. The blade has an orb and cross mark (Pl. 108) and is inscribed ANDRIA FERARA.

b. Scottish basket-hilted sword, *c.* 1730, with the mark of the Glasgow maker Robert Craig stamped on the quillon (Pl. 108). The single-edged German blade is inscribed ANDREA FERARA.

c. Scottish basket-hilted sword, *c.* 1750, the hilt inlaid with geometric patterns in brass. Under the quillon are the initials of John Allan (jr.) of Stirling, Pl. 108.

55

a. English hanger, *c.* 1630. The russet iron hilt is decorated with applied scroll and pattern-work in silver. The curved single-edged blade is probably German. Marks, Pl. 109.

b. English hanger, *c.* 1650. The iron hilt is decorated in silver *pointillé* work. The curved single-edged blade is pierced at the forte.

c. Hanger, probably English, *c.* 1630. The iron hilt is decorated with applied patterns in silver. The velvet-covered grip is a restoration. German blade, stamped with maker's marks, Pl. 109.

d. English hanger, *c.* 1680. The silver hilt is decorated with lions, Tudor roses and foliage. The grip is of stag antler, and the short curved blade is engraved at the forte with foliate designs. Mark, Pl. 109.

56

a. Forrester's sword, German, *c.* 1600, with a massive saw-backed blade. Near the tip of the blade is a circular hole, the purpose of which is uncertain. The grip is of stag horn, with a cap pommel.

b. English hanger, *c.* 1650. The hilt is formed from three lengths of stag antler, with silver terminals (one of which is missing). The curved single-edged blade is lightly etched at the forte with foliage patterns and stamped with an unidentified maker's mark.

c. English hanger, *c.* 1650, similar to the previous example. It has lost its quillon and pommel terminals. The blade bears a running wolf mark, Pl. 109.

57

a. Saxon hunting sword and scabbard, dated 1662. This comes from the armoury of the Electors of Saxony and is one of a group of similar hunting weapons. The grip is beaked and secured to the tang by large brass rivets. The wooden scabbard is covered in black tooled leather and contains two side knives and a bodkin-pointed file.

b. Saxon hunting trousse, *c.* 1662. This seems to be *en suite* with the sword *a* and has a similar beaked grip and brass rivets. The blade is of heavy chopper type. The wooden sheath is covered in tooled leather and contains four knives and a bodkin-pointed file. The mounts of the sheath are blued and chiselled, bearing the initials HGHZSGCVBC (Hans Georg, Herzog zu Sachsen, Gülich, Cleve und Berg Churfürst).

58

a. English silver-hilted hunting sword. It bears the London Assay marks and date letter for 1724–5. The pommel and shell are chiselled with bearded masks. The blade, which is associated, is from a military sword.

b. English silver-hilted hunting sword, bearing the date letter for 1750–1 and the initials J. C. of the maker, John Carman. The scabbard is of leather with silver mounts inscribed LOXHAM AT YE ROYAL EXCHANGE. William Loxham was Master of the Cutlers' Company in 1742.

c. Hunting sword, probably German, *c.* 1730. The hilt is of silver, with the grip agate. The blade is etched and gilt with decorative panels.

d. French hunting sword, dated 1733. The hilt is of gilt silver decorated with trophies, foliage, and animals. The blade is etched and gilt with hunting scenes, the royal arms of France, and the inscription MANUFACTURE ROYALE D'ALSACE, ANNO 1733.

59

a. German hunting sword, *c.* 1720. The hilt is brass, with a stag-horn grip. The blade is inscribed MANBERGER, FOURBISSEUR A FRANCFOURT. Two other hunting swords by Manberger, who died in 1734, are in the Historisches Museum at Frankfurt am Main. Mark, Pl. 109.

b. English silver-hilted hanger, bearing the date letter for 1783–4. The locket of the scabbard bears the motto and crest of the Hudson's Bay Company and the name of the cutler, Loxham. Edward Loxham was Master of the Cutlers' Company in 1758, *cf.* Pl. 58*b*.

c. English silver-hilted hanger, bearing the date letter for 1777–8 and the initials W. K., probably for William King. The scabbard is of leather with silver mounts inscribed CUTLER, CHARING CROSS.

60

a. Hunting sword, probably Dutch, of the mid seventeenth century. The ivory hilt is carved in the form of a lion; it was perhaps imported from the Dutch East Indies. The single-edged blade is stamped with a crowned head mark, used by Johannes Wundes of Solingen, Pl. 109.

b. German hunting sword, *c.* 1720, with an ivory hilt carved to represent hounds attacking beasts of the chase. The silver quillons are in the form of boars' trotters. The curved blade is etched and gilt at the forte.

61

a. Silver-hilted hunting sword, probably Dutch, of the second half of the seventeenth century. The hilt shows a lion fighting with hounds. Single-edged blade. Mark, Pl. 109.

b. Hunting sword, with a Brescian hilt of *c.* 1660 and an English blade of *c.* 1730. The iron hilt is chiselled into the form of dragons and signed by Carlo Botarello, a Brescian metalworker whose name appears on two pistols in the Royal Armoury at Turin which are dated 1665 and 1666. The two-edged blade is etched and gilt with the royal arms and the words VIVAT GEORGE II REX BRITANNIAE.

62

a. German hunting sword of *c.* 1686, with a calendar blade. This is one of a number of such blades etched with a perpetual Gregorian calendar. In a cartouche are instructions on how to use the calendar, based upon the year 1686. The blade is signed by Adam Ehinger, who is recorded as Landleutnant of Stadtamhof, near Regensburg, up to 1696.

b–c. Seventeenth-century calendar blade, converted into a British cavalry officer's sword *c.* 1760. The blade is etched with the portrait heads of Frederick V, King of Bohemia, Ernst, Count of Mansfeld, Prince Maurice of Nassau, and Prince Frederick Henry of Nassau, all of whom were prominent leaders of the Protestant faction in the Thirty Years War. The blade is also etched with a calendar and stamped with the crowned-head mark of Johannes Wundes of Solingen, Pl. 109.

63

a. Small sword, *c.* 1660, with an English hilt and a German blade. The hilt is of steel, decorated with silver encrustation. The blade has been etched with decorative patterns.

b. Small sword, probably French, the blade Spanish, *c.* 1670. The hilt is of silver, with a fluted pommel and quillons terminating in animals' heads. The blade is inscribed SEBASTIAN HERNANTEZ.

c. Small sword, with an Italian hilt of pierced and chiselled steel. The blade is German, dated 1712, and bears an inscription which may be translated 'I offer my life to the heart I serve, but my soul goes to the one who has given me victory.'

d. Small sword, probably French, *c.* 1720. The blued steel hilt is encrusted in gold with flowers, flags, and trophies of arms. The blade is etched and gilt at the forte with similar designs.

64

a. French small sword, *c.* 1720, the steel hilt chiselled with scenes from the Fables of La Fontaine. The blade is probably German, despite the fact that it is inscribed PEDRO DEL MONTE FECIT EN TOLEDO.

b. Small sword, probably Dutch, *c.* 1750. The hilt is cast with scenes of the Labours of Hercules. The blade is German, in imitation of an Italian one, hence the signature ANTONIO PICHINIO.

c. Small sword, French, *c.* 1740. The hilt is of steel, with the pommel and shells pierced and chiselled.

d. French small sword, *c.* 1750, with a steel hilt of fine quality. The blade is blued and gilt with foliage patterns.

65

The Collingwood Sword. Presented by the City of London to Lord Collingwood after the Battle of Trafalgar, this is one of several swords which the City bestowed upon notable warriors during the Napoleonic wars. The City Council voted Collingwood a sword, value 200 guineas, in November, 1805, and the commission was given to one Thomas Harper of 207, Fleet Street.

The sword was presented to Collingwood's widow in 1810, after he had died at sea before returning to London to receive it. The hilt is of gold, the grip set with enamel plaques surrounded by diamonds. The knuckle guard is inscribed in diamonds against a blue enamel ground: ENGLAND EXPECTS EVERY MAN TO DO HIS DUTY. TRAFALGAR. The shell guards are inscribed with the City Council resolution of 1805 awarding the sword. The shagreen scabbard has gold mounts, one of which gives the name and address of the furbisher, Harper.

66

a. English silver-hilted small sword, bearing the London Assay marks and date letter for 1758-9.

b. French small sword, *c.* 1820, with a bright steel beaded hilt. The triangular-sectioned blade is blued and gilt and engraved at the forte with the name of the furbisher, Le Court, of the Rue St. Honoré, Paris.

c. Small sword with its scabbard and case. English, or perhaps German, *c.* 1830.

67

a. English brass-hilted hanger. There is a group of such hangers in the Tower collection, which may perhaps be identified with those ordered for 'matrosses' in 1692. This example is signed Hollier on the blade, and from 1715 one Thomas Hollier is recorded as working for the Board of Ordnance. One of his tasks was the re-blading of old weapons.

b. English hanger of the second half of the eighteenth century. The cast brass hilt has a pommel in the form of an eagle's head and the grip simulates cord binding. The short, curved single-edged blade is stamped with various marks and with 48 on the back, Pl. 109.

c. English hanger, similar in type to *a.* The grip has been partly decorated in white enamel, but this is probably not original. The blade bears the maker's name, GRVSON.

68

a. English infantry hanger of the early eighteenth century, with a brass hilt. The blade bears the running fox mark of the Shotley Bridge factory, Pl. 109.

b. Infantry hanger, of similar type and date to the previous example. The blade also has the fox mark of Shotley Bridge, Pl. 109.

c. English brass-hilted infantry hanger, inscribed on the shell guard TOTTENHAM ASSOCIATION, 1782. The blade has the fox mark of Shotley Bridge, Pl. 109.

d. English brass-hilted hanger of the late eighteenth century. On the blade is the fox mark of Shotley Bridge, Pl. 109.

69

a. English dragoon sword of the mid eighteenth century, with a pierced steel basket hilt. The single-edged blade is engraved with interlace patterns at the forte.

b. English cavalry sword of the mid eighteenth century, with a gilt brass basket hilt decorated with trophies and classical figures. The single-edged blade bears the monogram GR surmounted by a crown.

c. English cavalry sword of the mid eighteenth century, with a brass basket hilt. The single-edged blade is stamped with a broad arrow mark.

d. Dragoon sword, *c.* 1790, with a steel basket hilt and a single-edged blade. The blade is etched with the word INCONQUERABLE and the crowned GR monogram. The motto Unconquerable was awarded to the Second Irish Horse (later the Fifth Dragoon Guards) in 1788.

70

a. English cavalry sword, *c.* 1780-90. The hilt has a knuckle bow and back guard linked by three horizontal bars. The blade is single edged, the back sharpened for 20 cms. from the point, and inscribed at the forte GILLS WARRANTED. Gills of Birmingham were one of the major manufacturers of cavalry swords in the later eighteenth century.

b. English cavalry trooper's sword, mid eighteenth century, with large open basket guard and long curved single-edged blade. Mark, Pl. 109.

c. English light dragoon sword, *c.* 1750–60. The hilt consists of a dish, two side bars, and a triangular guard on the knuckle bow. Straight single-edged blade.

d. English light dragoon sword, *c.* 1777–88, with brass stirrup hilt, with a fish-skin covered grip, and a long, very slightly curved blade. The scabbard is also of brass.

71

a. British dragoon sword, dated 1795, with a stirrup hilt and a curved hollow-ground blade. The blade bears the crowned GR cypher, the maker's name, Wooley and Co., Birmingham, and the date on one face; on the reverse it is inscribed 20/7/LD. The Seventh (Queen's Own) Light Dragoons were constituted in 1783.

b. British dragoon officer's sword, *c.* 1780, with steel hilt, on which two side bars pivot out from the knuckle bow and lock with a spring catch. The single-edged blade is etched with trophies of arms and the words KINGS LIGHT DRAGOONS, with the maker's name, Cullum (of Charing Cross). The King's Light Dragoons became the Fifteenth (King's) Hussars in 1806.

c. American sabre and scabbard, *c.* 1795. The steel hilt is based upon the English pattern seen in Pl. 70*a*. The curved blade, of exceptional length, is blued and gilt, with a scroll bearing the word WARRANTED and an eagle with a scroll reading E PLURIBUS UNUM, surrounded by sixteen stars.

72

a. The Light Dragoon trooper's pattern sword of 1796, with stirrup hilt, with a broad curved blade stamped OSBORN AND GRUNDY on the back.

b. Light Dragoon sword, 1796 pattern, for an officer. The blade is etched with the royal arms, figures and foliage, and bears the words THOS. GILL, WARRANTED NEVER TO FAIL, 1798.

c. Similar to the previous example, the blade inscribed T. BATE'S WARRANTED.

73

a. Light Cavalry officer's sword, with a silver hilt bearing the date letter for 1806–7. The scabbard is of black leather with silver mounts.

b. Sabre and scabbard, probably for an officer in a volunteer regiment, *c.* 1796. The scabbard is inscribed KNUBLEY AND CO, NO. 7, CHARING CROSS, LONDON. John Knubley, a sword cutler, was at this address from 1794–1799.

c. Sabre for an officer, *c.* 1800. The blade, which is similar to that on the previous example, is etched with spurious arabic inscriptions and signed on the back JEAN KNEGT MANUFACTURIER DE SABRES A SOHLINGEN.

74

Watercolour commemorating the comparative testing of light cavalry swords by Wooley and Osborn carried out at the Tower in 1804. The German, who 'did not think proper to attend', was John Justus Runkel of Solingen, who was resident in London and a Freeman of the Cutlers' Company from 1796–1806.

75

a–b. British officer's pattern sword of 1803. The hilt is of gilt bronze, with a lion's head pommel and the knuckle bow fretted and engraved with the GR monogram. The curved single-edged blade is blued and gilt, bearing the royal arms and cypher, trophies, and foliage. The scabbard is of black leather covered with red silk and bearing a seal stamped Pattern Ordnance. This is therefore one of the sealed pattern swords of 1803.

c. Officer's sword, pattern of 1803, the blade signed J. J. RUNKEL, SOLINGEN (*see* Pl. 74).

76

a. Sword which belonged to the first Duke of Wellington. The hilt with boat-shaped shell guards is of brass. The blade is blued and gilt, with the royal arms as borne from 1801 to 1816, and signed by Runkel (*see* Pl. 74).

b. Presentation sword, dated 1804/5, with a gold hilt, the blade blued and etched. The black fish-skin scabbard has gold fittings and is inscribed: THE GIFT OF HIS MAJESTY KING GEORGE III TO COLONEL PRINCE HIS AIDE DE CAMP AND LIEUT COLONEL OF THE 6TH OR INNISKILLING REGIMENT OF DRAGOONS, FOR HIS ACTIVITY AND JUDGMENT IN CHOOSING THE HORSES FOR HIS MAJESTY'S GERMAN LEGION.

c. British infantry officer's sword, pattern of 1822, with a half basket-hilt in brass. The guard incorporates two scrolls, bearing the words ROYAL SCOTS FUSILIERS and their motto NEMO ME IMPUNE LACESSIT. The curved 'pipe-backed' blade is also engraved with the name and motto.

77

a. Sabre for officers of the 10th Hussars, *c.* 1810. The hilt is of brass, and the remains of a seal can be seen on the grip. The large langets are inset with the Prince of Wales feathers in silver and the motto ICH DIEN.

b. British officer's pattern sword of 1822, with gilt brass half basket hilt incorporating the cypher G IV R.

c. Sealed pattern sword for rifle regiments, 1827. The pipe-backed blade is inscribed on one face THE LX RIFLES and on the other 1ST DUKE OF YORKS OWN RIFLE CORPS (a title born by the 60th Rifles from 1824–30).

d. British staff sergeant's sword, *c.* 1825, with a cast brass hilt bearing the cypher of George IV.

78

a. British pioneer's sword, *c.* 1820, brass hilted, the blade slightly curved and with a saw back, stamped OSBORN AND GRUNDY.

b. British pioneer's sword, pattern of 1856, stamped with the maker's name WATTS and inscribed 3A &SH (3rd. Argyll and Sutherland Highlanders).

c. Sword of the Land Transport Corps, 1855–7. The blade bears the mark of Carl Reinhardt Kirschbaum of Solingen.

79

a. British heavy cavalry trooper's pattern sword of 1796. Engraved on the knuckle guard is the inscription THIS SWORD BELONGED TO SERGT. SHAW OF THE LIFE GUARDS WHO KILLED 13 MEN AT THE BATTLE OF WATERLOO. PRESENTED BY COL. MC VICAR TO E. YOUNG ESQRE. M.D. WHO NOW GIVES IT TO HIS G.SON HENRY WILEY MIDDLETON, JANUARY 1ST 1864. No doubt the sword did belong to Shaw, but it is not the one he used at Waterloo since that broke during the battle and he killed the thirteenth man with his helmet.

b. Household Cavalry trooper's sword of *c.* 1805. One of a large group of such brass-hilted swords which has remained in the Tower, probably because the swords were found unsuitable for service use. This example is stamped on the blade DAWES, BIRMINGHAM.

c. British cavalry trooper's sword, pattern of 1856. The blade is stamped REEVES and the steel scabbard 5L152 (5th Lancers).

80

a. Sabre, probably the German pattern which formed the basis for the brass-hilted Household Cavalry sword of *c.* 1805.

b. Hilt of the Household Cavalry sword seen full length in Pl. 79*b*.

c. Sword for a trooper of the First Life Guards, *c.* 1825.

d. British heavy cavalry trooper's sword, pattern of 1821, dated 1843. The blade is stamped ENFIELD.

81

a. British cavalry trooper's sword, pattern of 1884. The hilt has a steel bowl guard pierced with a Maltese cross. The guard is stamped 5DG (5th Dragoon Guards).

b. British cavalry trooper's sword, pattern of 1899, converted from the pattern of 1890.

c. British cavalry trooper's sword, pattern of 1908. The blade is stamped WILKINSON.

d. Sword for a cavalry officer, pattern of 1796. The shell guard is pierced and engraved with foliage.

e. Sabre for the British East India Company, *c.* 1860. The hilt is similar to that of the heavy cavalry and Royal Engineers officer's pattern of 1857. The blade bears the maker's name, GARDEN AND SON (London), and the crest of the East India Company.

f. Sword for an officer in the Royal Artillery, late nineteenth century. The blade bears the maker's name, HAMBURGER ROGERS & CO. (London), and is etched with the VR cypher and the words ROYAL ARTILLERY. Mark, Pl. 109.

82

a. British cavalry band sword, *c.* 1820. The hilt is of cast brass, with a horse's head pommel. The grip is stamped H48.

b. British band sword, early nineteenth century, with cast brass hilt with a lion's head pommel. The single-edged blade is stamped HERBERT on the back.

c. British band sword, *c.* 1850, with a mameluke hilt. The tang bears the maker's name, HERBERT & CO., 8 PALL MALL EAST, LONDON.

83

a. British bugler's sword, pattern of 1895. The hilt is of steel, and the ricasso is stamped MOLE, BIRMINGHAM.

b. British bugler's sword, pattern of 1857. The steel hilt is stamped 4RIR (Royal Irish Rifles).

c. British drummer's sword, pattern of 1895. The hilt is brass.

d. British drummer's sword, pattern of 1857. The hilt is brass.

84

a. Sword of the kind carried by the Yeomen of the Guard and the Yeomen Warders of the Tower in the nineteenth century. The hilt is brass.

b. British coastguard's sword, *c.* 1860. The hilt is brass and the blade is stamped REEVES.

c. Police sword, dating between 1821–9. The blade is etched DISMOUNTED HORSE PATROL and W. PARKER HOL[BORN]. This patrol, with headquarters at Bow Street, existed from 1821–9.

d. Sword for a prison officer, *c.* 1850. The blade is etched WORMWOOD SCRUBBS PRISON and PARKER FIELD AND SONS, 233 HOLBORN, LONDON.

85

a–b. Sword of Napoleon I, presented to him by his comrade-in-arms Alexandre Desmazis, as a souvenir of their service together at Valence. The hilt is brass and is inscribed on the shells DESMAZIS, OFF[ICI]ER AU REG[IMEN]T DE LA FERE NO. 4/1780 and CORPS D'ARTILLERIE. The blade is engraved A SON AMI N. DE BUONAPARTE, SOUVENIR 1786, VALENCE.

c. Boy's sword, with a brass hilt and a blued blade etched GARDE IMPERIAL DU ROI DE ROME. In 1814 Le Sieur Goubaud, an art teacher at the Lycée Bonaparte, proposed the creation of the Garde du Roi de Rome, to be formed of pupils from the four Paris lycées. There is no evidence that the project was ever developed, but this sword was presumably designed for it.

86

a. French cavalry sword, *c.* 1750. The blade is etched with various devices, including the French royal arms and the words VIVE LE ROY, which have been deliberately defaced, presumably during the Revolution.

b. French cavalry sword, *c.* 1780. The blade bears the royal arms and is inscribed GARDES DU CORPS DU ROY. Mark, Pl. 109.

c. French cavalry sword, *c.* 1780. The brass shell guard is decorated in relief with the royal arms. The blade is engraved with various devices and the words VIVAT REGUM CARISSIMUS. REGIMENT DES CARABINIERS DE MONSIEURS. MANUF^{re} DE KLINGENTHAL. Marks, Pl. 109.

87

a. French sword of honour, *c.* 1800, one of a series presented by the Minister of War to the men of the 3rd Company of the 19th Demi-Brigade. The hilt is brass and bears an inscription recording the presentation together with the words MANUFACTURE A VERSAILLES. BOUTET. The single-edged blade is lightly etched and inscribed KLINGENTHAL on the back. Marks, Pl. 109.

b. French sword for an artillery officer, pattern of 1829. The hilt is of brass, and the curved single-edged blade is inscribed on the back COULAUX AINE ET CIE A KLINGENTHAL.

c. French cavalry sword, pattern of 1816. The hilt is of brass, and the straight single-edged blade is of Klingenthal manufacture. Marks, Pl. 109.

88

a. Sword of a cadet of the French military academy in the Champs de Mars, Paris, *c.* 1790. Marks, Pl. 106.

b. Sword of the Ecole de Mars, *c.* 1795. The hilt is brass, but with the subsidiary quillons and knuckle guard in steel. The wooden scabbard is covered in red cloth.

89

a. Sword of a French army sapper, *c.* 1800, with the brass hilt in the form of a cock.

b. French infantry sword, pattern of 1831, with a brass hilt and leaf-shaped blade stamped JEAN on one face. Marks, Pl. 109.

c. French infantry sword, pattern of 1816. The blade is of Klingenthal manufacture and dated 1824. Marks, Pl. 109.

90

a. German rifleman's sword, late eighteenth century. The hilt is brass, and the single-edged blade is etched with strapwork and a boar at the forte.

b. Dress sword, probably Prussian, *c.* 1820, with the pommel in the form of a plumed helmet. The single-edged blade is blued and gilt with trophies of arms and flowers.

c. Bavarian cavalry sword of the late eighteenth century. The curved single-edged blade bears the words FUR DAS VATERLAND and the arms of Bavaria, with the crowned cypher CT (probably for Charles Theodore, Duke of Bavaria 1778–99).

d. German light cavalry sword, *c.* 1820, similar in form to the British Light Dragoon pattern of 1796 (*cf.* Pl. 72*a*). Mark, Pl. 109.

e. German artillery sword, *c.* 1820, with a brass hilt and a curved single-edged blade stamped at the forte GEBR WEYERSBERG, SOLINGEN.

f. Austrian cavalry sword, dated 1881, the blade inscribed GOTT MIT UNS.

91

a. Spanish officer's sword, dated 1802. The brass hilt bears a crowned monogram of the letters RCDG (Real Cuerpo de Guardias).

b. Spanish infantry officer's sword. The brass hilt is inscribed on the shell guard APPROVADA POR S.M. EN 1818. The Toledo blade bears a similar inscription.

c. Spanish cavalry sword, with a brass hilt. The shell bears the words MODELO APPROVADA EN 1825, and the blade MODELO DE ESPADA DE CABALL. DE LINEAS.

d. Spanish infantry sword with a brass hilt. The blade is inscribed REAL FABRICA DE TOLEDO ANO DE 1818.

e. Military sword, probably Neapolitan, *c.* 1800. The brass hilt is of the Bilbo type (*cf.* Pl. 42 *a–b*). The blade is signed SEBASTIAN ERNANDEZ EN TOLEDO and bears the name SCORZA, perhaps that of the owner, on the ricasso. The blade is etched on both faces with Italian inscriptions, which may be translated: 'He who can defend himself and strike needs no other aid in peril. Who can repress the proud and comfort the faint hearted, defend the innocent and punish the impious. May your vigilance subdue all human disorder so that nothing can oppose you. Let luck and arms judge between us, the sole light of our race.'

f. Italian cavalry sword, *c.* 1820, with a brass hilt and the blade inscribed VIVA FERDINANDO IV RE DELLE DUE SICILIE. Ferdinand ruled as king of the Two Sicilies from 1759–1825.

92

a. Sword of King George II (1683–1760). This is a fine example of an early eighteenth-century military sword. The blade is etched with a calendar (*cf.* Pl. 62) and signed by Iohannes Brach (of Solingen).

b. Sword of King George III (1738–1820), officer's pattern of *c.* 1790, the blade blued and gilt, with the royal arms.

c. Sword of King George IV (1762–1830), officer's pattern of 1814.

d. Sword of King William IV (1765–1837), worn by him as Admiral of the Fleet.

93

a. Sword of King Edward VII (1841–1910), carried by him as Colonel of the 10th Hussars (Prince of Wales' Own). The blade is by Wilkinson.

b. Sword of King George V (1865–1936), worn by him as Admiral of the Fleet. The blade is etched CARTER & CO., PALL MALL, LONDON.

c. Sword of King George VI (1895–1952), carried by him when Duke of York, as Colonel-in-

Chief of the Scots Guards. The blade is engraved EDWARD SMITH, 5 BOYLE STREET, LONDON W.I.

94

a. Sword of the first Duke of York (1763–1827), officer's pattern of 1822. The blade bears the cypher of George IV and the words PROSSER, SWORD CUTLER TO THE KING. CHARING CROSS.

b. Sword of the Duke of Connaught (1850–1942), as Honorary Colonel of the Cazadores de Arapiles. The weapon is a fine example of modern Toledo workmanship.

DAGGERS

95

a. Dagger of the type known as a baselard, with an I-shaped hilt. Probably Tuscan, late fifteenth century.

b. German dagger of the late fifteenth century, with a narrow grip and small, sloping quillons.

c. Rondel dagger, probably English, early fifteenth century. The grip is a restoration.

d. English rondel dagger of the early fifteenth century.

96

a–b. Italian 'ear' dagger of *c.* 1500. The grip is of gilt brass and ivory. The blade, which has an asymmetrical ricasso, is etched with foliage patterns and masks.

97

a. Gunner's stiletto, Italian, *c.* 1650. The blade bears a sequence of irregular gradations, each with a number; these are intended to enable a gunner to calculate the weight of a shot from the bore of the gun.

b. Gunner's stiletto similar to *a.* In this and the preceding example the grips are of cowhorn.

c. Schiavona dagger and sheath. The hilt is decorated in silver and gilt and with semi-precious stones. The blade is deeply grooved and pierced, and the sheath is of silver. Probably Dalmatian, late eighteenth century.

98

a–f. Italian stiletti of the late sixteenth century.

99

a. Spanish left-hand dagger, *c.* 1650, with a bright steel hilt, pierced and chiselled.

b. Spanish left-hand dagger, *c.* 1650. The guard is of excellent workmanship.

c. Spanish left-hand dagger, dated 1780. The hilt is plain, and the blade is inscribed TOLEDO and dated. It has a sheath of black leather.

100

a. German left-hand dagger, *c.* 1610. The hilt is of chiselled iron, the decoration including classical figures. The leaf-shaped blade has a pierced fuller.

b. German left-hand dagger, *c.* 1610. The quillons and pommel are chiselled with foliage patterns against a gilt ground.

101

a. Italian left-hand dagger, late sixteenth century. The ebony grip is a restoration.

b. Italian left-hand dagger, *c.* 1600, with a flamboyant blade.

c. Left-hand dagger, probably German, *c.* 1600, with a saw-edged blade.

102

a. Steel sheath for a Landsknecht dagger, German, *c.* 1530.

b. Dutch sheath, dated 1597, made of boxwood and carved with saints, scenes of the parable of the prodigal son and representations of the six works of mercy.

c. Sheath for a large knife and set of tools, of leather enclosed in a chiselled metal casing. Perhaps English, dated 1643.

103

a. Ballock knife, of the late fifteenth century, with a bone grip. Found in the Scheldt at Antwerp.

b–c. Colonel Blood's daggers. English or Scottish ballock daggers and sheaths, dated 1620. Traditionally those carried by Colonel Blood when he attempted to steal the Crown Jewels in 1671.

104

a. Scottish dirk, *c.* 1740, with a wooden grip carved with interlace patterns.

b. British dirk, *c.* 1880, of the pattern issued to N.C.O.'s in Highland regiments. The blade is stamped by the maker, Robert Mole.

c. British naval dirk, carried by Midshipman Benjamin Patey at the Battle of Copenhagen in 1801.

105

a. English dagger and sheath, dated 1628. The dagger, with a saw-backed blade, is inscribed OMNIA VINCIT AMOR and FEARE GOD HONOR Y KING. The tooled leather sheath includes two side pockets, one of which contains a bodkin.

b. English dagger and sheath. This is a rare relic of the 'Popish Plot' stirred up by Titus Oates in 1678. The blade is inscribed with the following words, placed beneath a skull: MEMENTO GODFREY OCT. 12. 1678/PRO RELIGION PROTESTANTIVM. Sir Edmund Berry Godfrey was the Protestant magistrate to whom Oates first took his story of the Popish Plot. A few weeks later, on October 12, Sir Edmund disappeared and his body was found on October 17 on Primrose Hill, transfixed with his own sword. The Catholics were immediately blamed for the crime and two alleged plotters were eventually hanged at Tyburn for the murder. The truth of the matter is still in doubt. One theory is that Godfrey was murdered at the instigation of Oates to provide dramatic proof of the supposed plot.

c. Dagger, probably English, *c.* 1600. The pommel and quillons are inlaid with silver and damascened in gold, forming foliage patterns and cherubs' heads. The blade bears a crowned F mark.

SWORDS

a b c
Early mediaeval swords, *c.* 950–1100.

PLATE I

a b c d

Swords of the 12th and 13th centuries.

PLATE 2

a b c d

Swords of the 13th and 14th centuries.

PLATE 3

a b c d e f

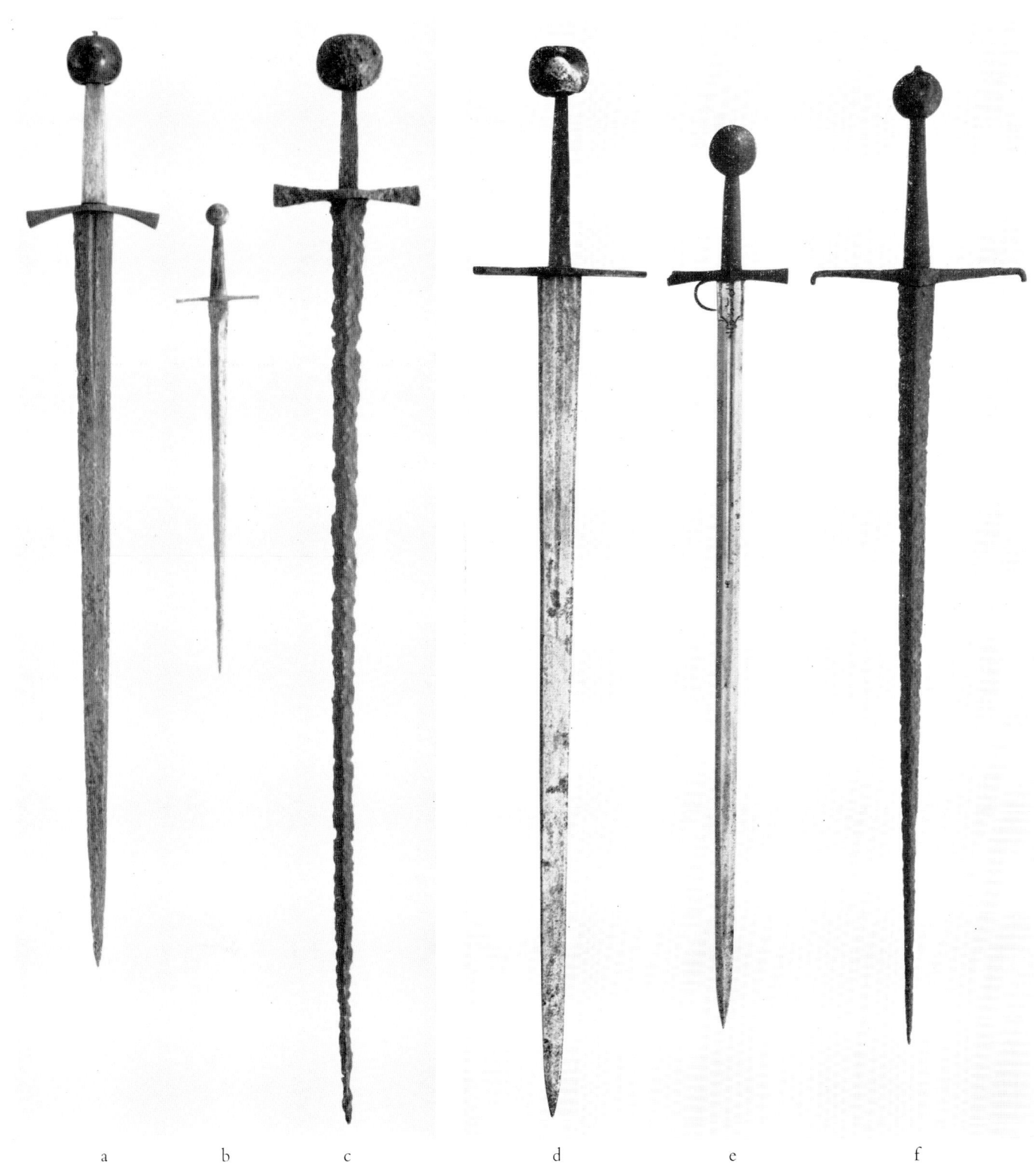

Swords of the 14th century.

PLATE 4

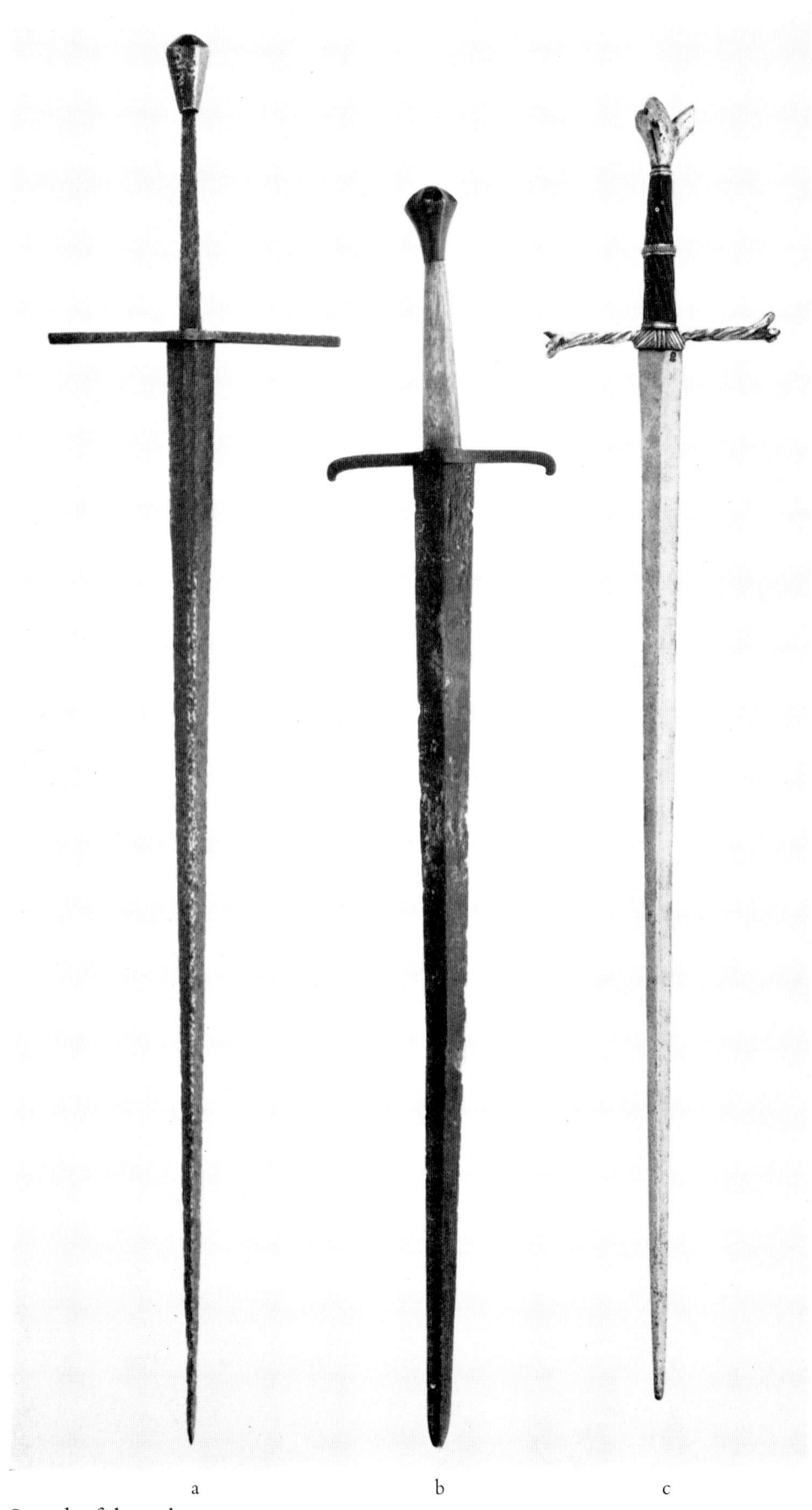

a b c
Swords of the 15th century.

PLATE 5

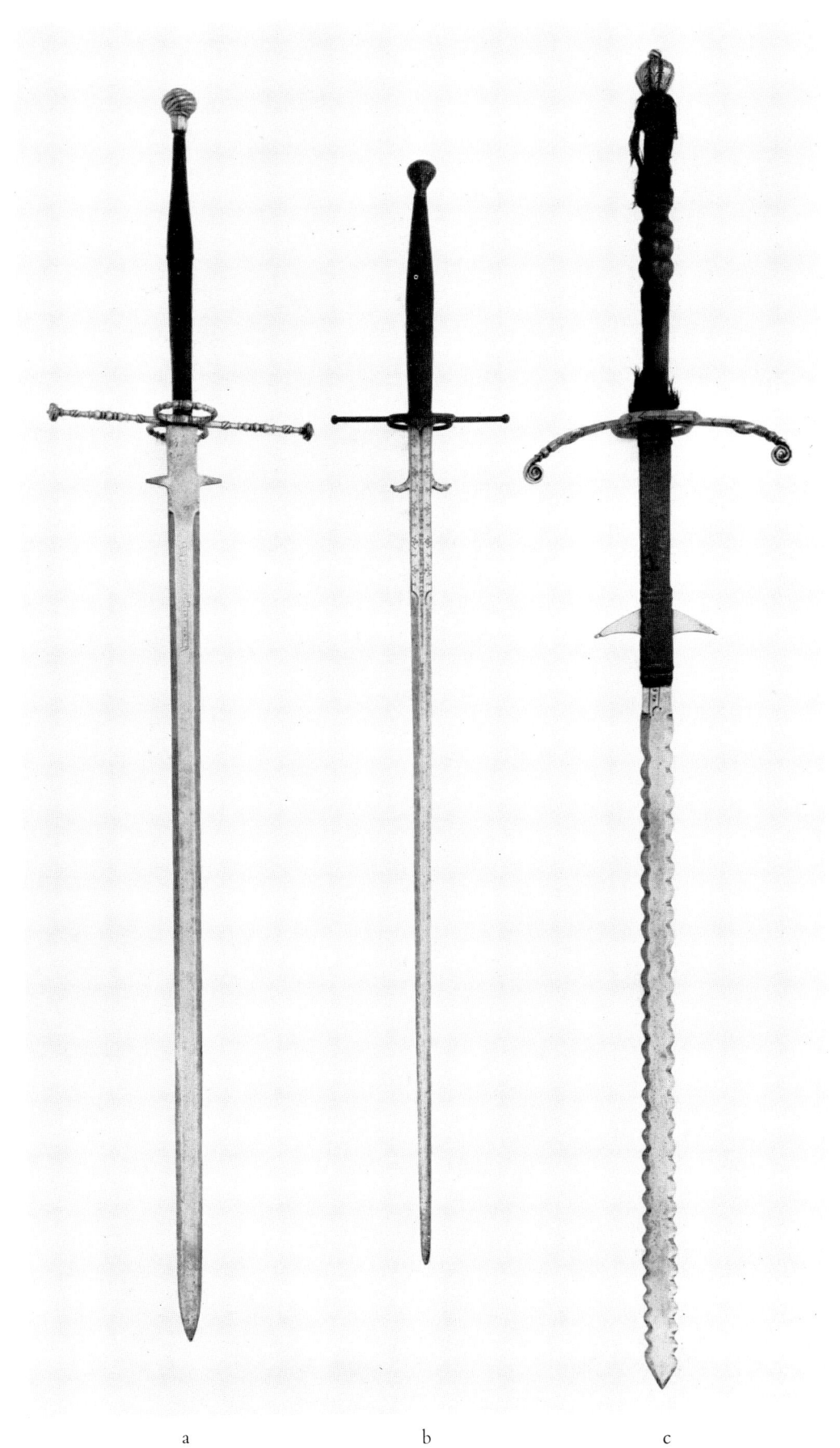

a b c
German two-hand swords, 16th century.

PLATE 6

a b c

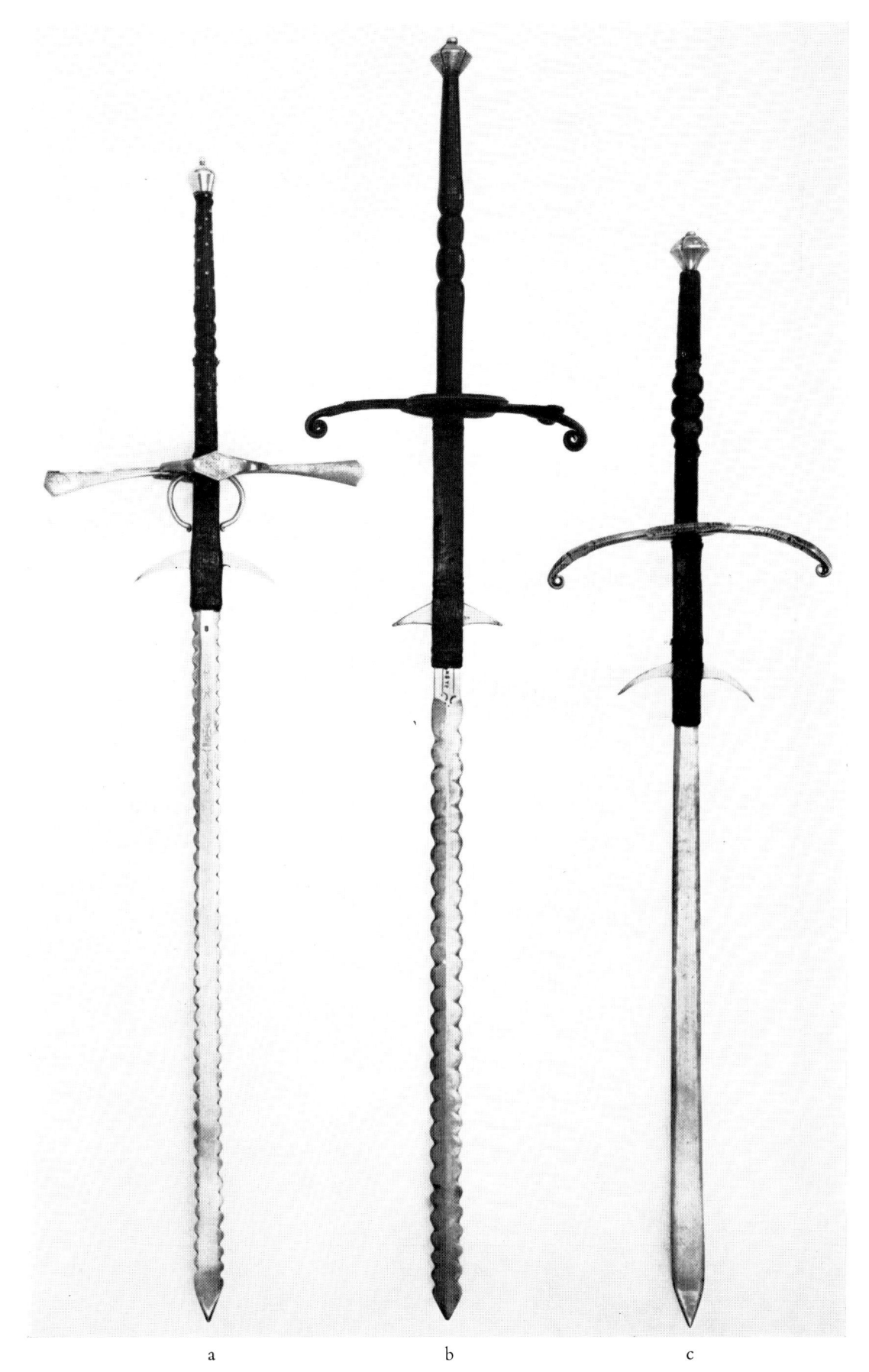

German two-hand swords, 16th century.

PLATE 7

b

Sword for the State Guard of the Duke of Brunswick, dated 1573.

PLATE 8

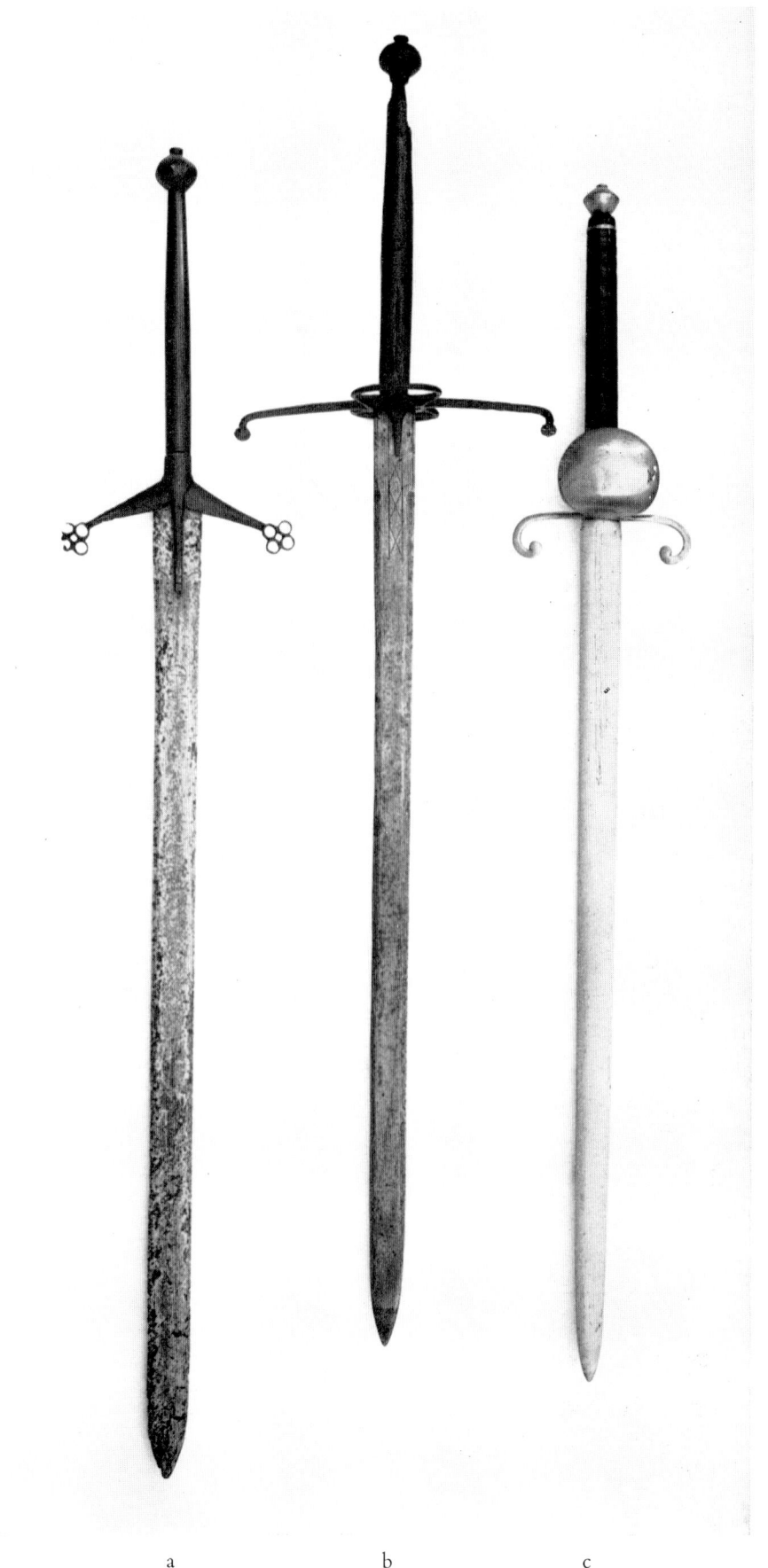

a   b   c
Scottish claymores, 16th–17th centuries.

a b c

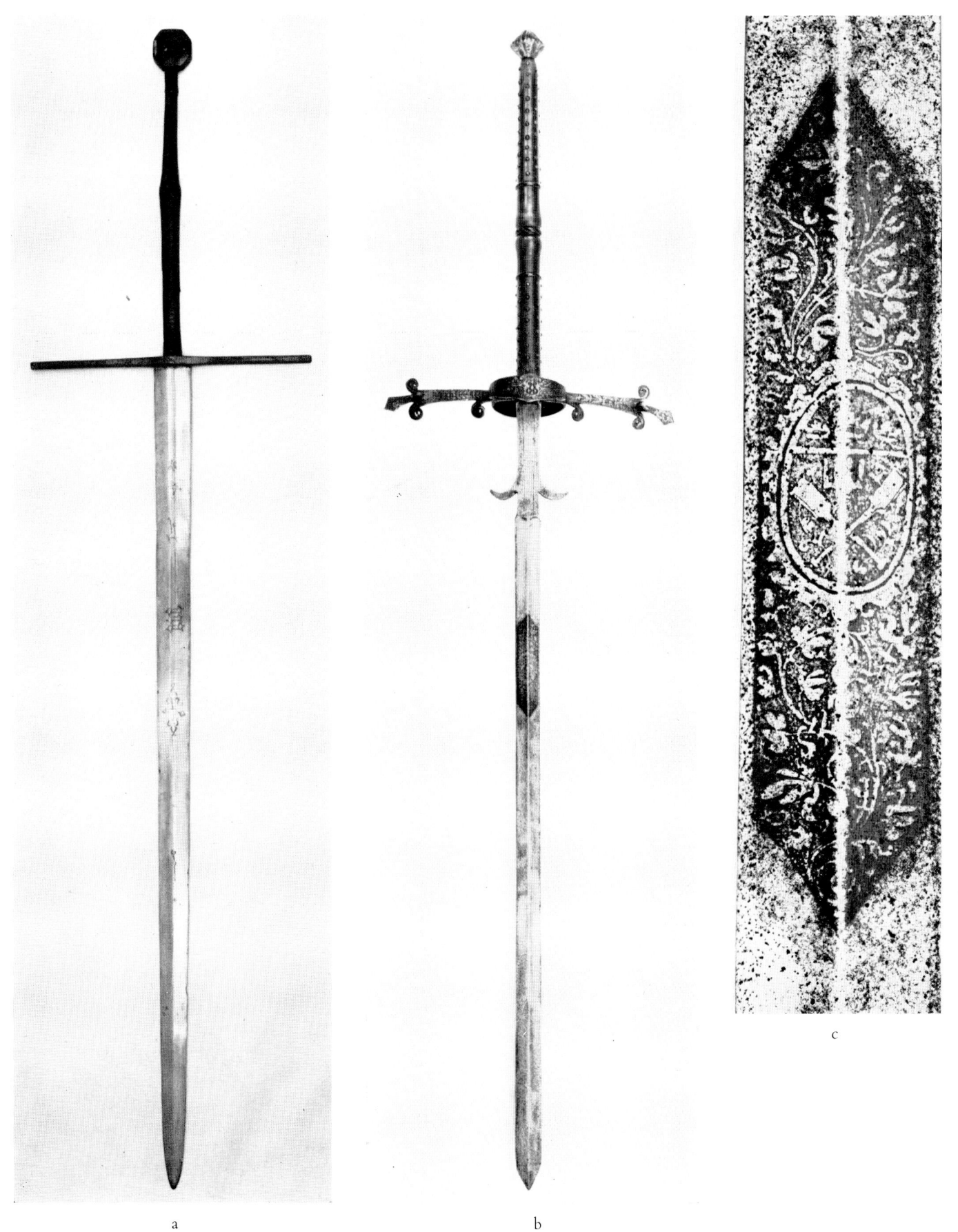

Processional swords of the 15th and 17th centuries.

PLATE 10

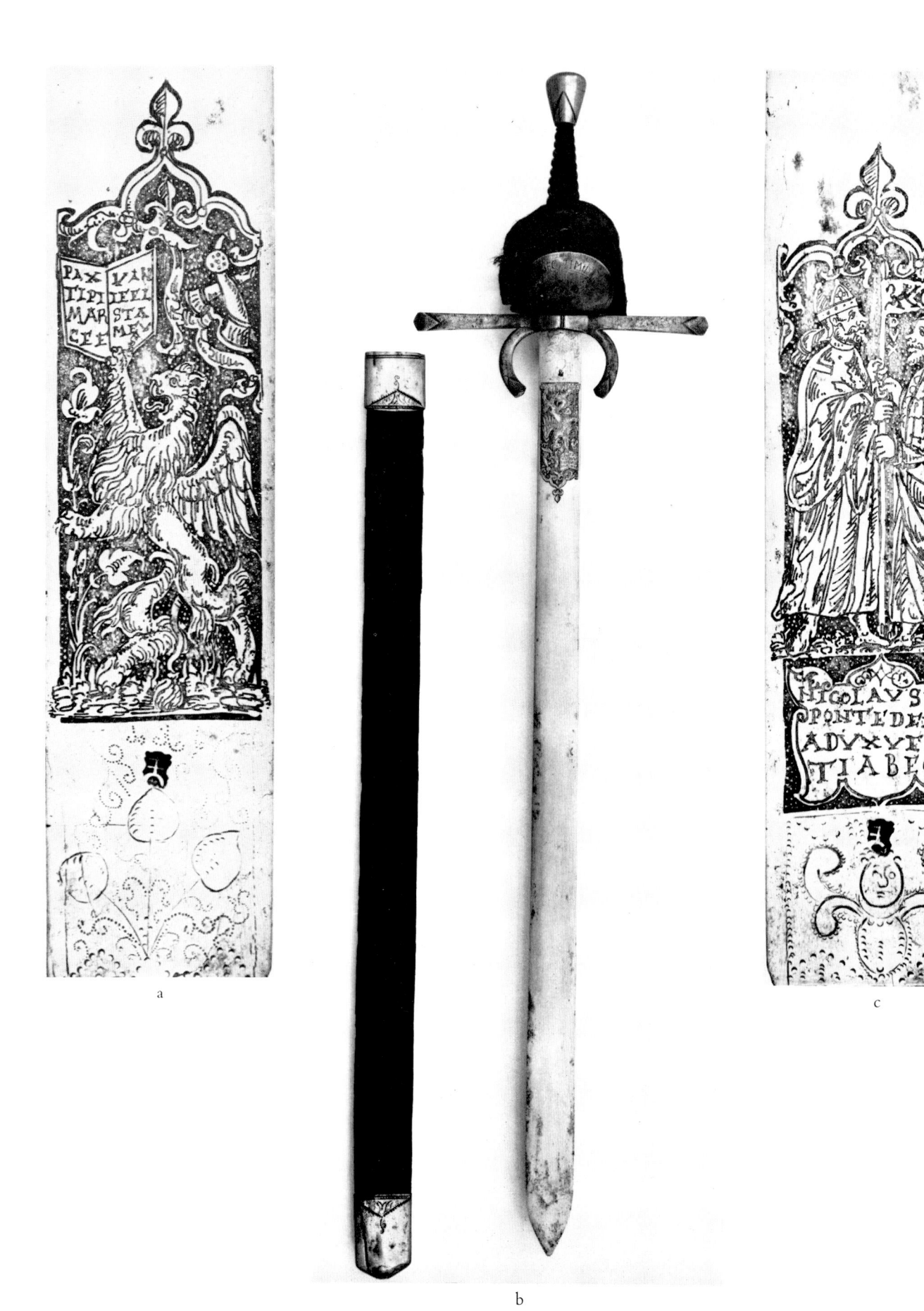

Processional sword for a Doge of Venice, *c.* 1580.

PLATE 11

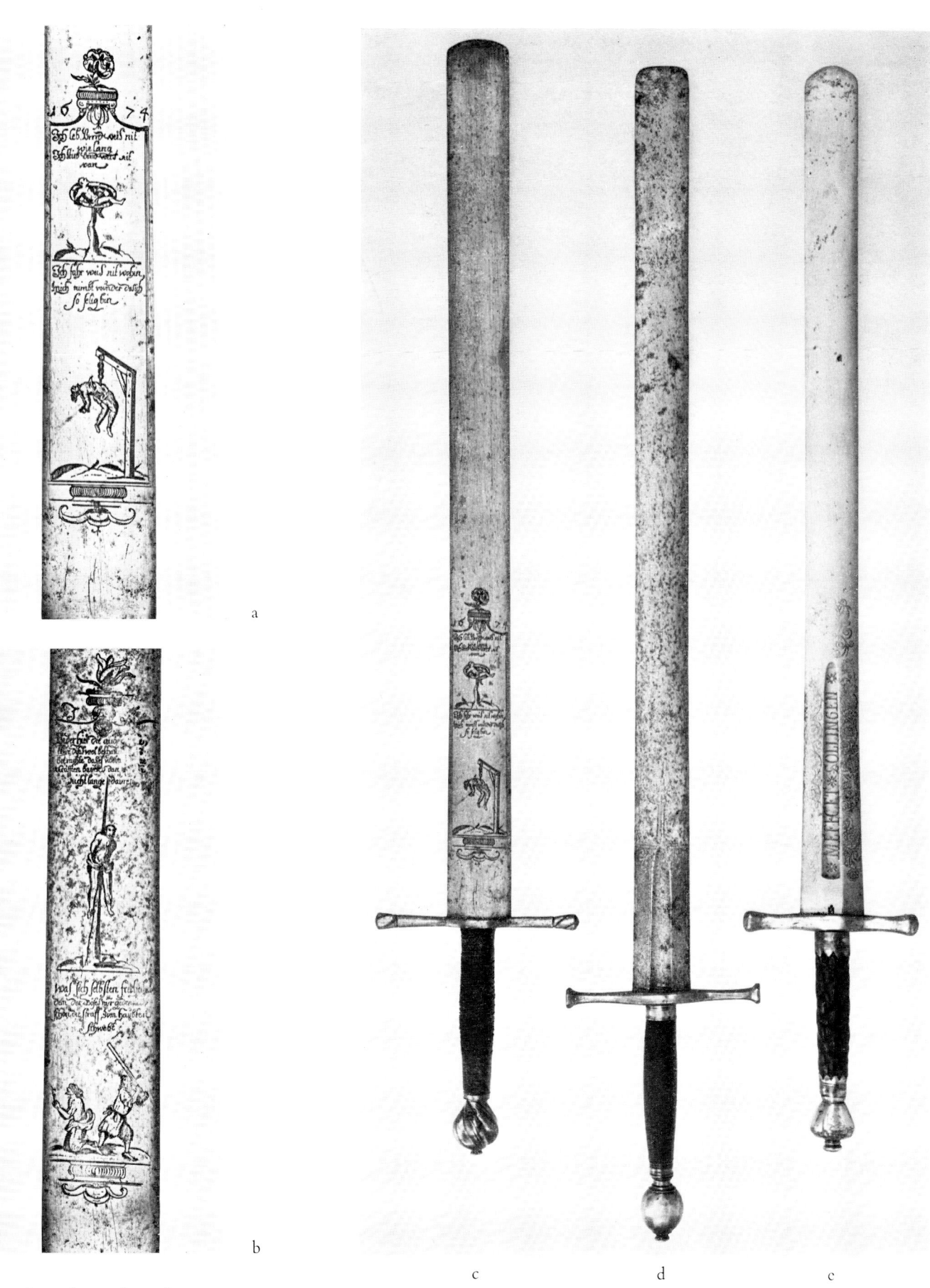

Executioners' swords, 17th century.
PLATE 12

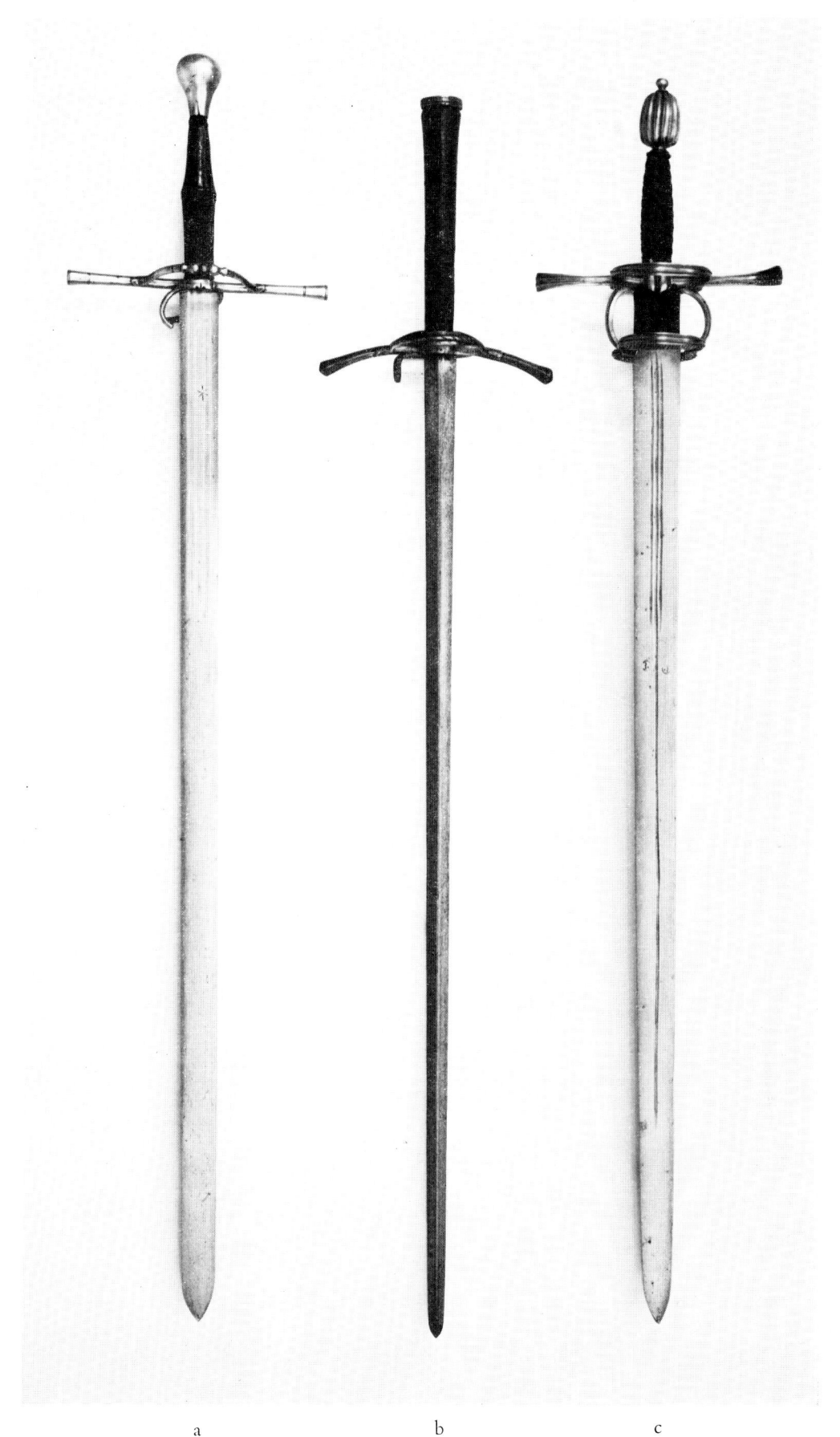

a b c
German hand-and-half swords, 16th century.

PLATE 13

a b c
Hand-and-half swords: (a) German, *c.* 1550; (b) German, *c.* 1600; (c) Italian, *c.* 1550.

PLATE 14

a b c
Short swords, 15th–16th centuries.

PLATE 15

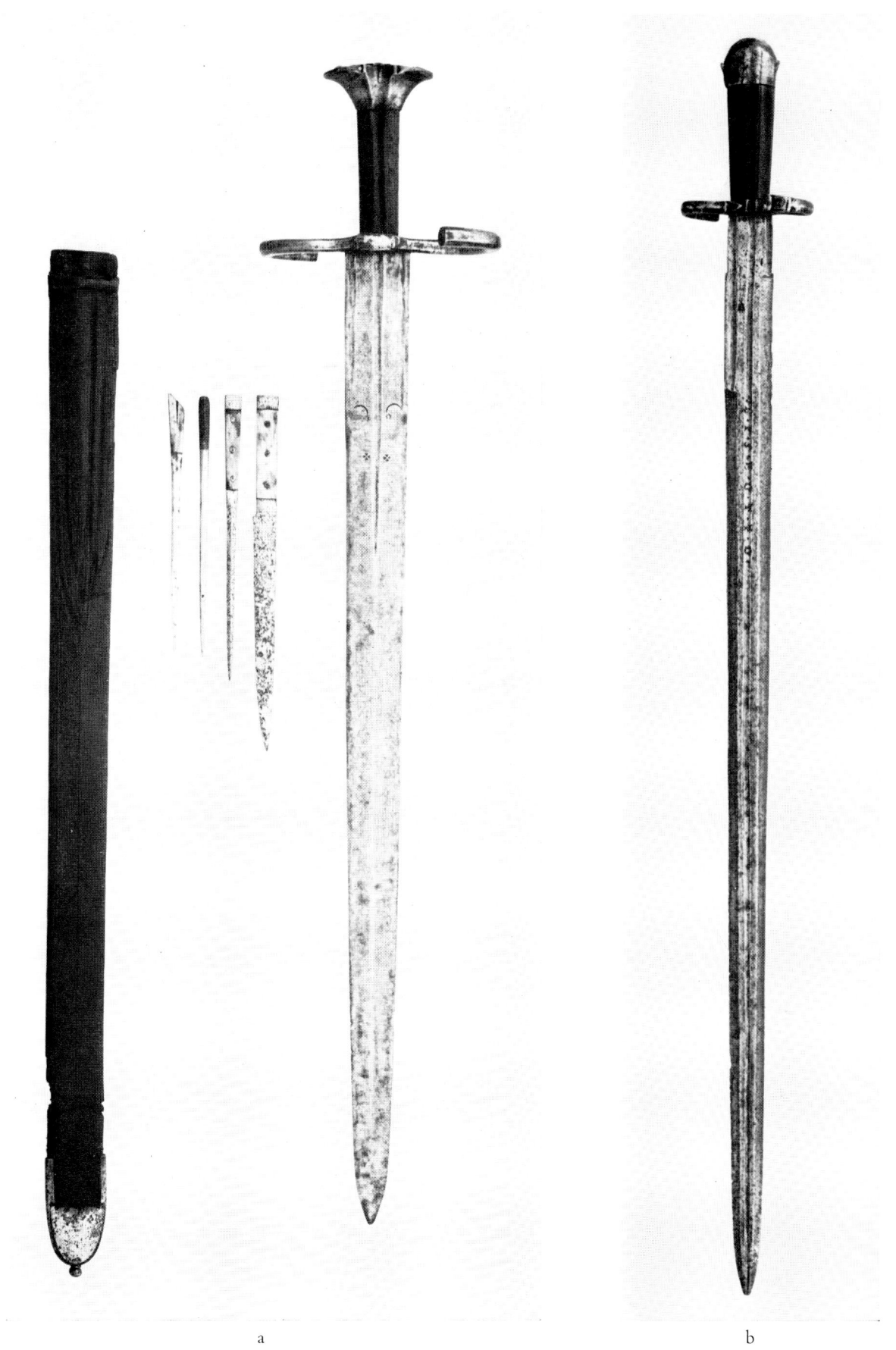

a b
Landsknecht swords, early 16th century.

PLATE 16

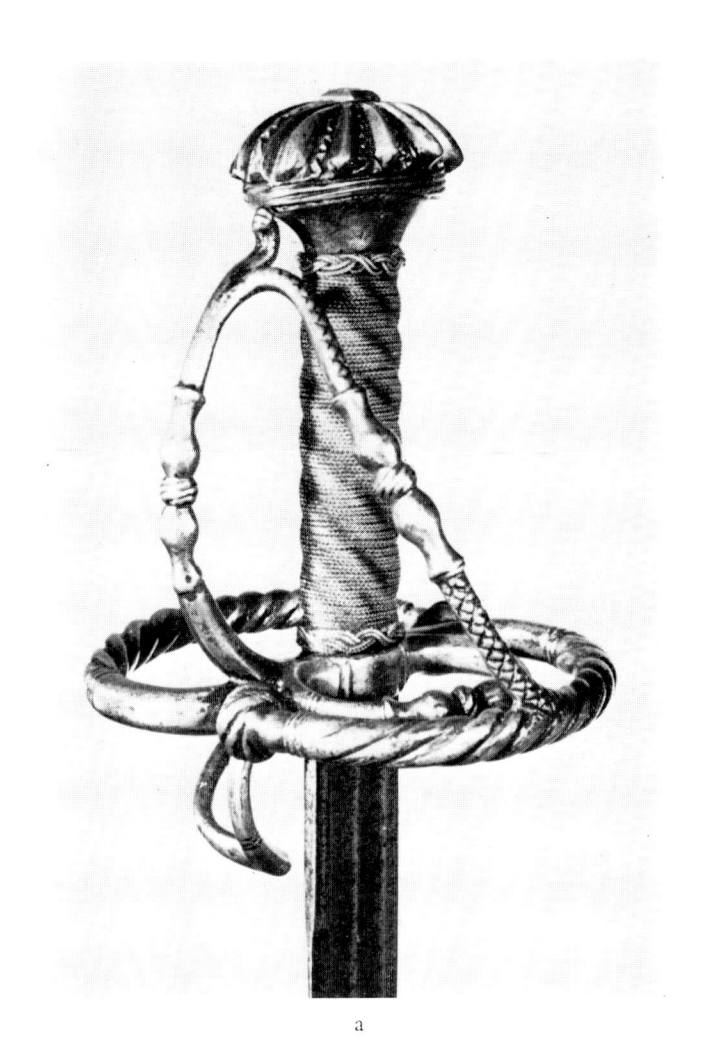

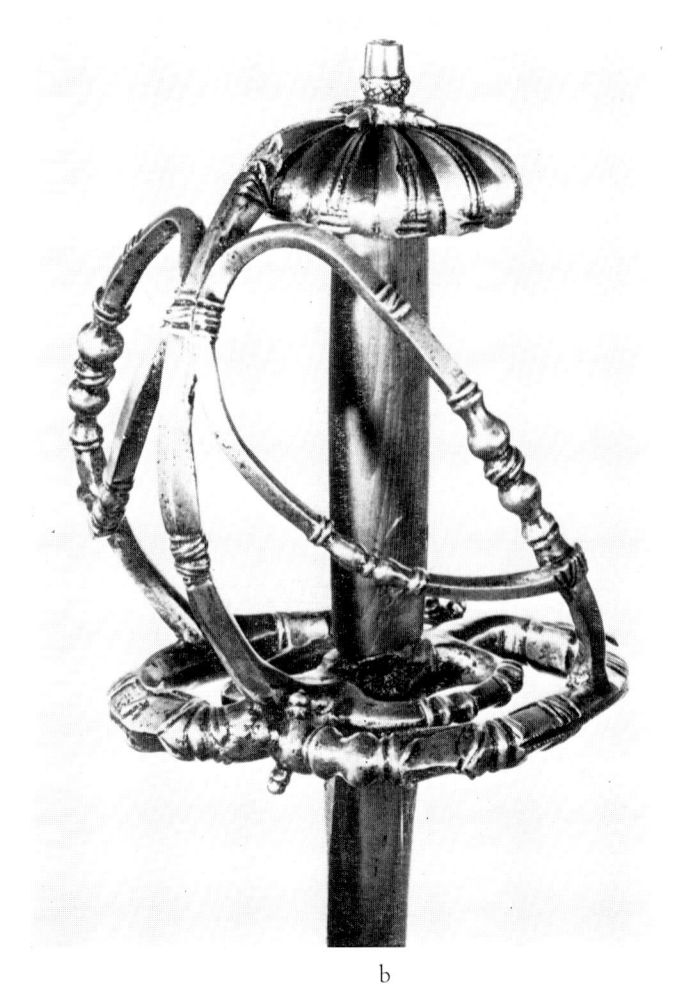

Landsknecht swords.
(a) c.1540; (b) early 17th century

PLATE 17

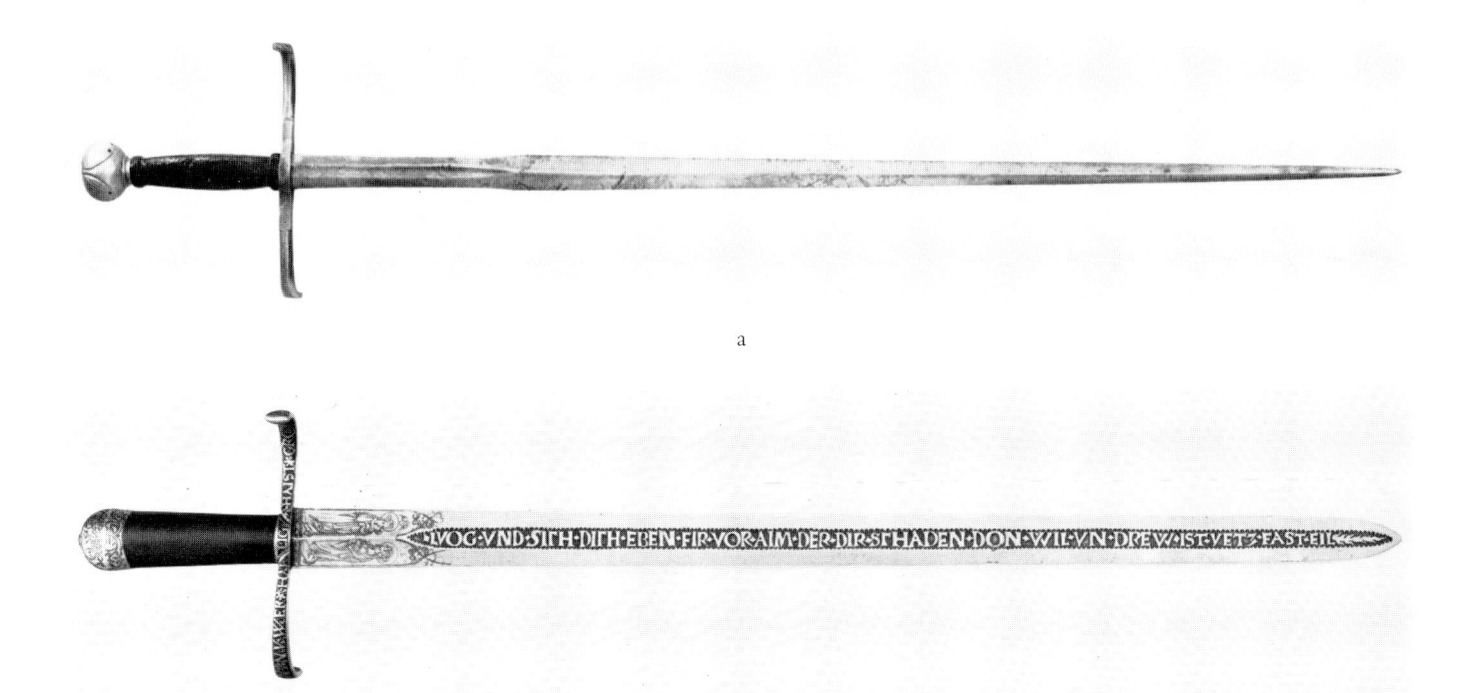

(a) Estoc, *c.* 1500; (b, c) Landsknecht sword, *c.* 1500; (d) Italian sword, *c.* 1540.
PLATE 18

(a) Italian sword, c. 1560; (b, c) Cinquedeas, early 16th century.

PLATE 19

a b

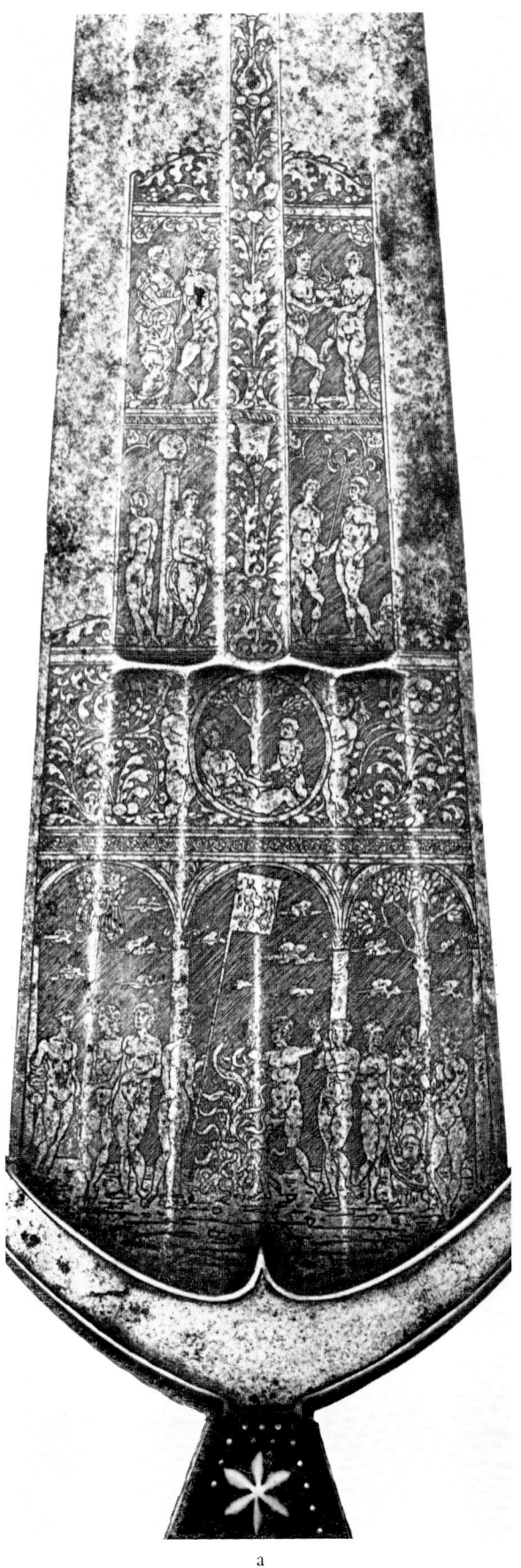

Cinquedeas, early 16th century.

PLATE 20

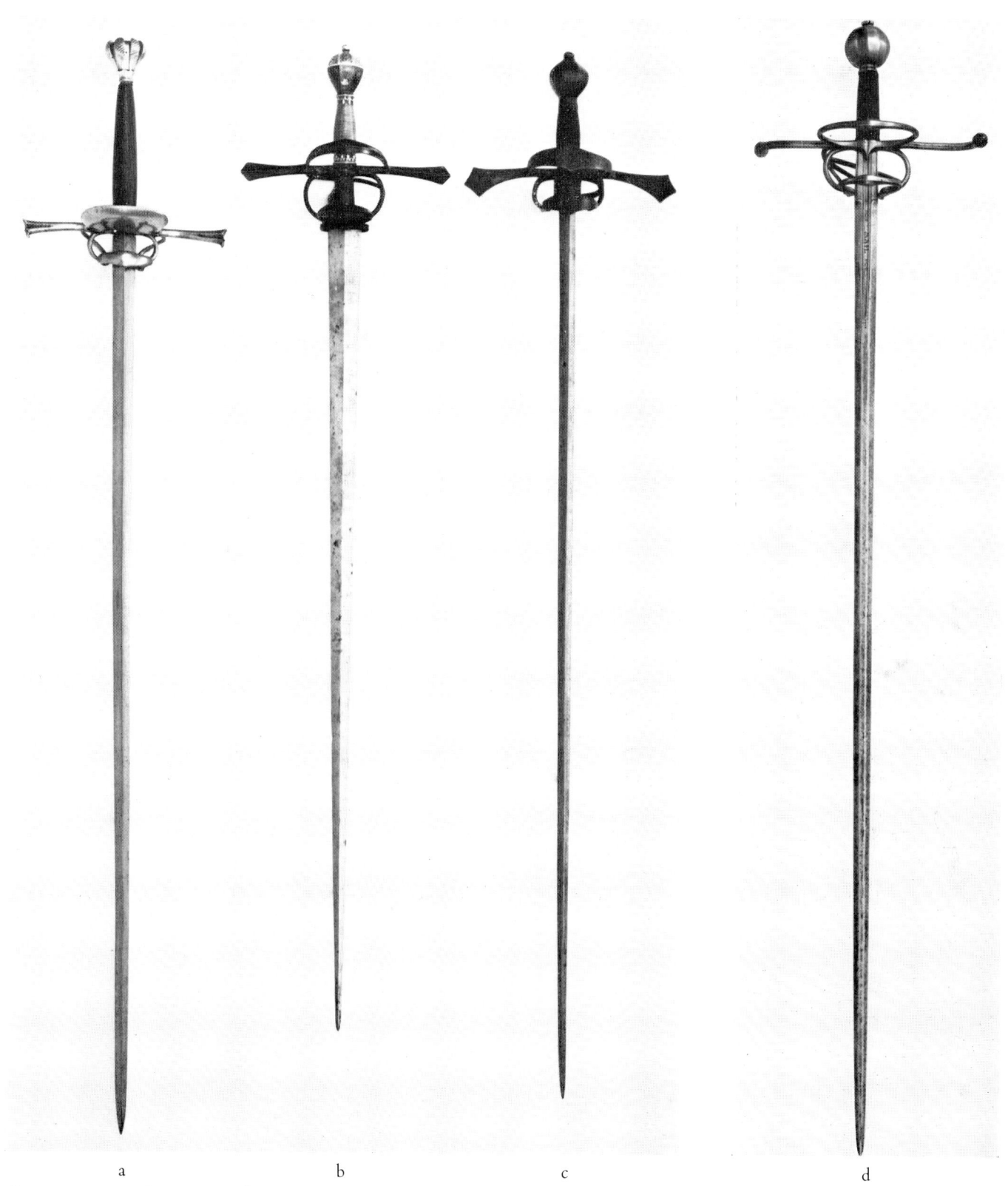

a b c d
German estocs and rapiers, 16th century.

PLATE 21

Saxon sword-rapier, late 16th century.

PLATE 22

a

b

(a) Three mediaeval sword pommels; (b) 16th-century pommel and sword hangers.

PLATE 23

a

b

c

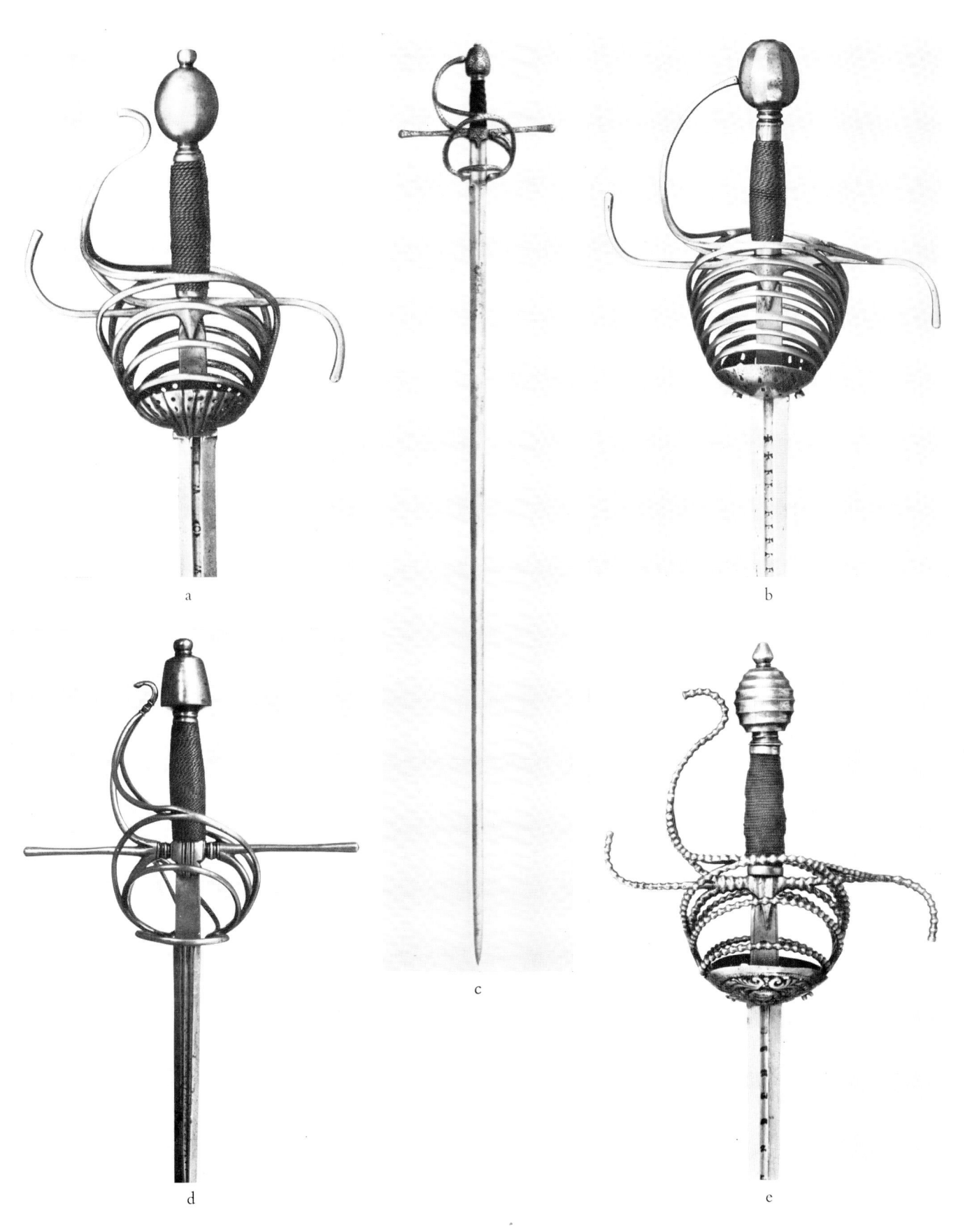

d

e

Military rapiers, late 16th century.

PLATE 24

a

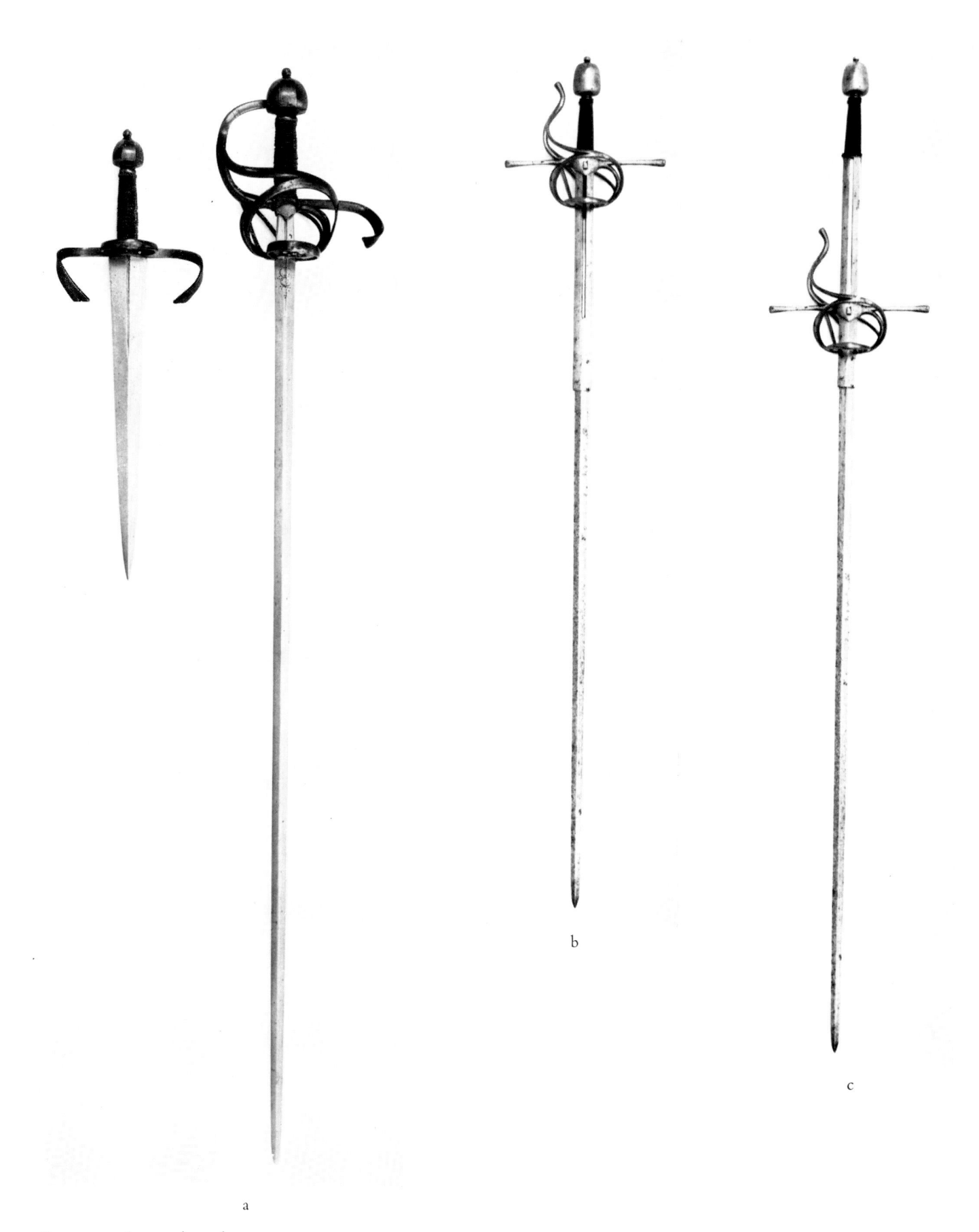

German rapiers, early 17th century.

b

c

PLATE 25

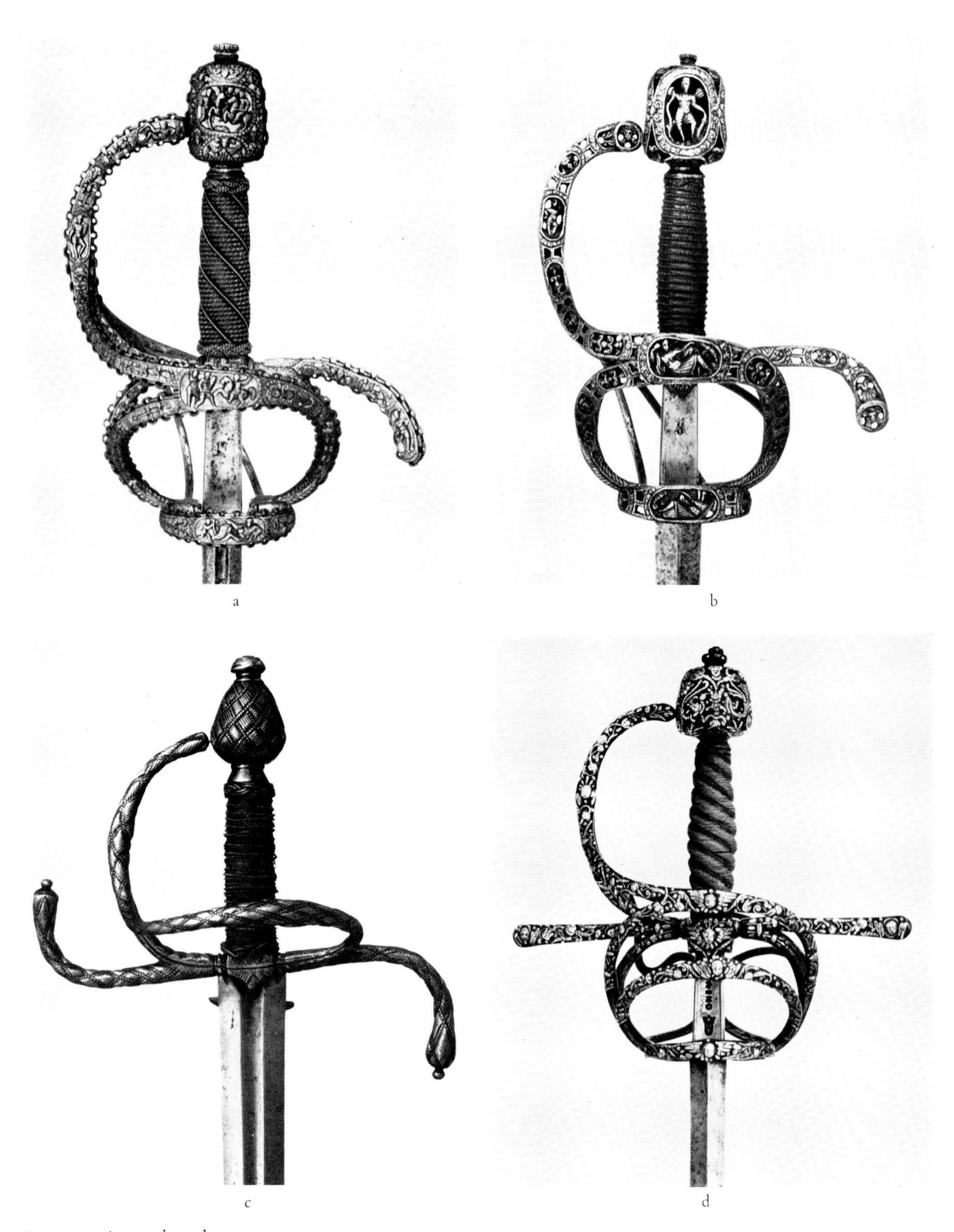

German rapiers, early 17th century.

PLATE 26

a

b

c

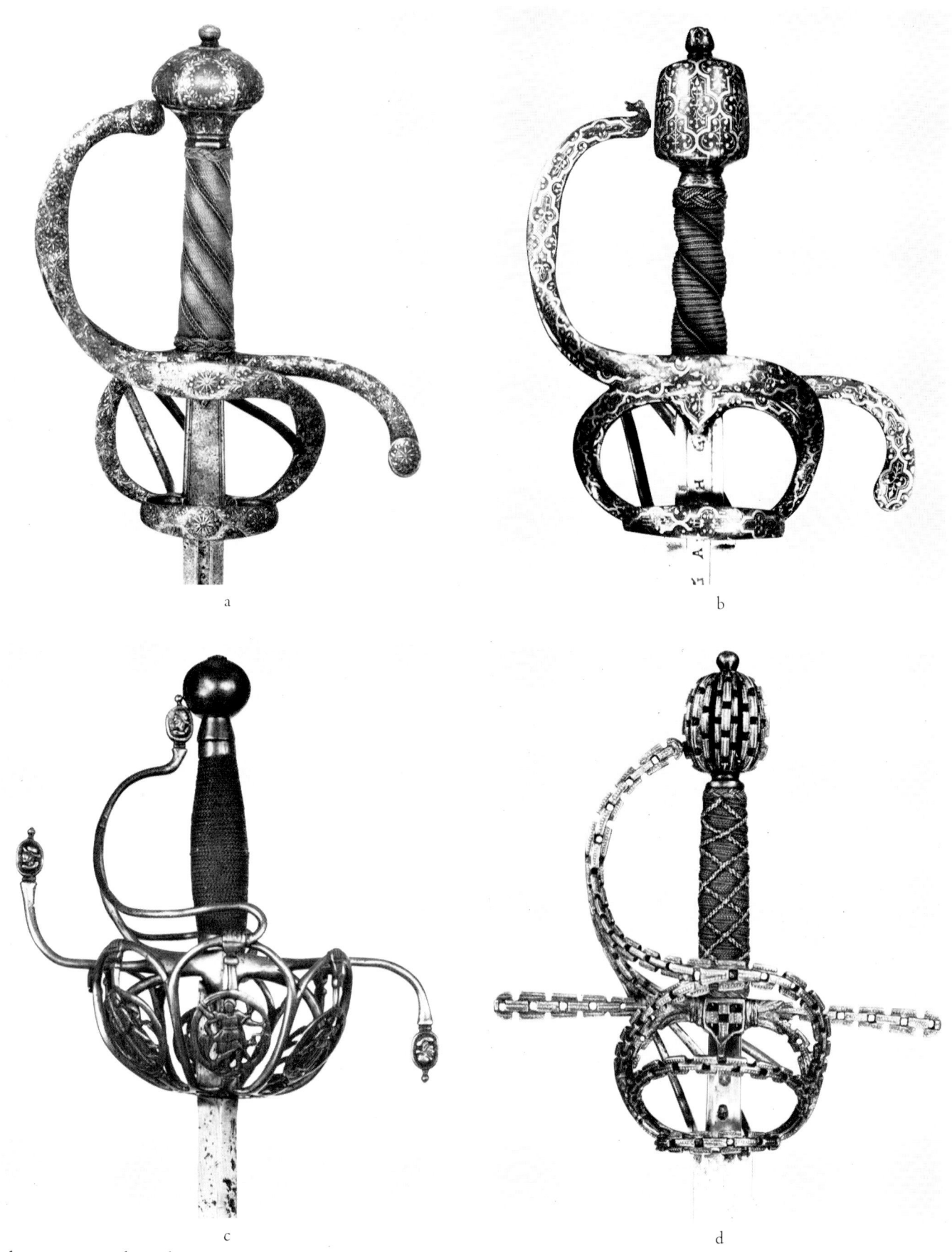

d

Italian rapiers, early 17th century.

PLATE 27

a b

c d

English rapiers, first half of the 17th century.

PLATE 28

Rapiers of the first half of the 17th century: (a–c) English, (d) Dutch.

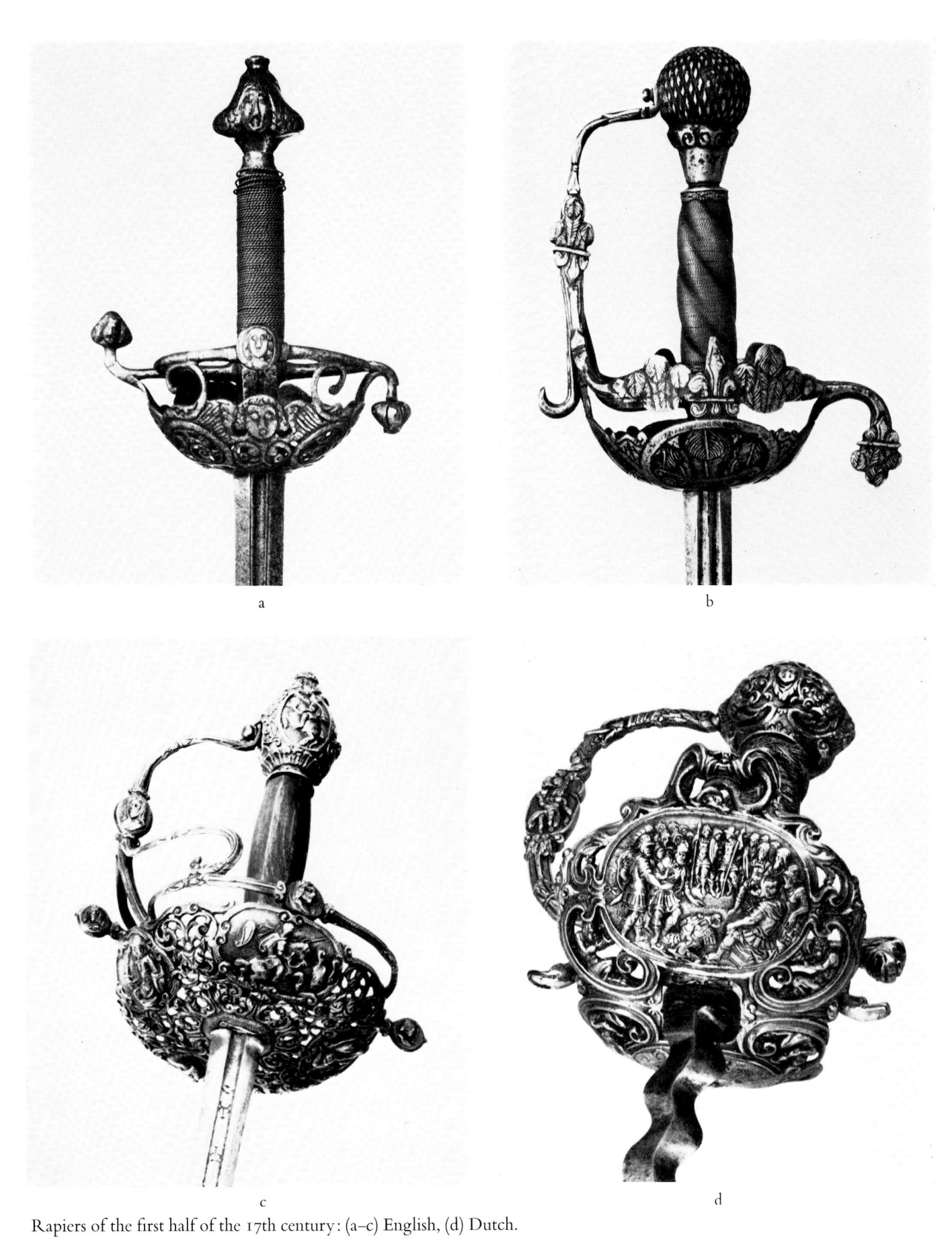

a

b

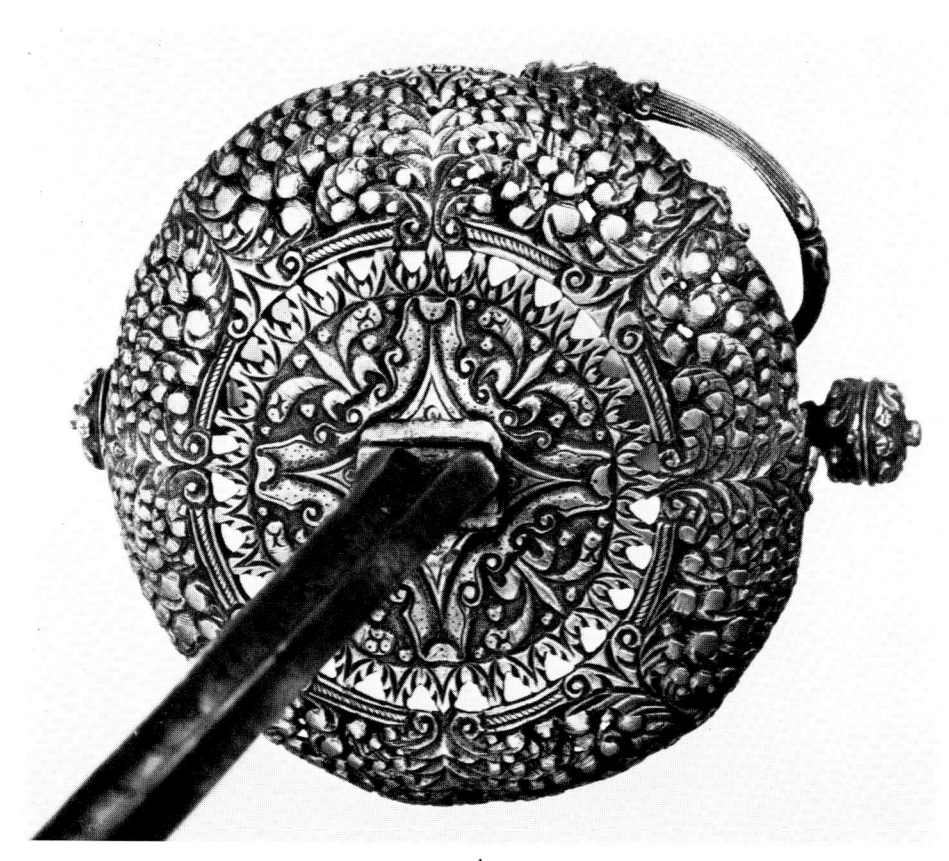

English rapiers, mid 17th century.

PLATE 30

Sword rapiers, 17th century.

PLATE 31

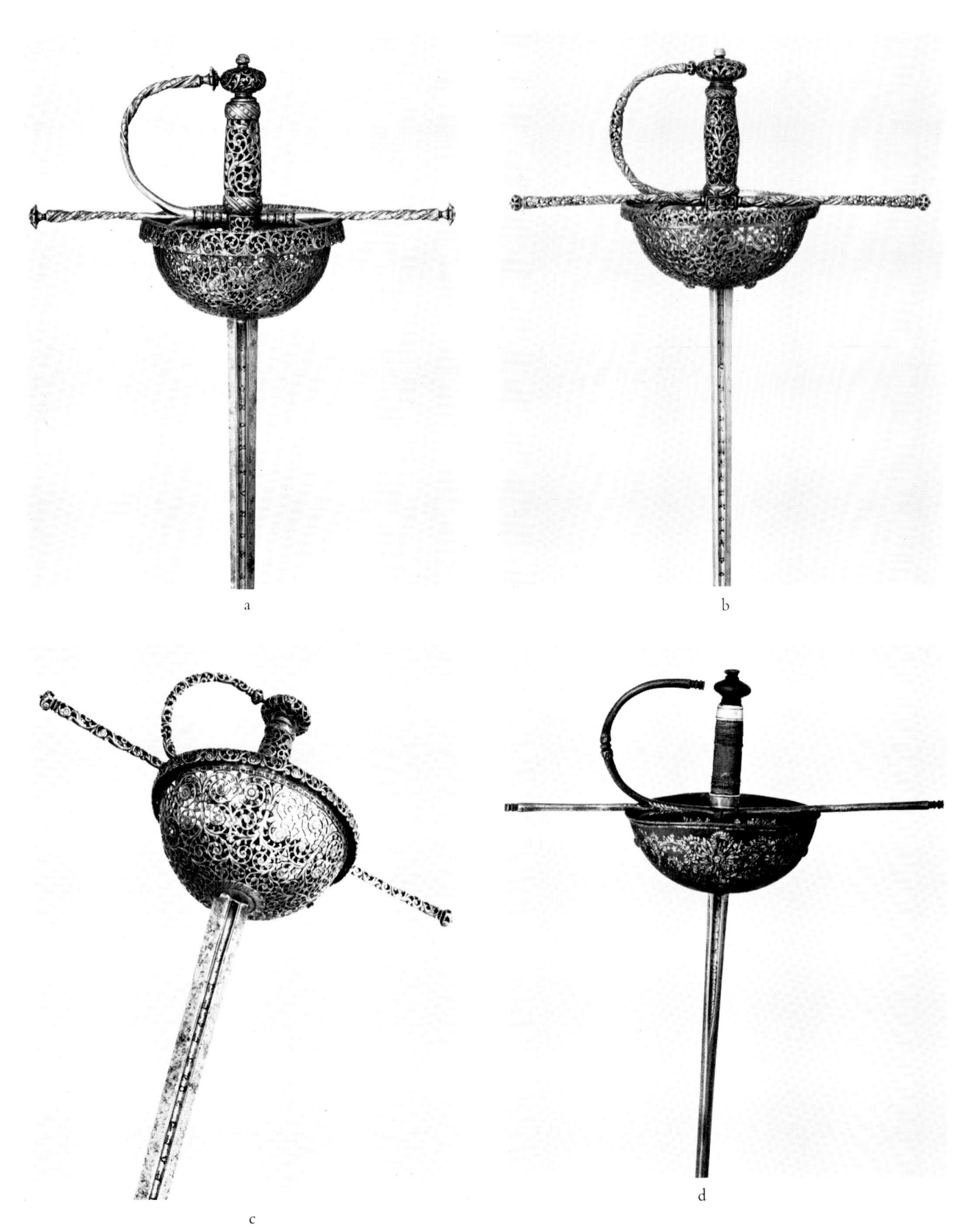

a

b

c

d

Spanish cup-hilt rapiers, 17th century.

PLATE 32

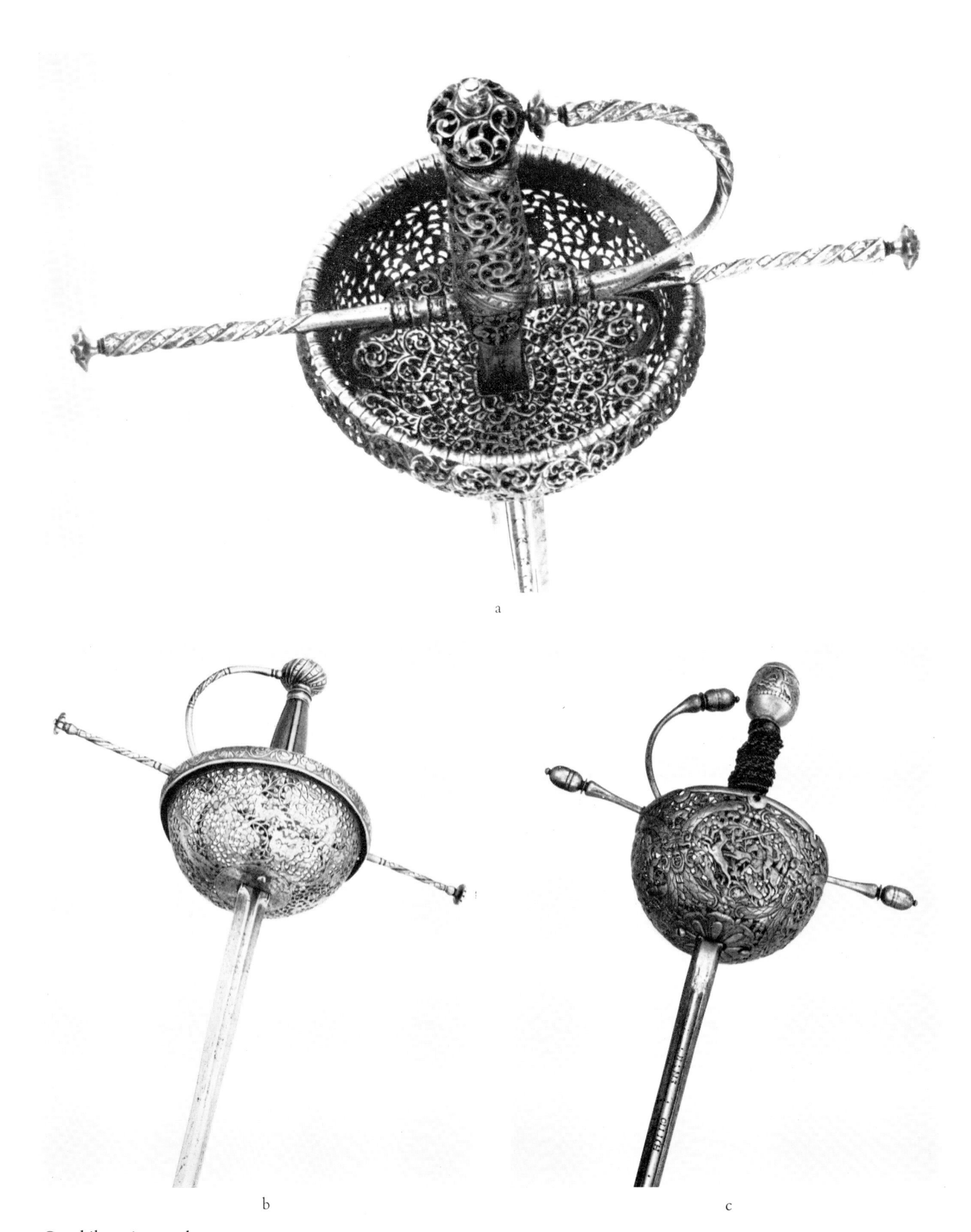

Cup-hilt rapiers, 17th century.

PLATE 33

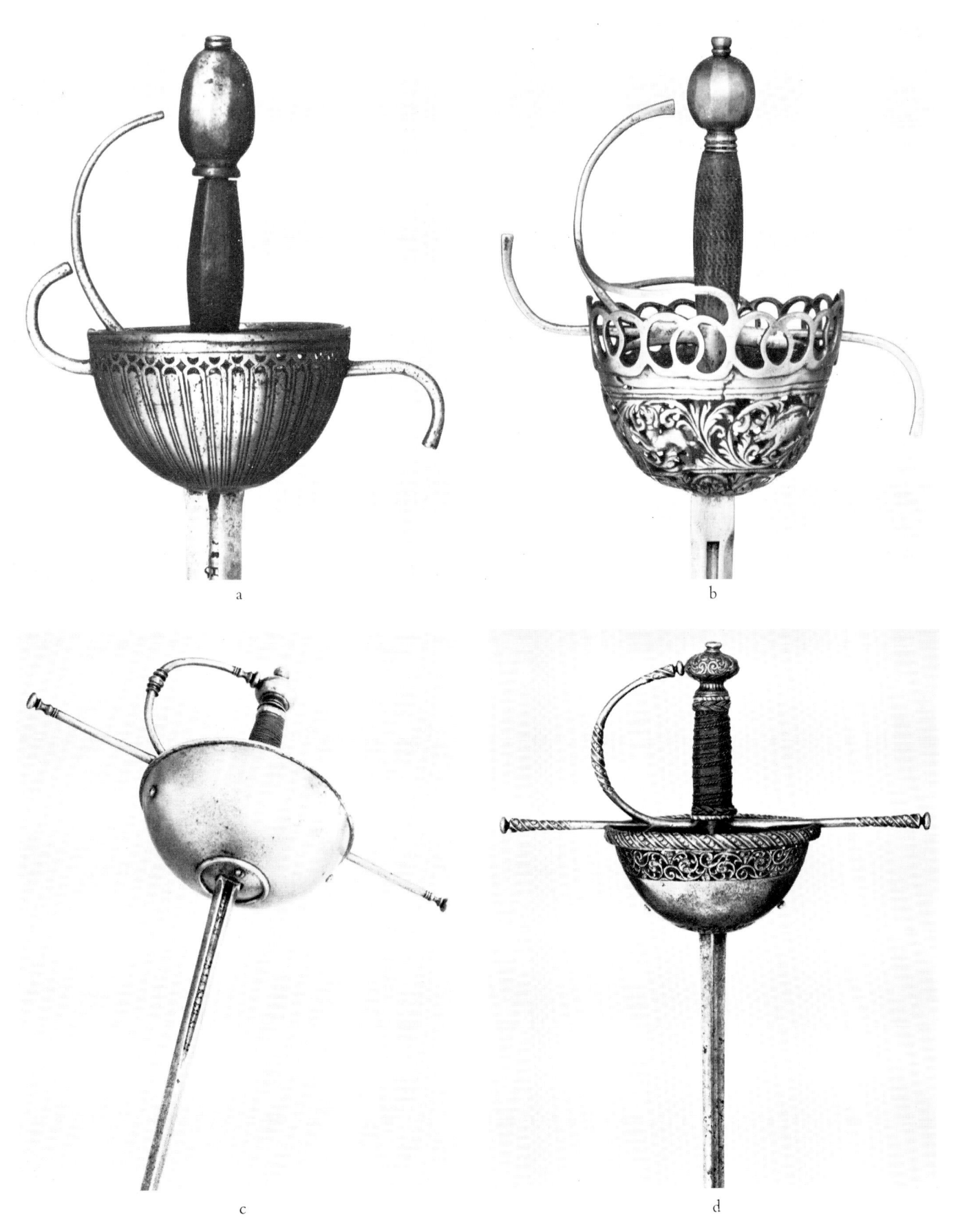

a

b

c

d

Cup-hilt rapiers, 17th century.

PLATE 34

Sword pommels, 16th century.

PLATE 37

a

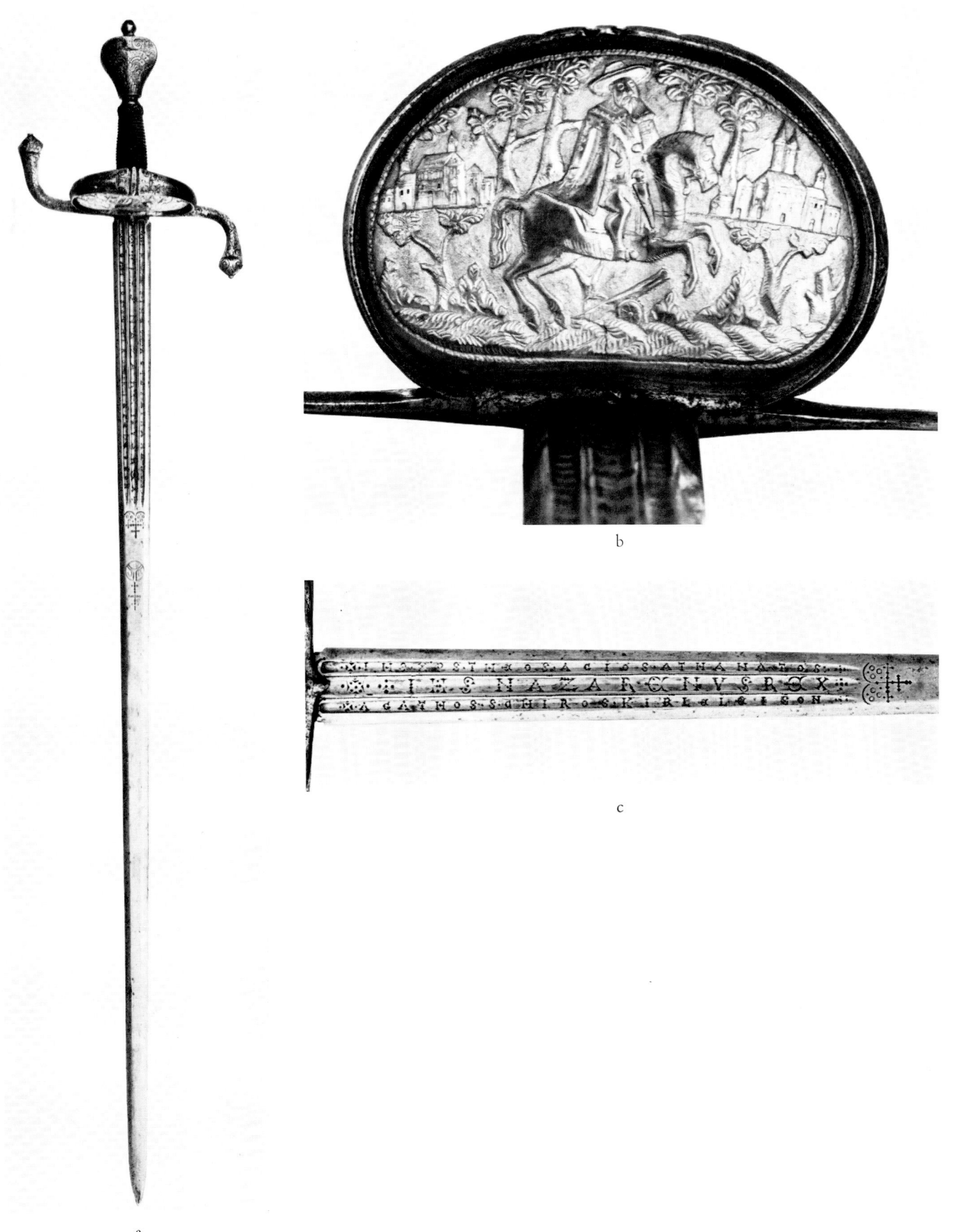

Broadsword, possibly Swedish, c. 1650.

PLATE 38

b

c

German broadswords, second half of 17th century.

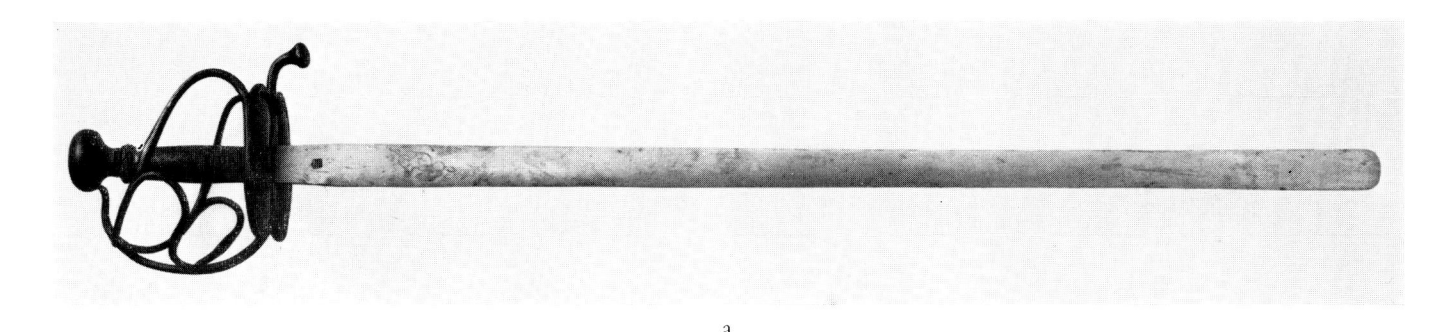

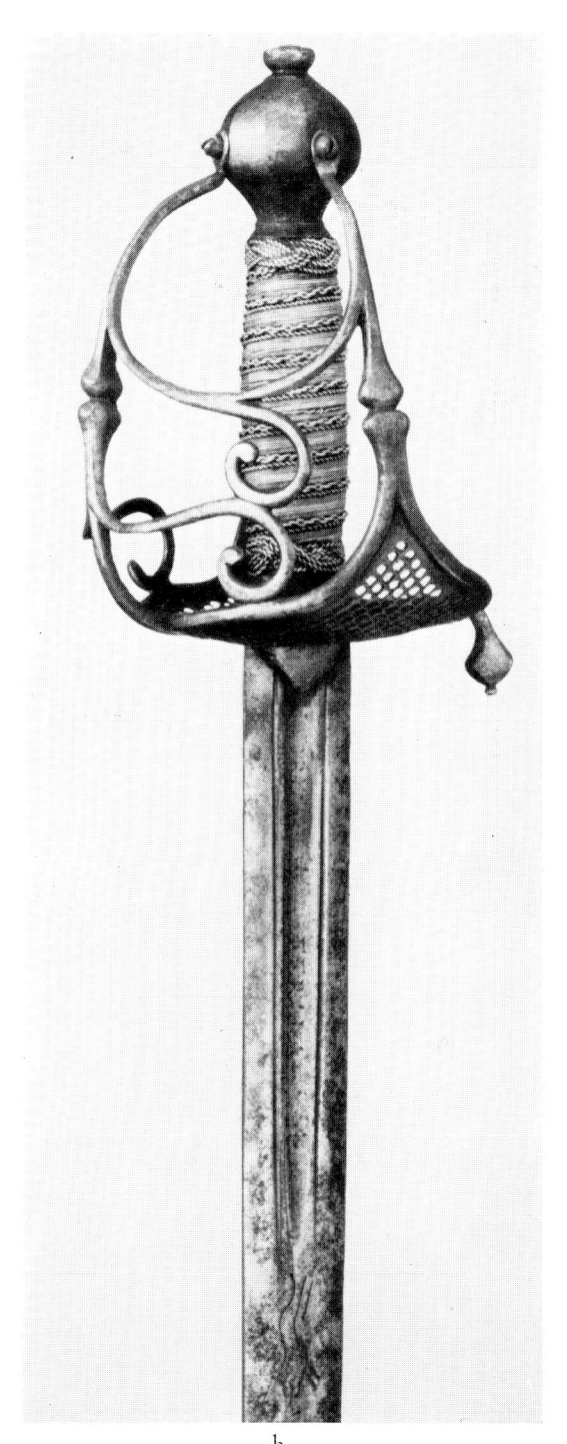

PLATE 39

a

b c d

German broadswords, mid 17th century.

PLATE 40

a

b

c

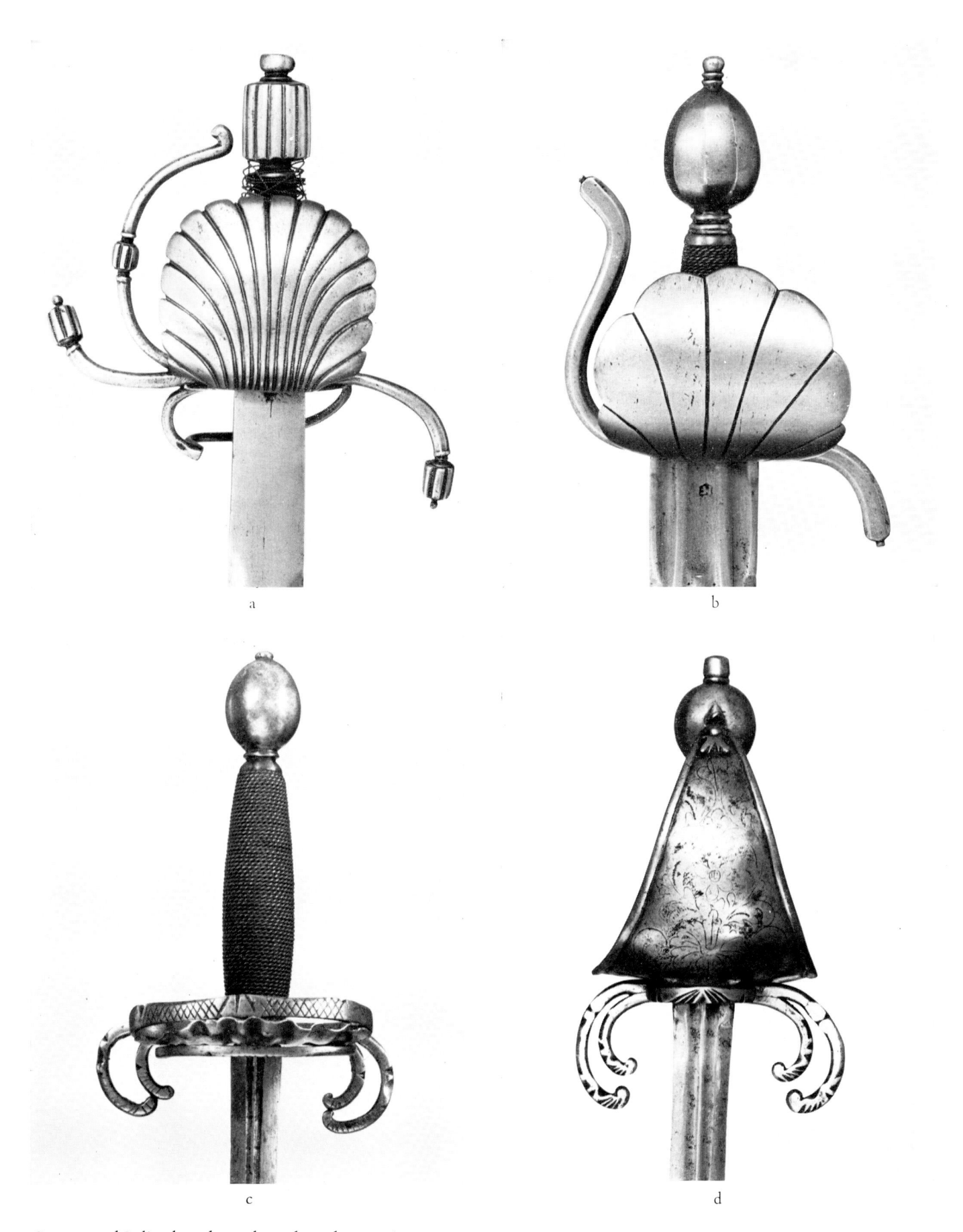

d

German and Italian broadswords, 16th–17th centuries.

PLATE 41

a

b

c

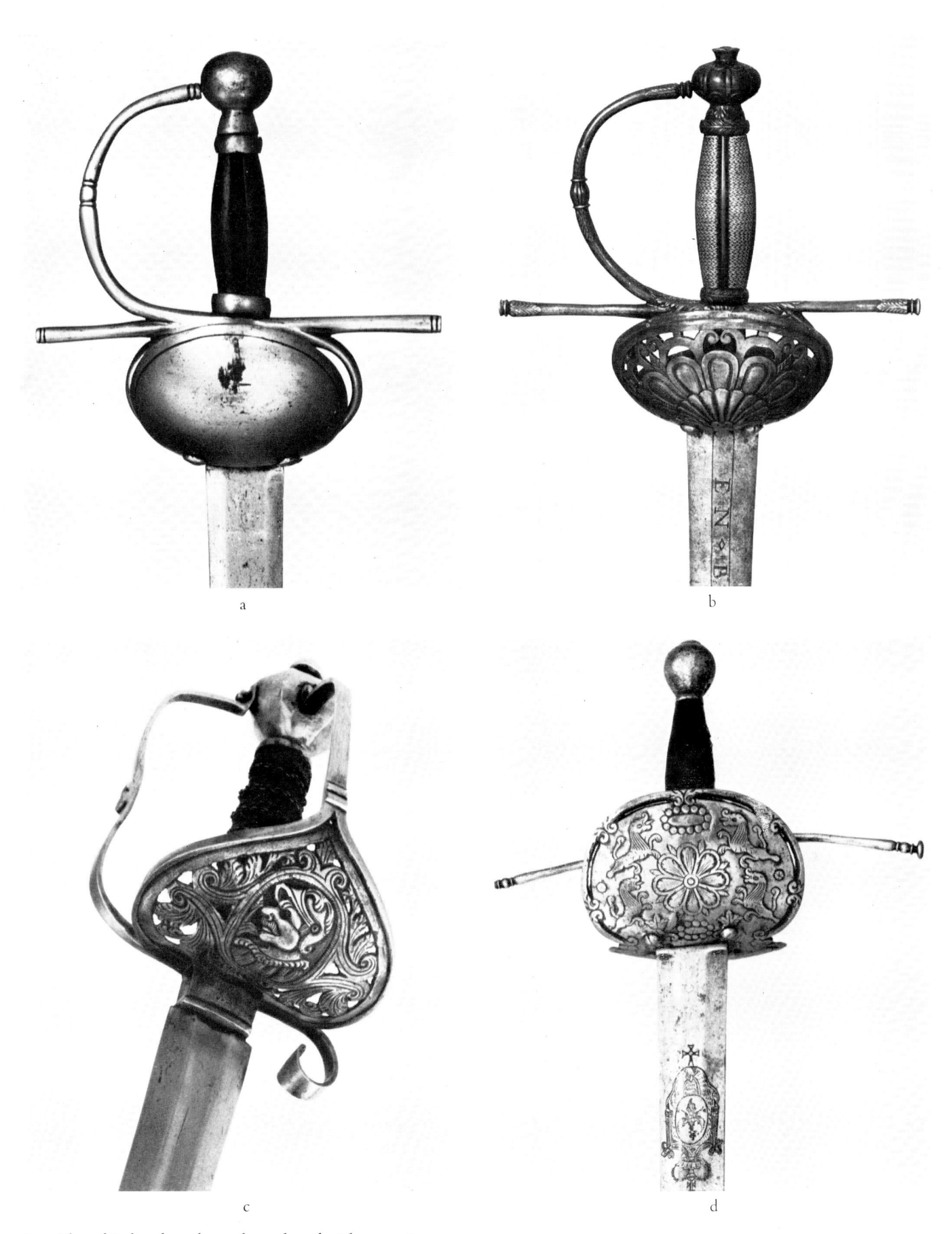

d

Spanish and Italian broadswords, 17th and 18th centuries.

PLATE 42

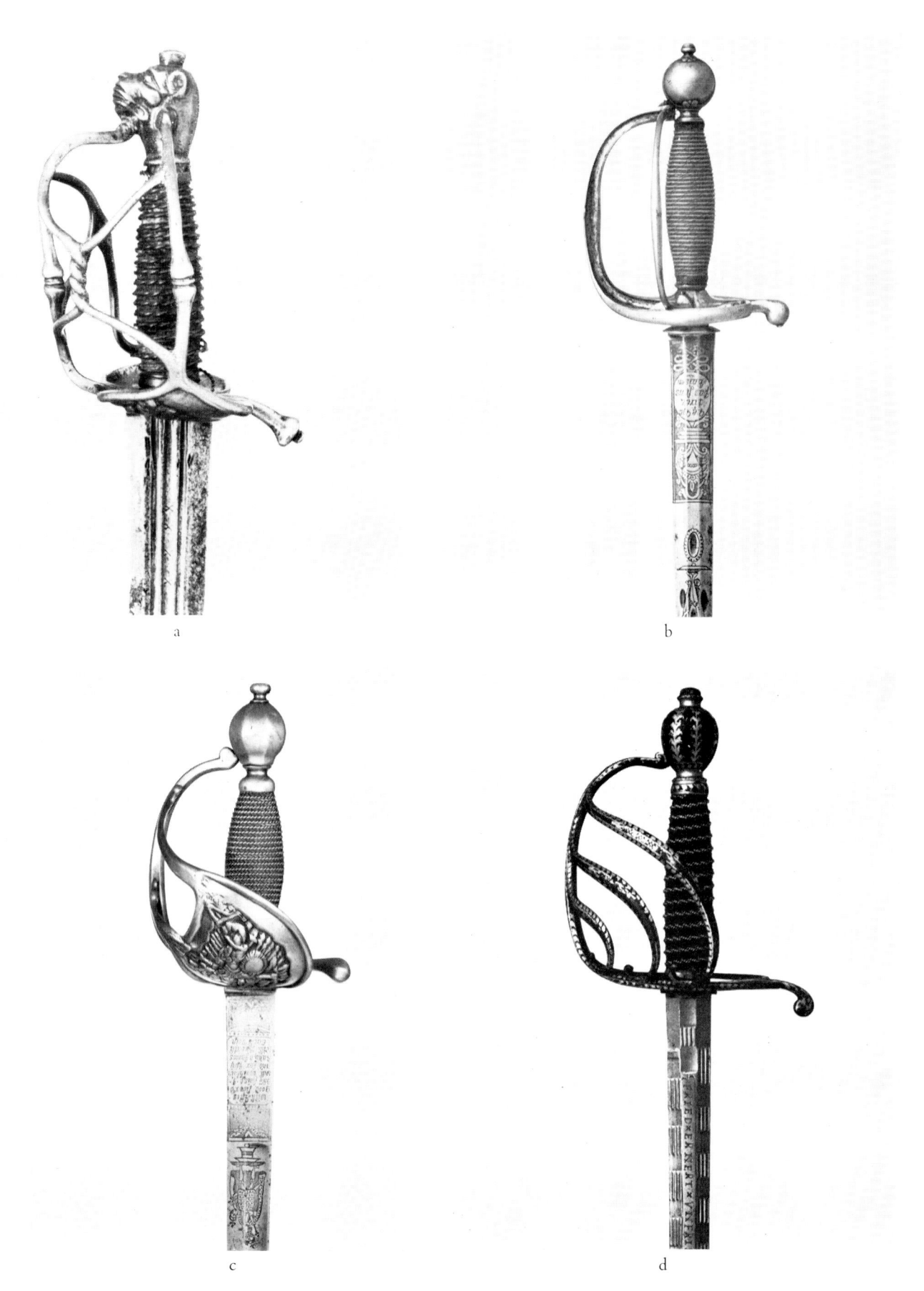

Broadswords: (a) Swiss, *c.* 1700; (b) French, *c.* 1720; (c) French, *c.* 1720; (d) Indian hilted sword, *c.* 1770.

PLATE 43

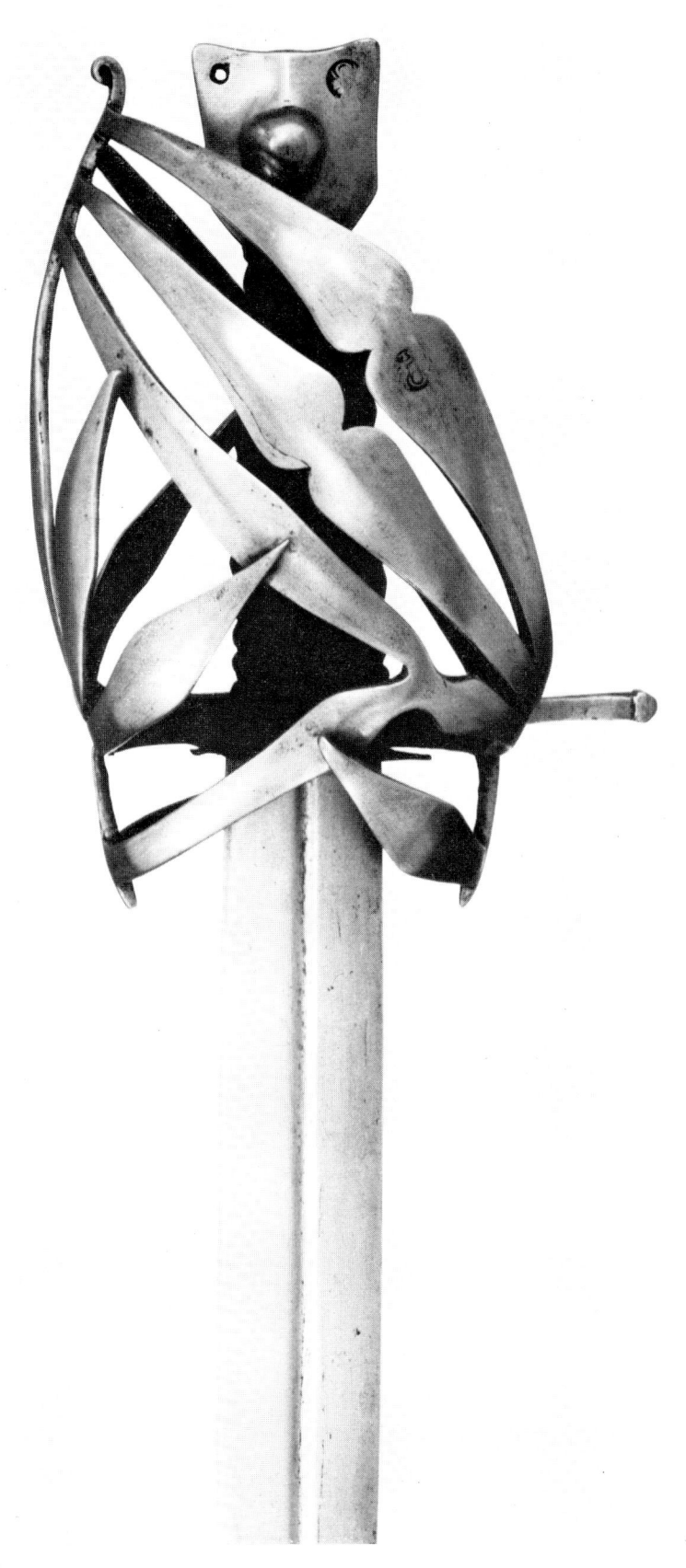

Italian schiavona, c. 1700.

PLATE 44

a  b
Italian schiavonas, 18th century.

PLATE 45

a

b

English sword, c. 1649.

PLATE 46

a

b

c

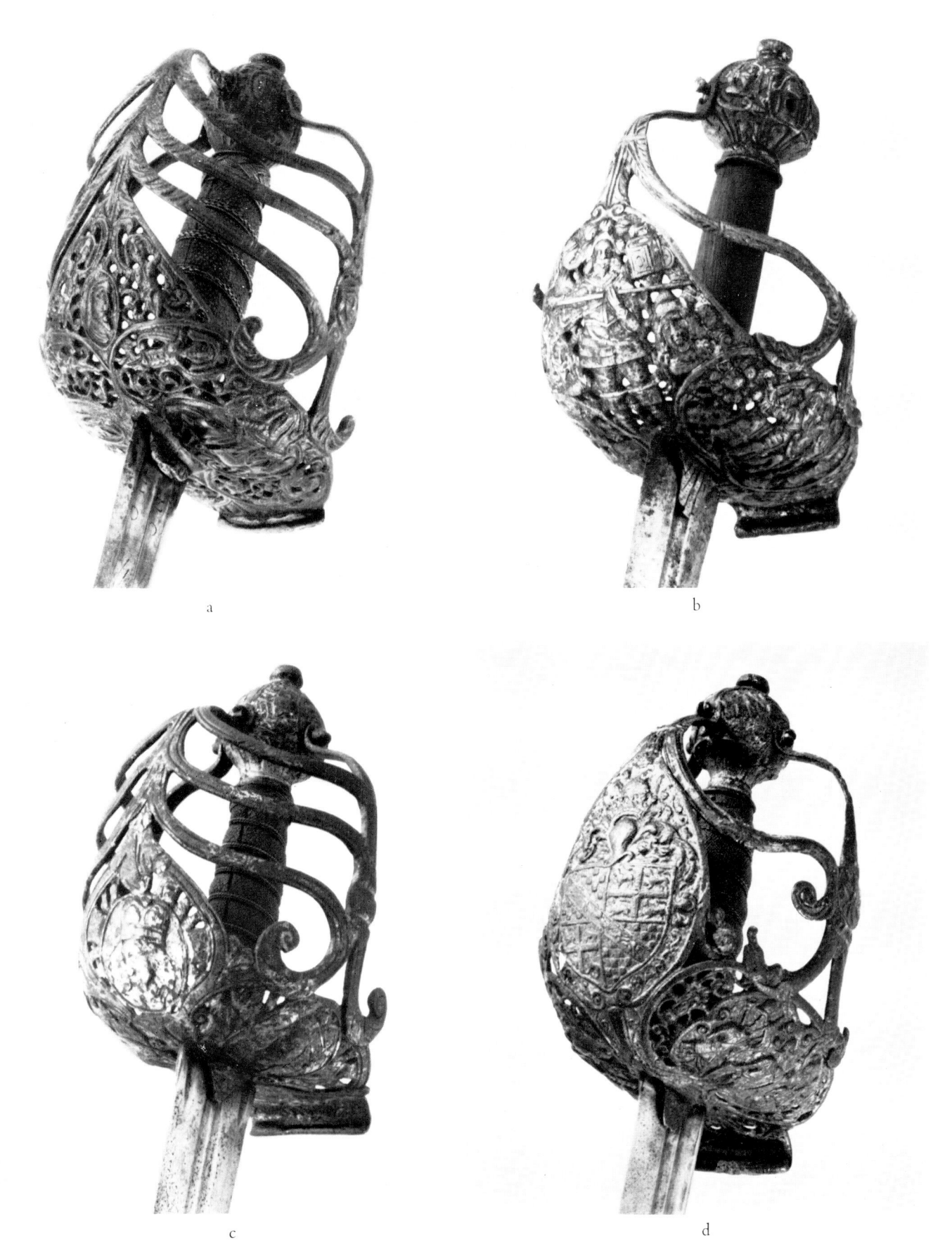

d

English broadswords, mid 17th century.

PLATE 47

a

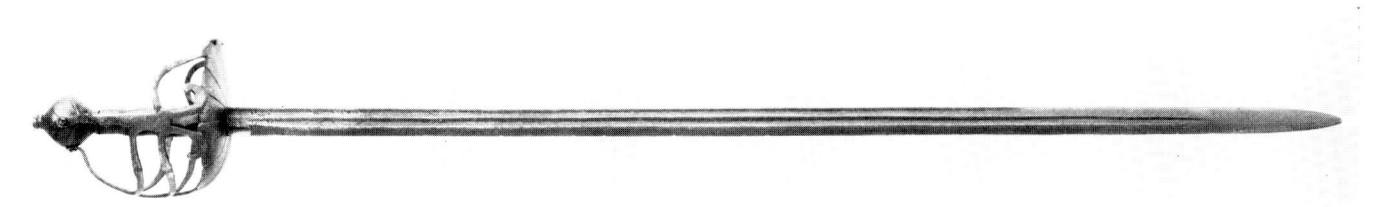

b

English swords, mid 17th century.

PLATE 48

a

b

c

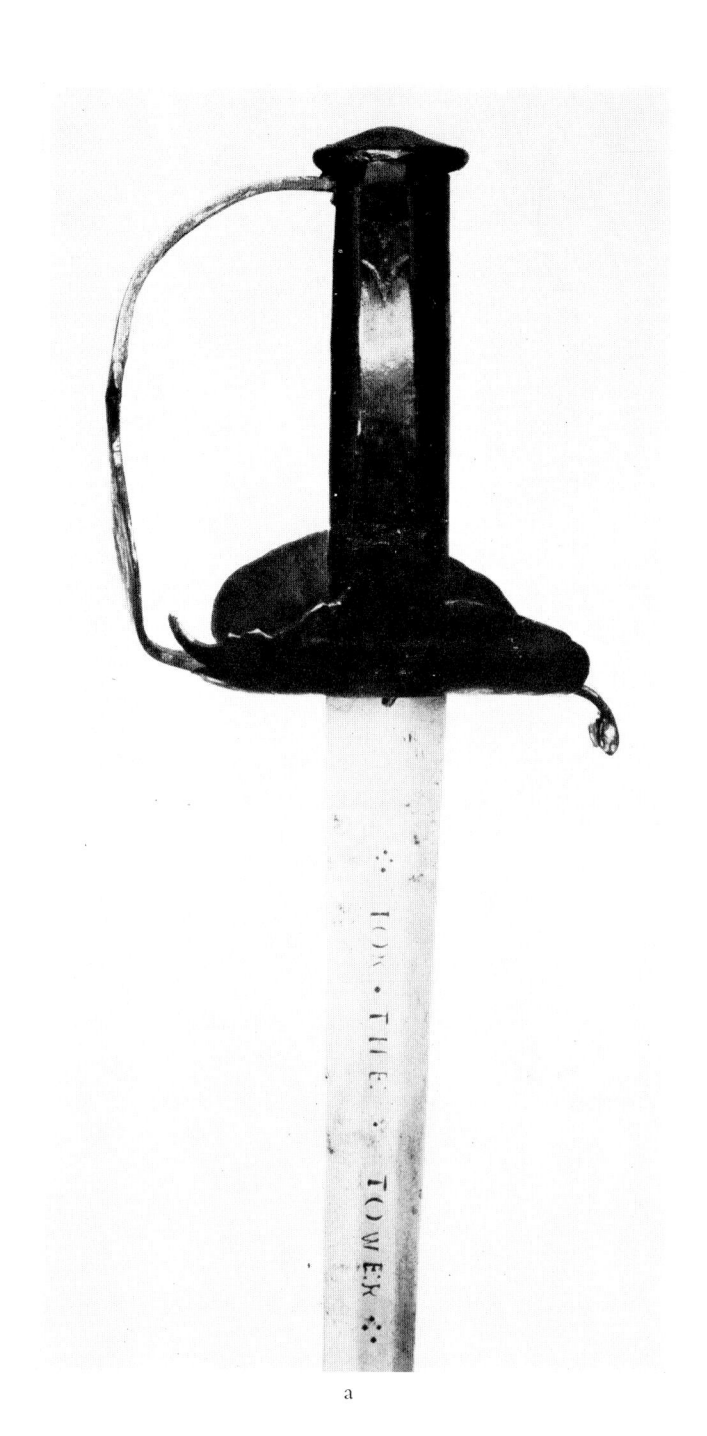

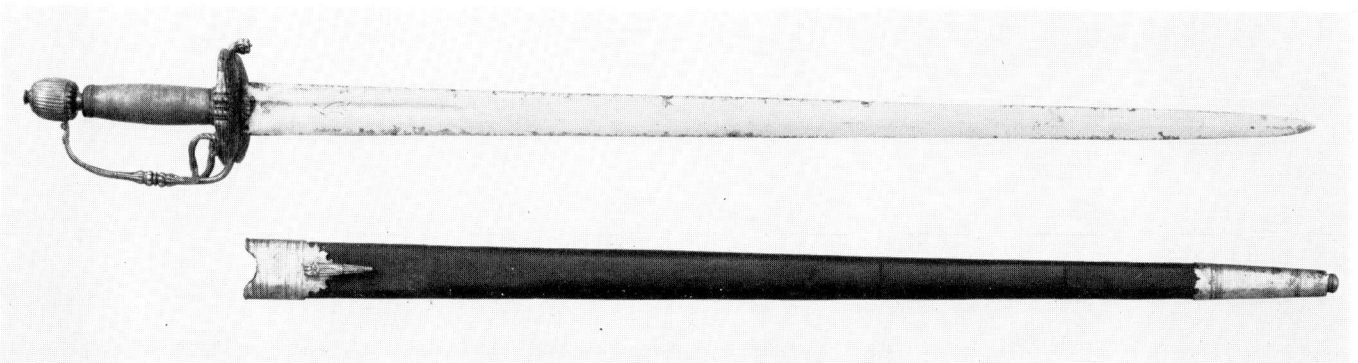

English broadswords, second half of the 17th century.

PLATE 49

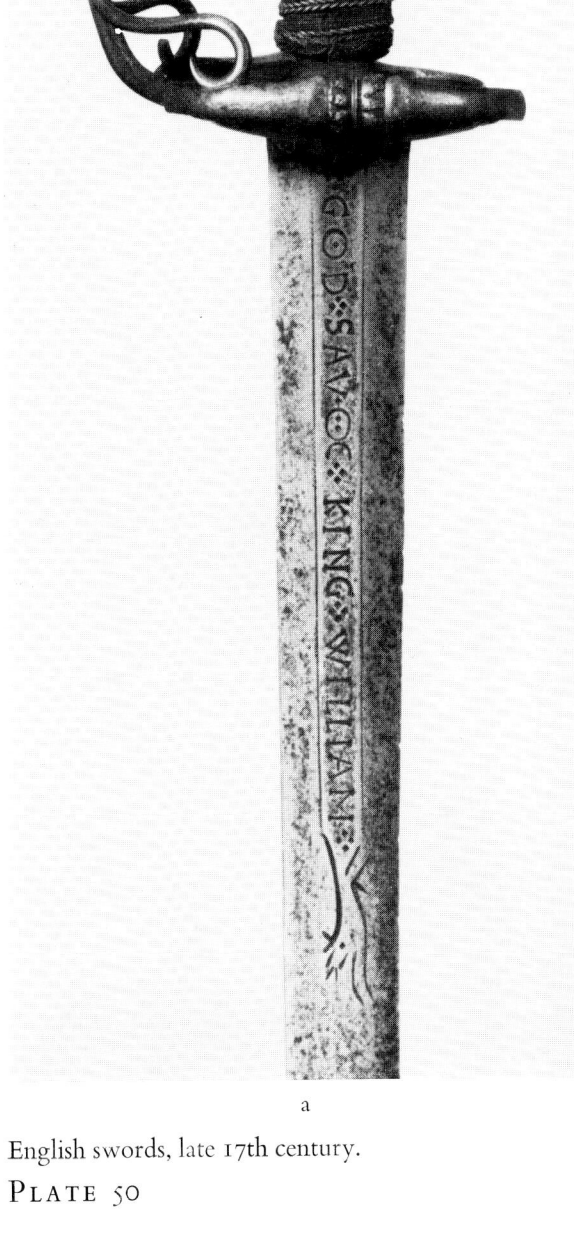

a

English swords, late 17th century.
PLATE 50

a

b

c

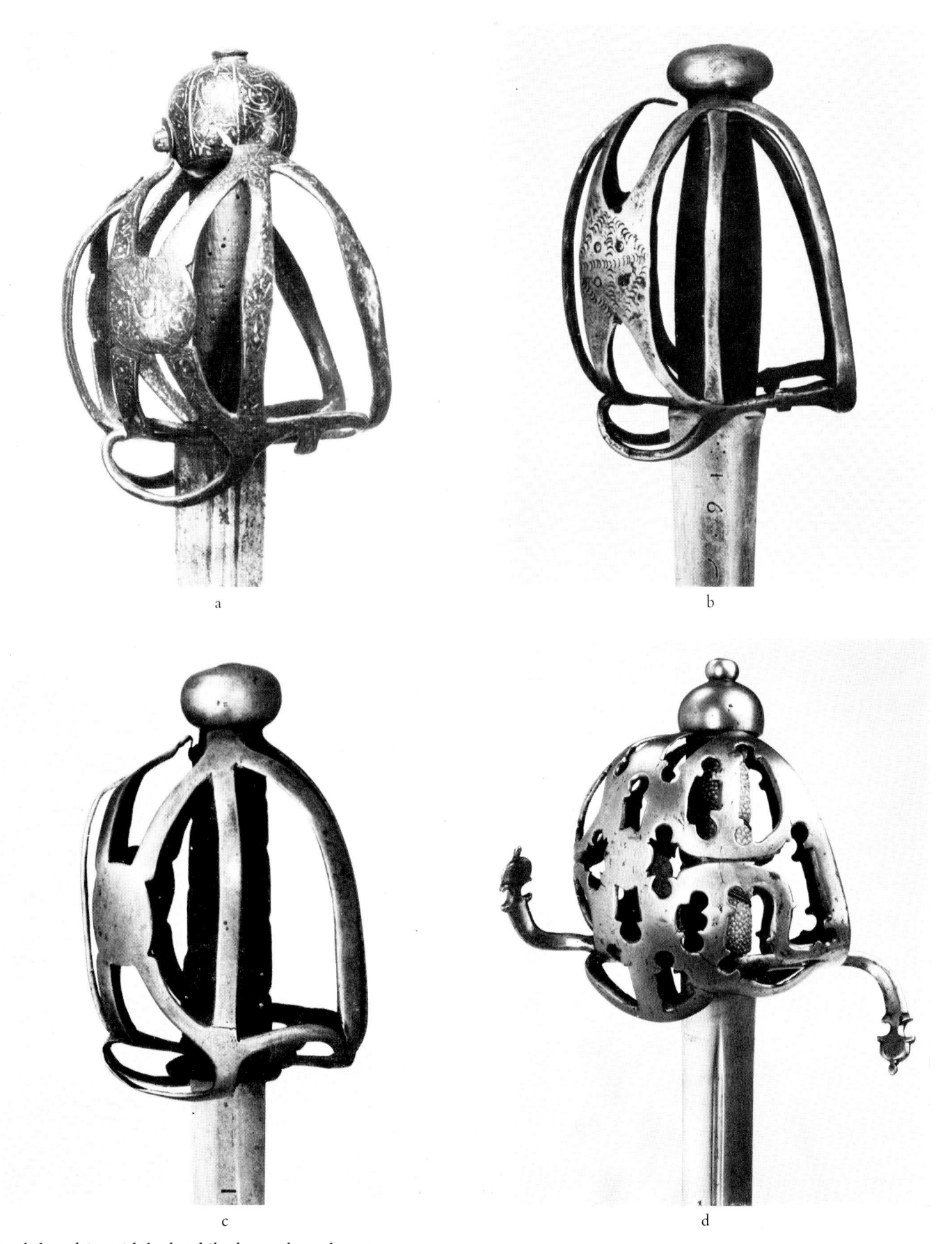

d

English and Scottish basket-hilted swords, 17th century.

PLATE 51

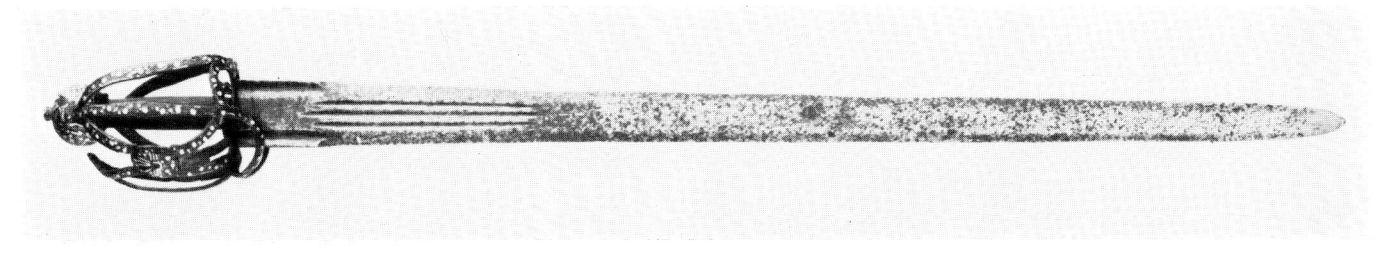

English and Scottish basket-hilted swords, early 17th century.

PLATE 52

a

b

c

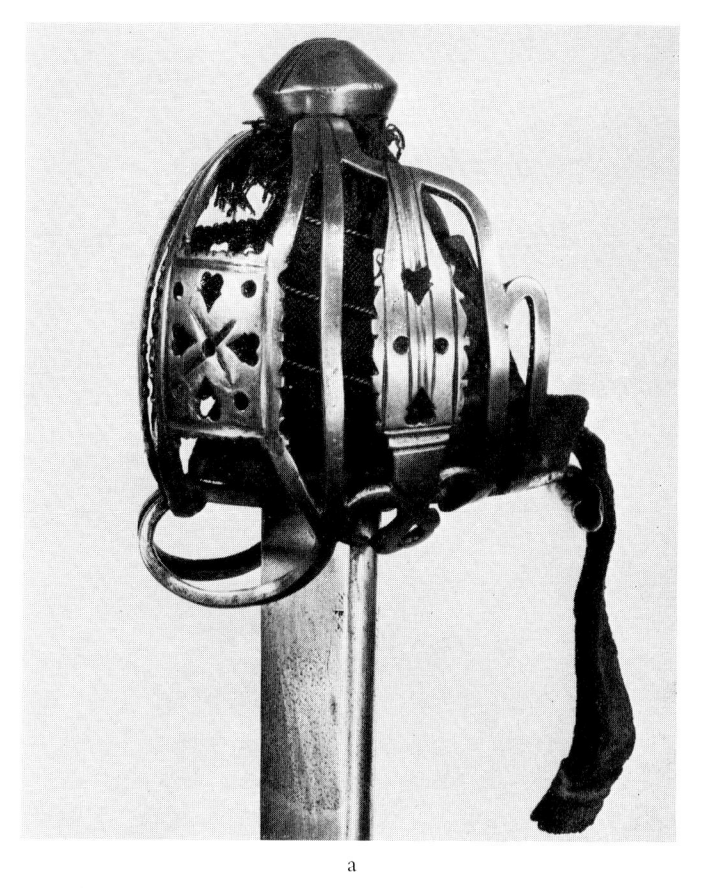

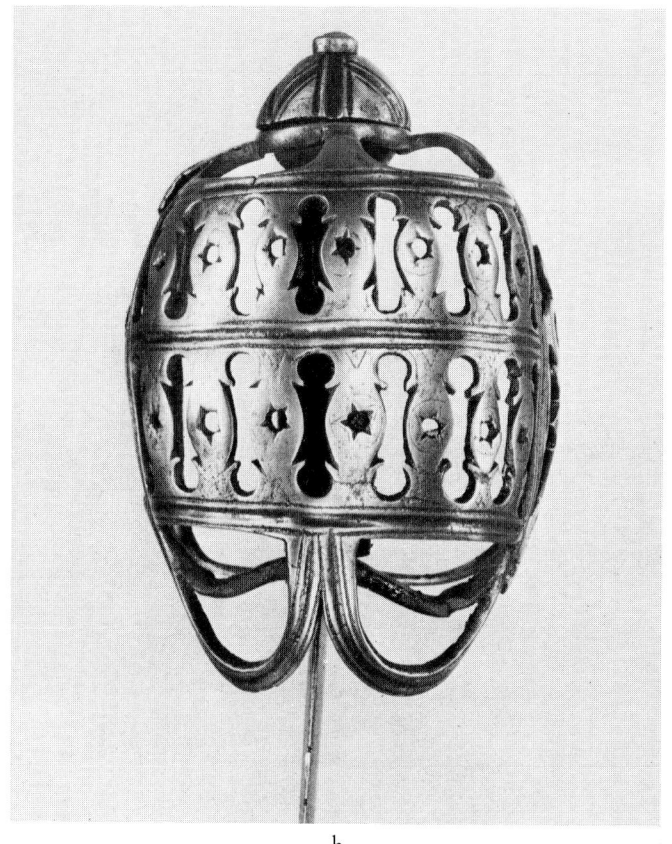

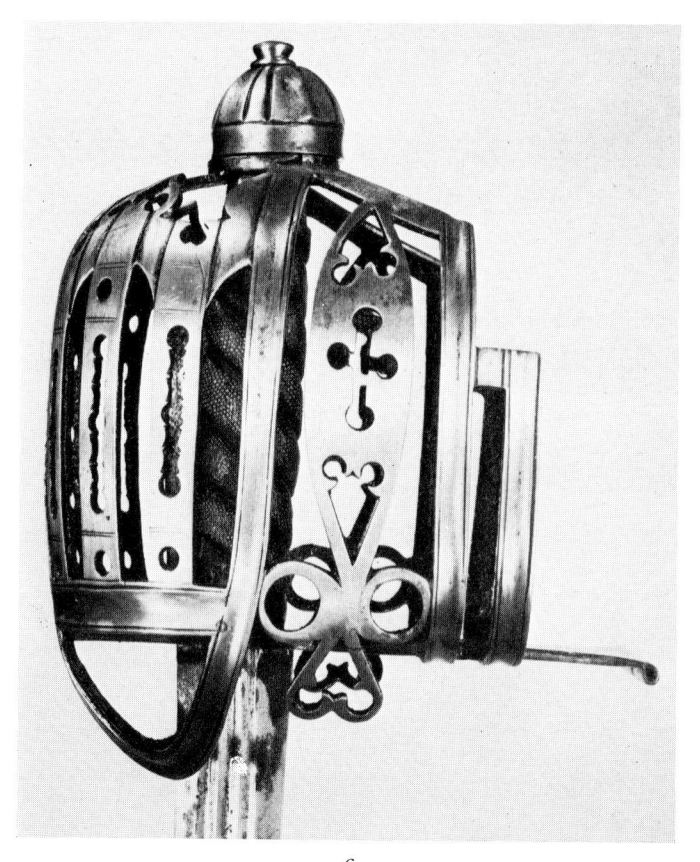

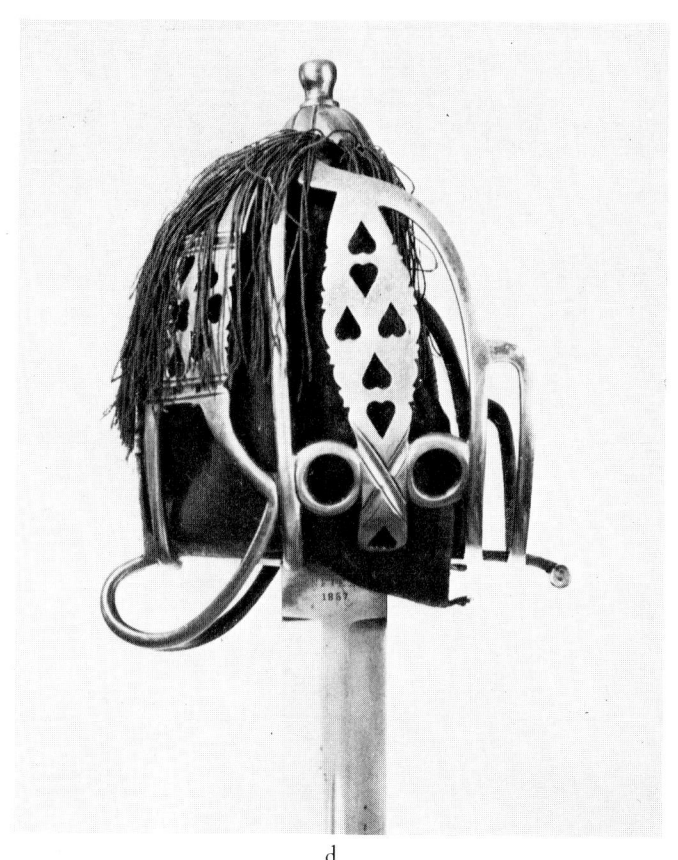

d

English and Scottish basket-hilted swords, 18th–19th centuries.

PLATE 53

a

b

c

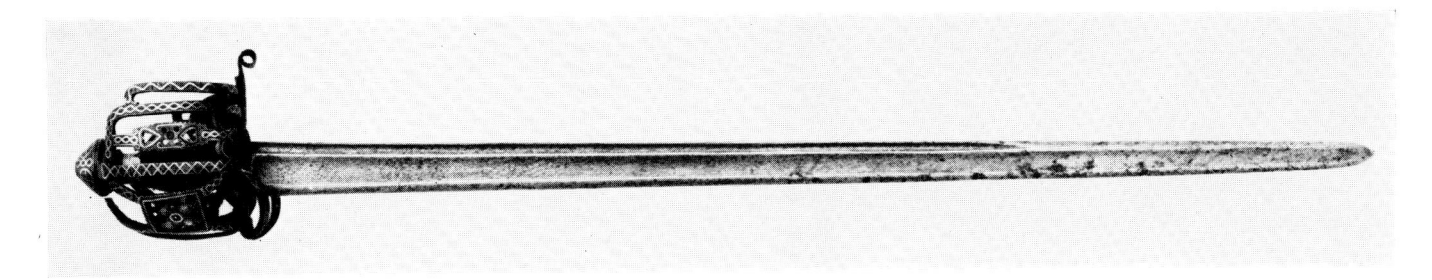

Scottish basket-hilted swords, 18th century.

PLATE 54

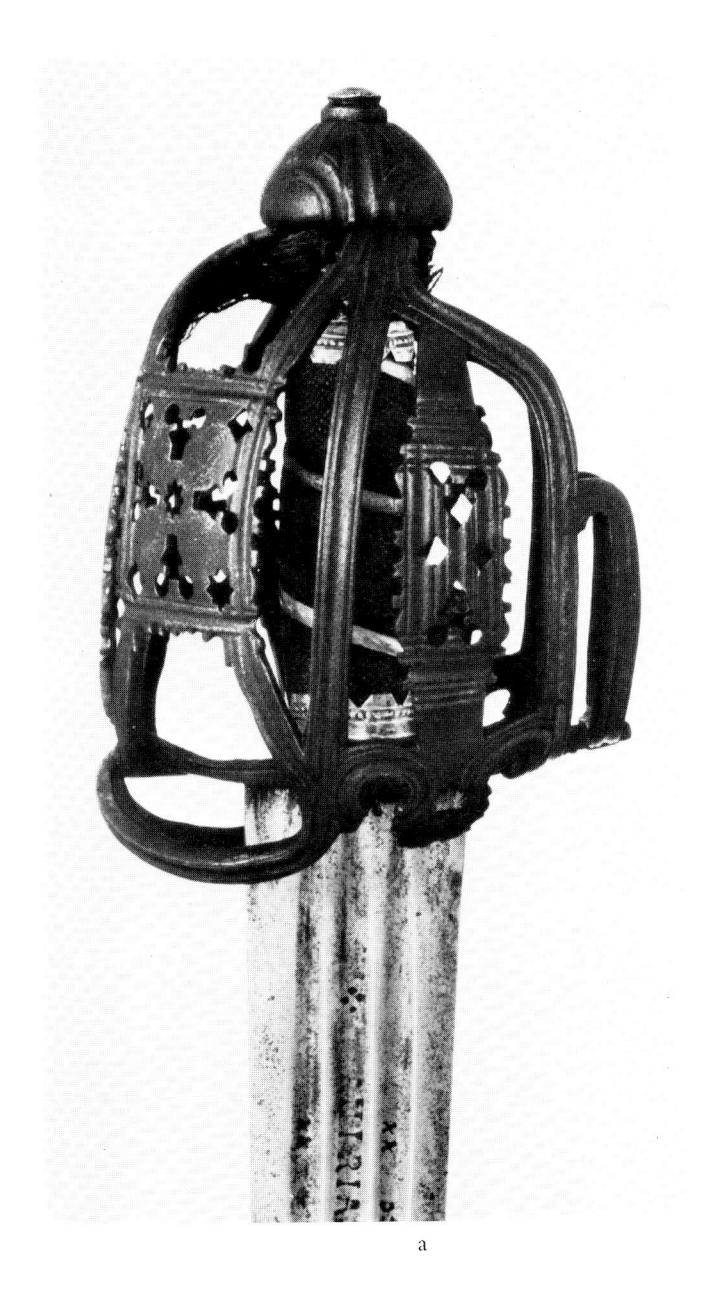

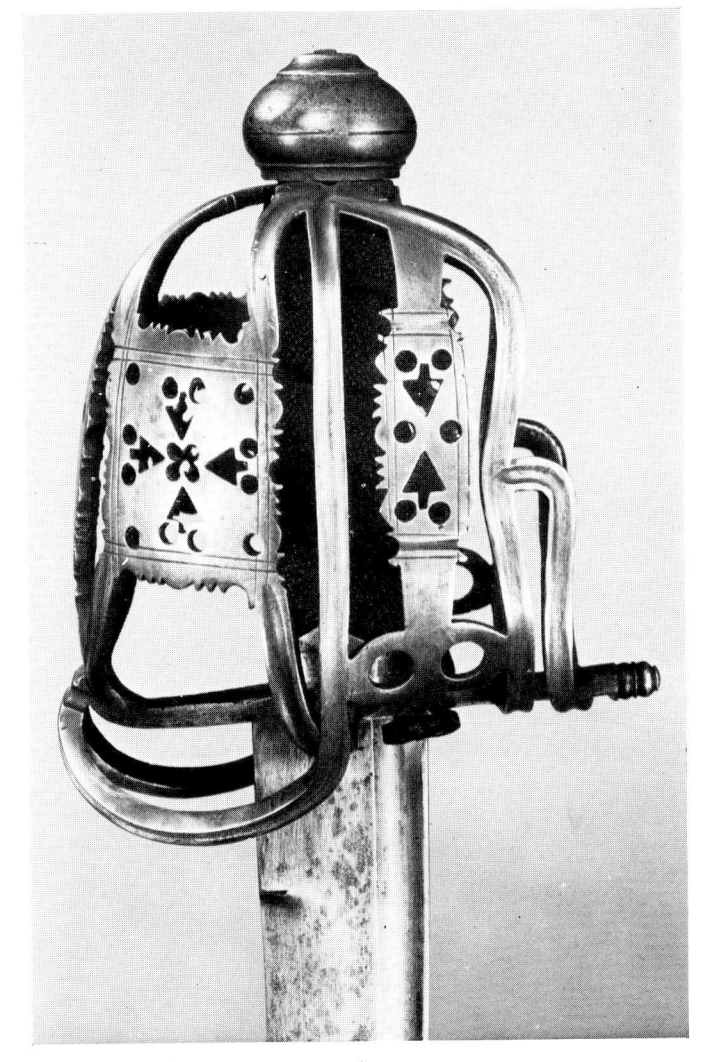

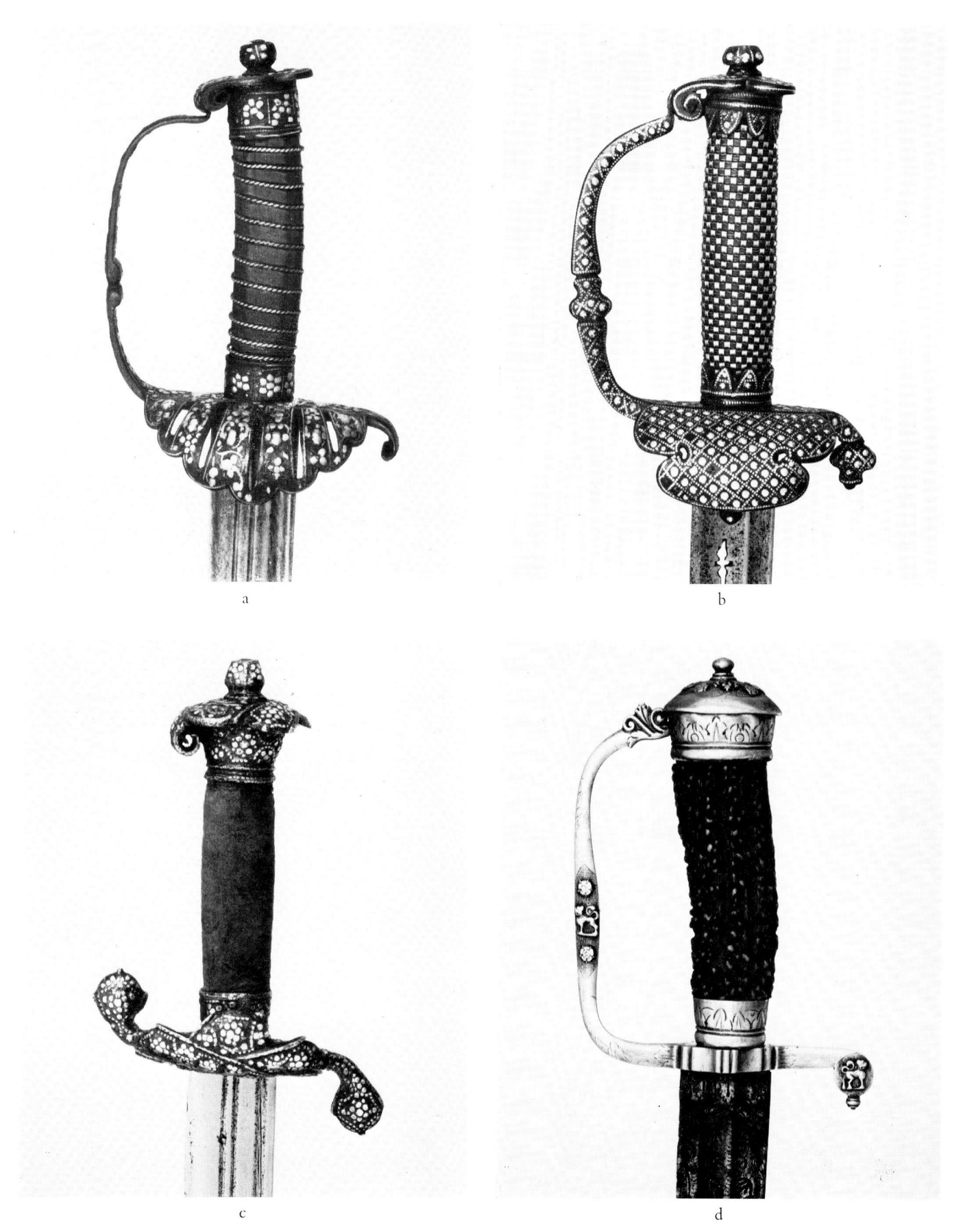

English hangers, 17th century.

PLATE 55

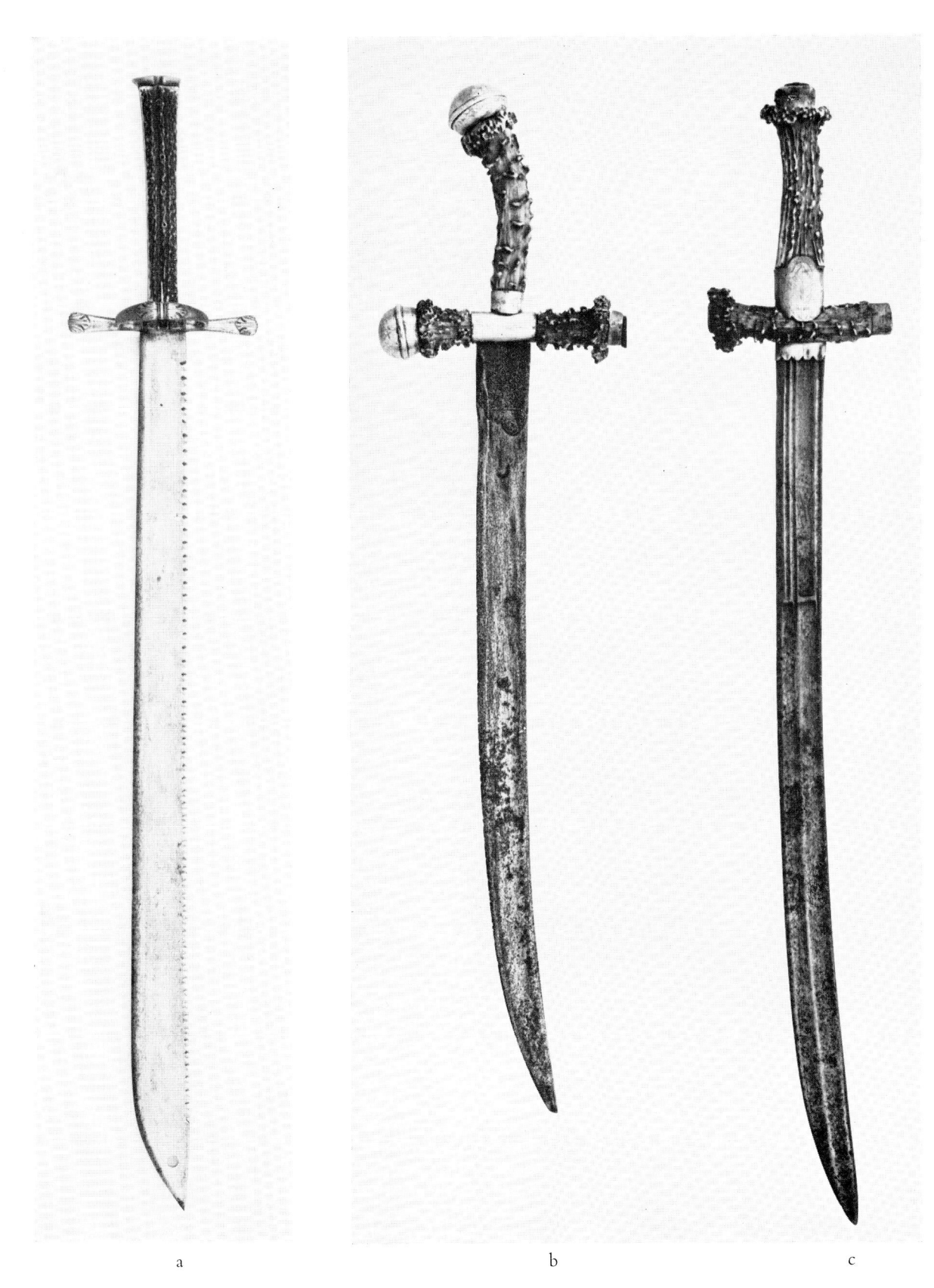

(a) German forrester's sword, *c.* 1600, (b–c) English hangers, *c.* 1650.

PLATE 56

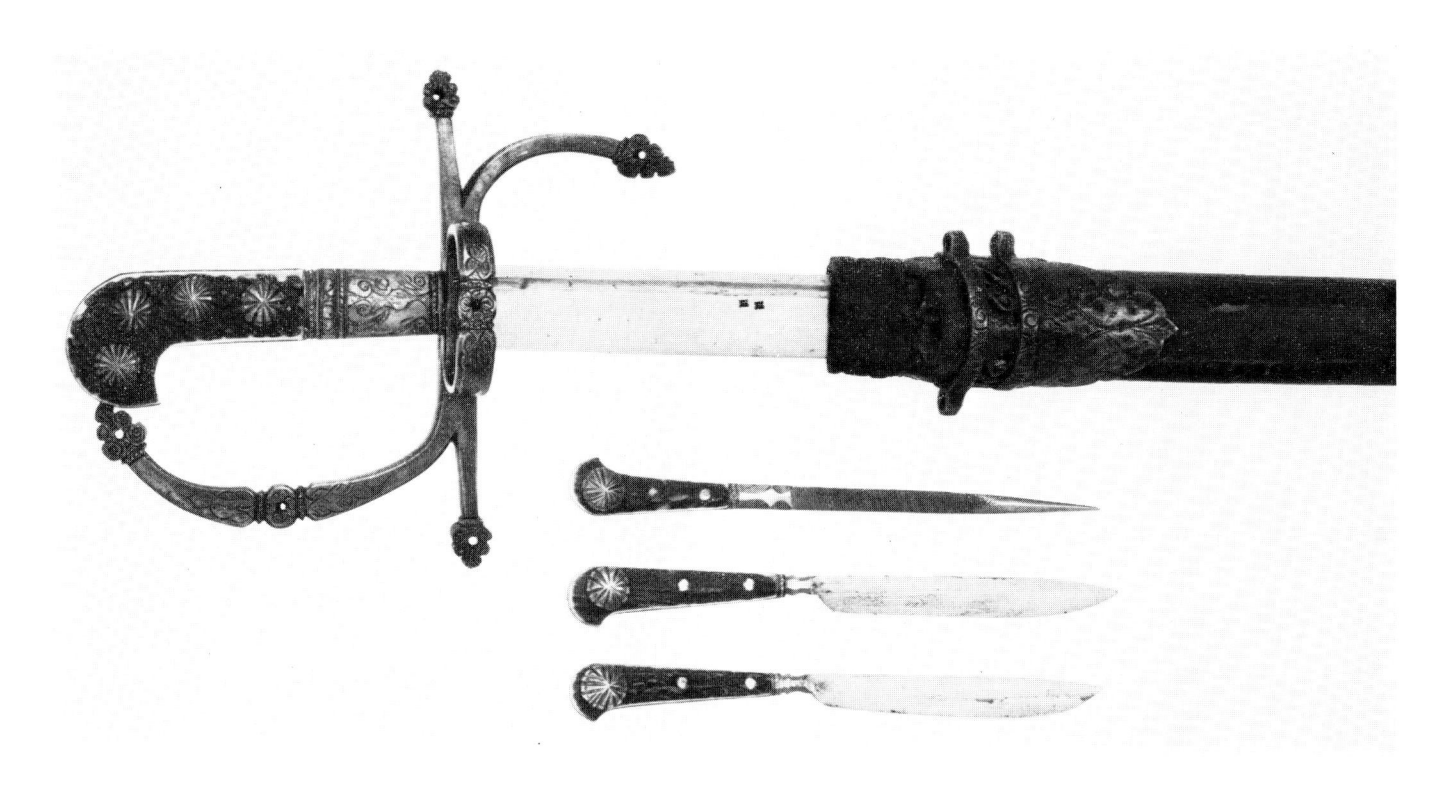

a

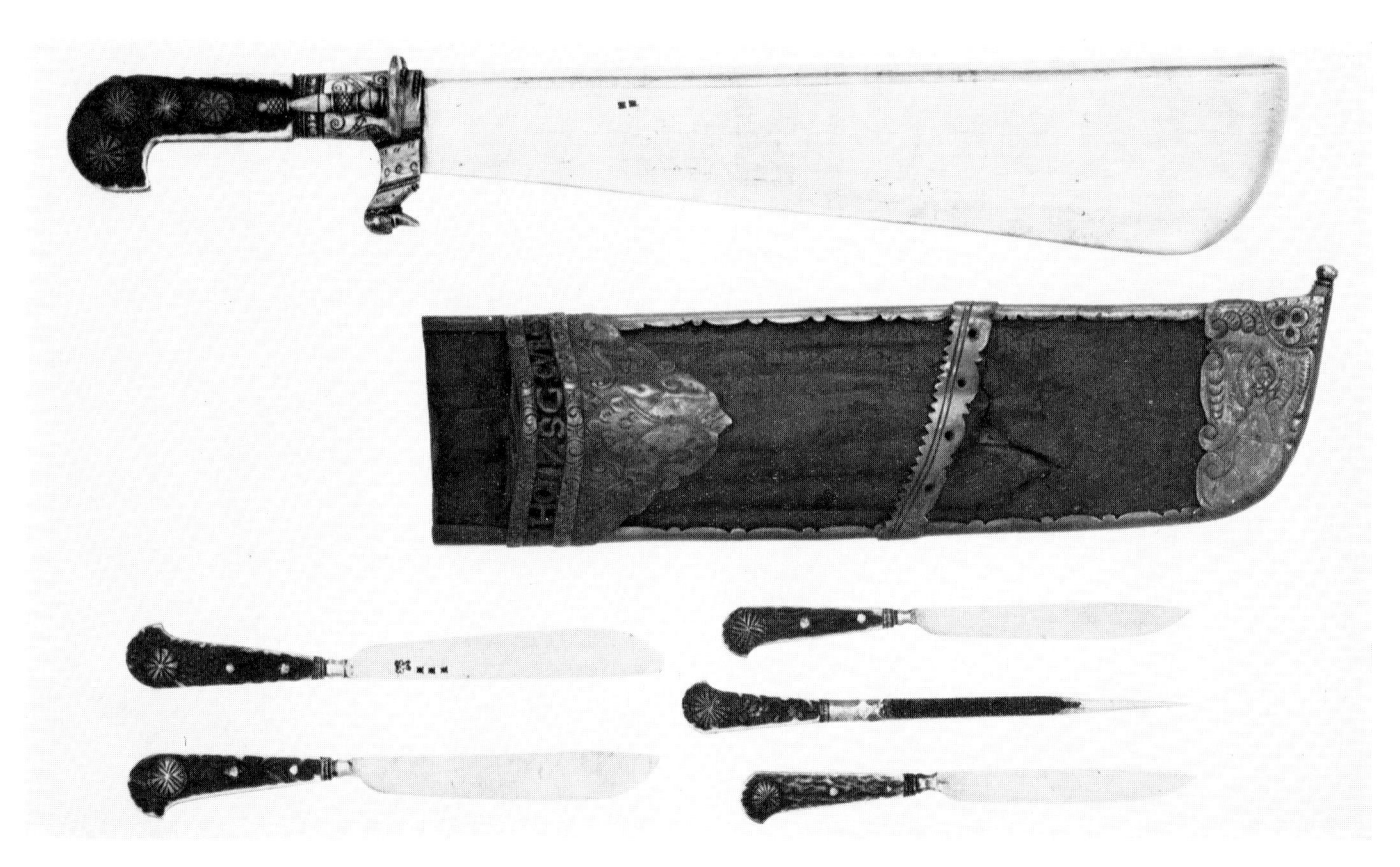

b

Saxon hunting sword and trousse, 1662.

PLATE 57

a b

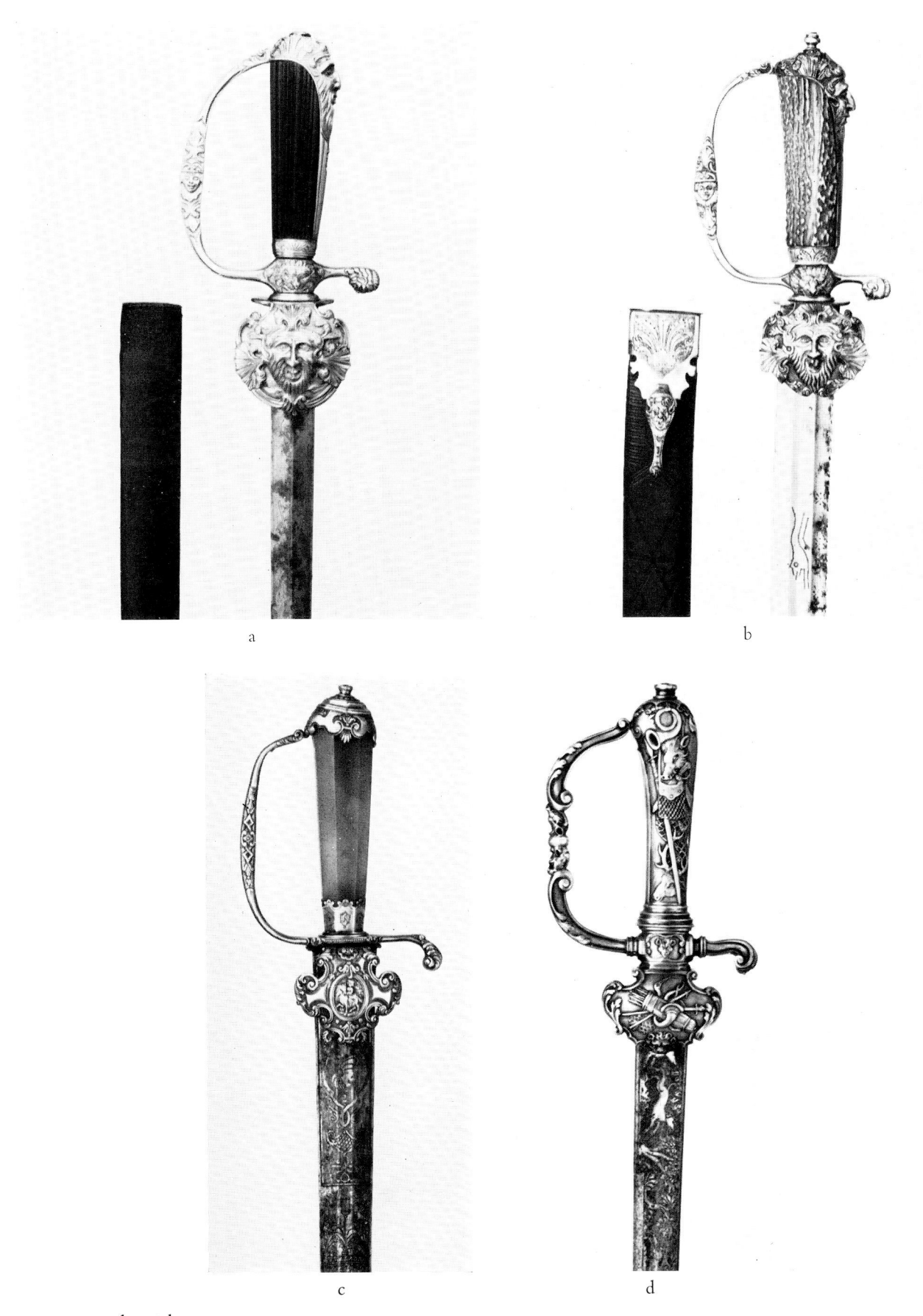

c d

Hunting swords, 18th century.

PLATE 58

a   b   c

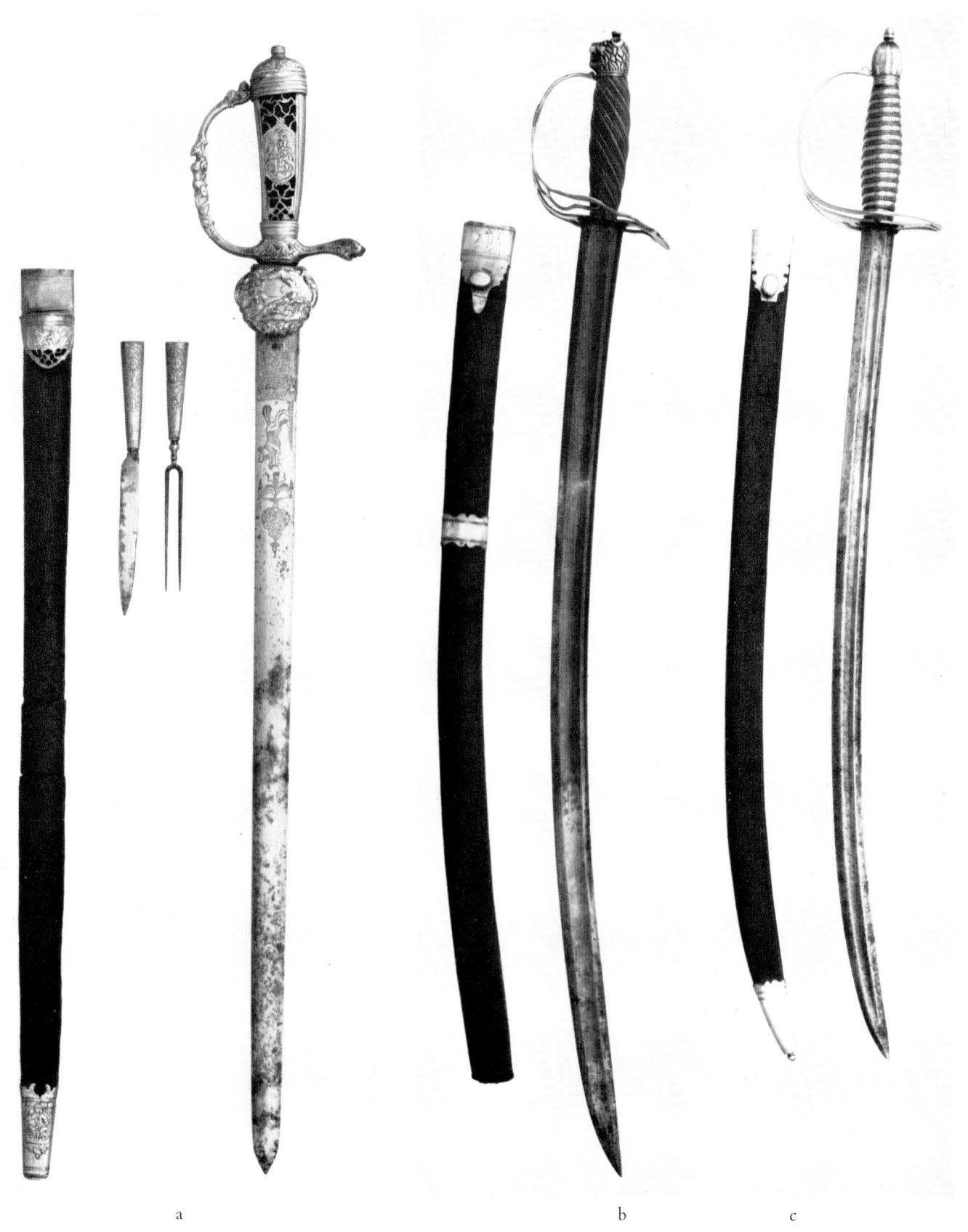

German hunting sword and English hangers, 18th century.

PLATE 59

(a) Hunting sword, mid 17th century; (b) German hunting sword, c. 1720.

PLATE 60

a b

(a) Hunting sword, second half of 17th century; (b) Italian (Brescian) hunting sword, hilt c. 1660.

PLATE 61

a b c

Swords with calendar blades.

PLATE 62

a

b

c

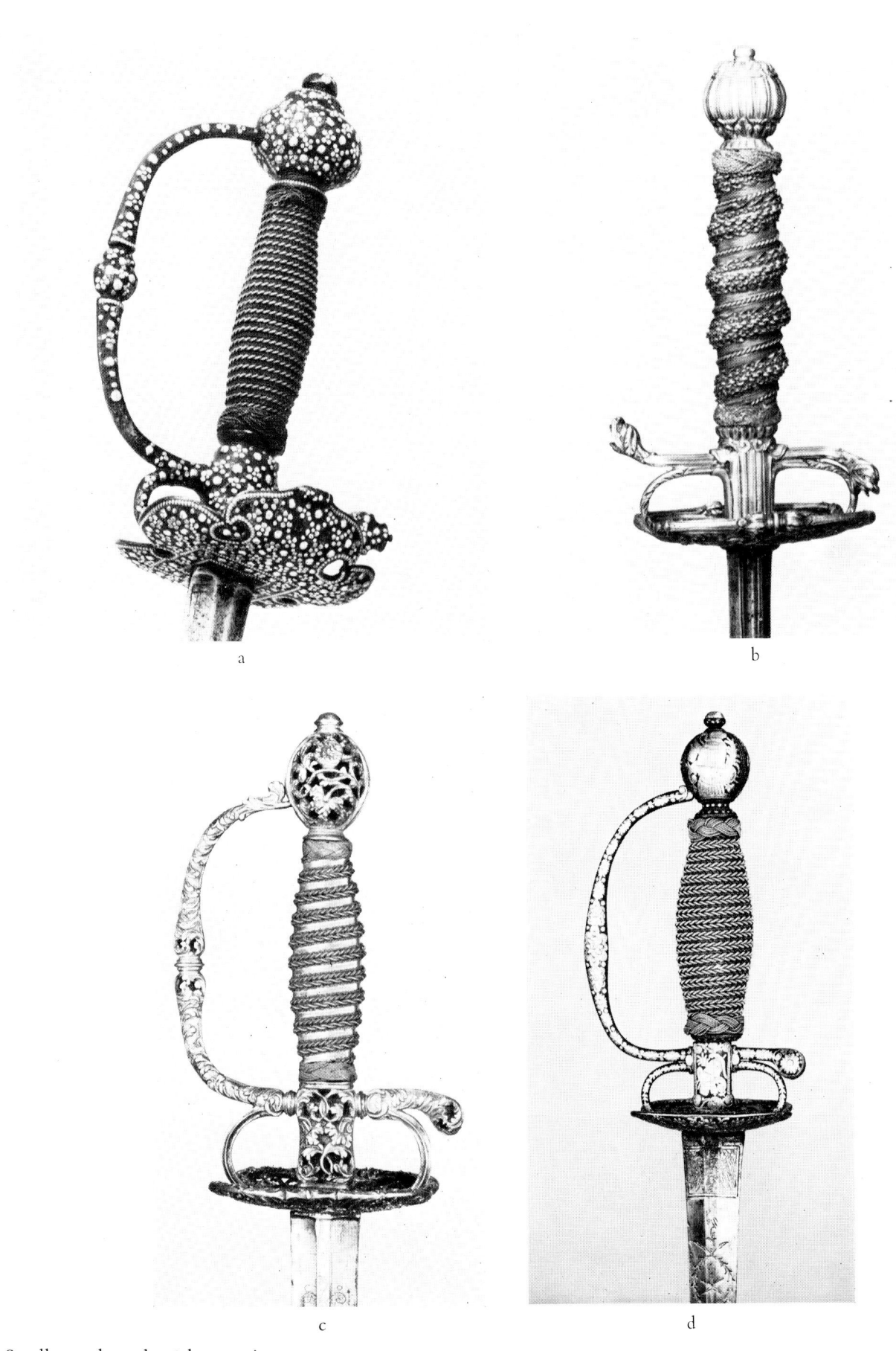

d

Small swords, 17th–18th centuries.

PLATE 63

a

b

c

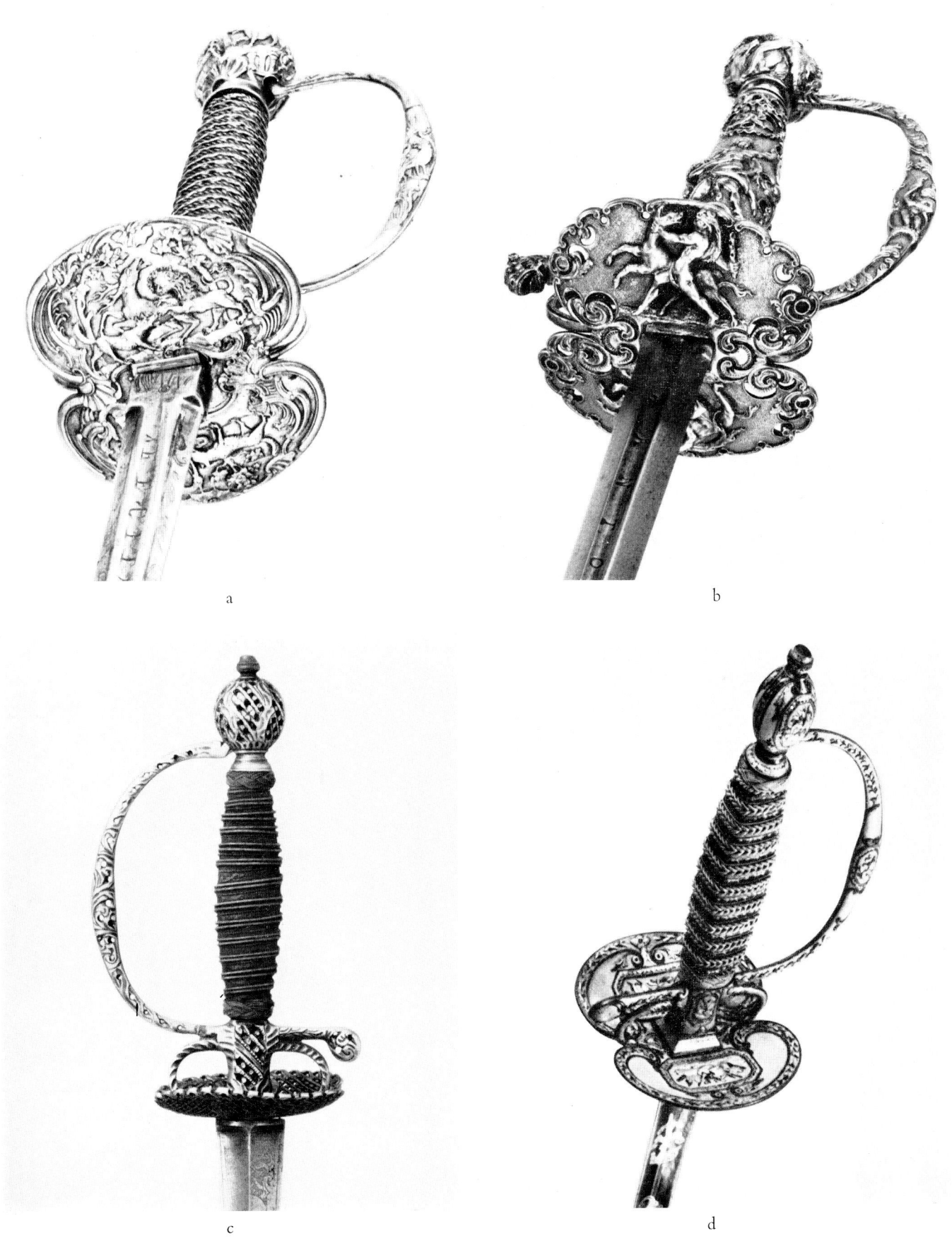

d

Small swords, 18th century.

PLATE 64

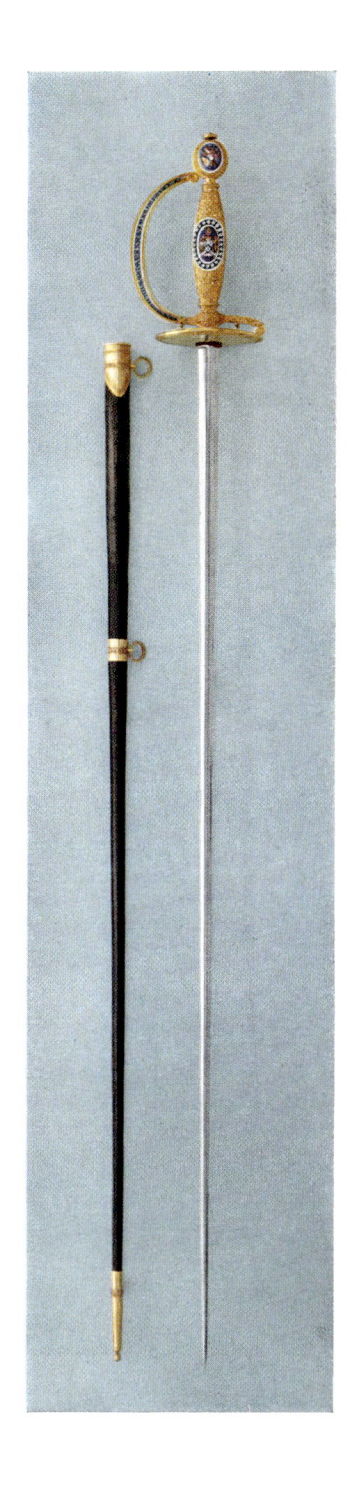

The Collingwood sword.

PLATE 65

a

b

c

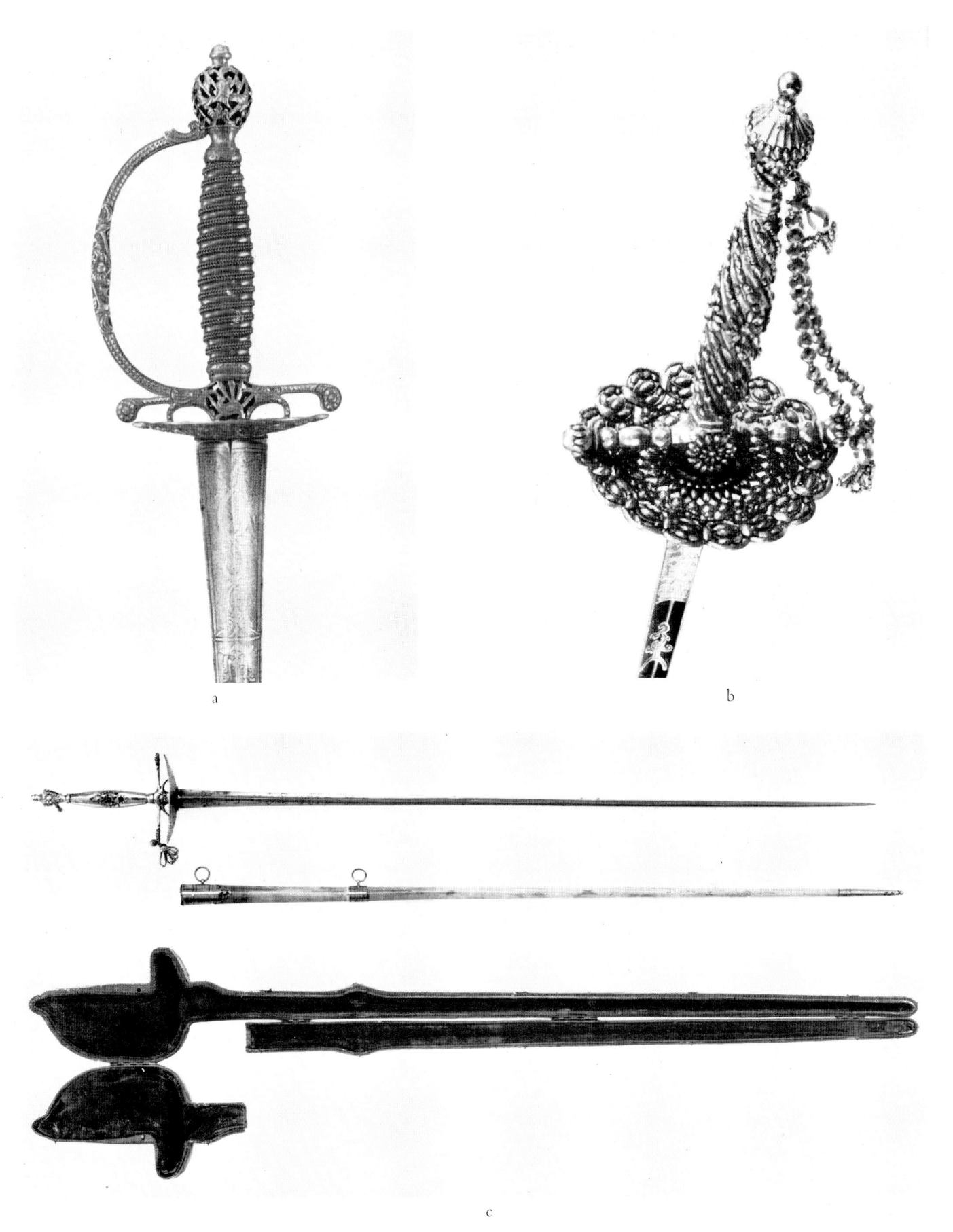

Small swords, 18th–19th centuries.
PLATE 66

a

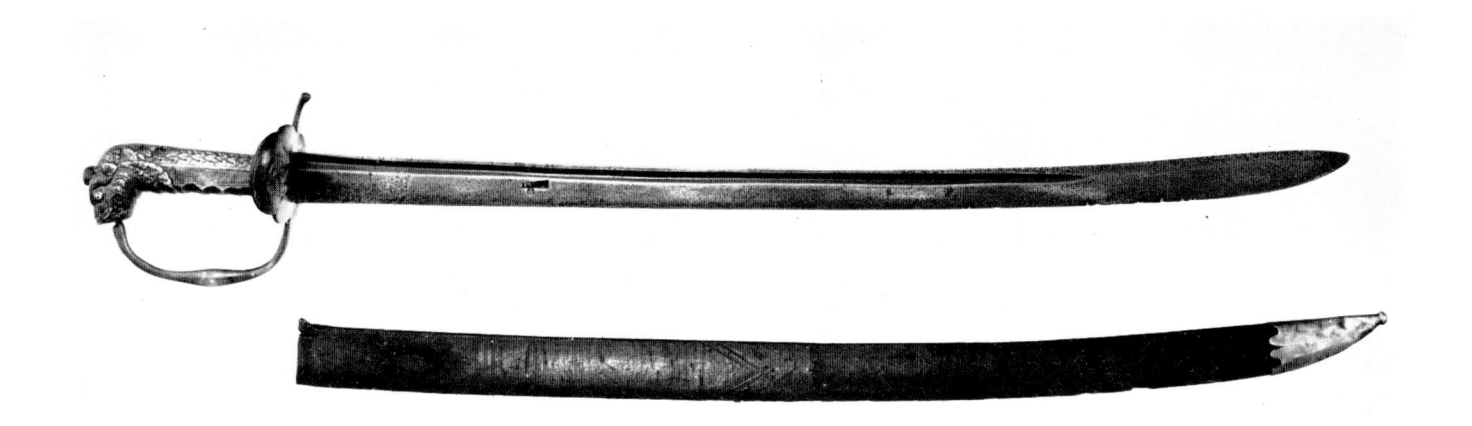

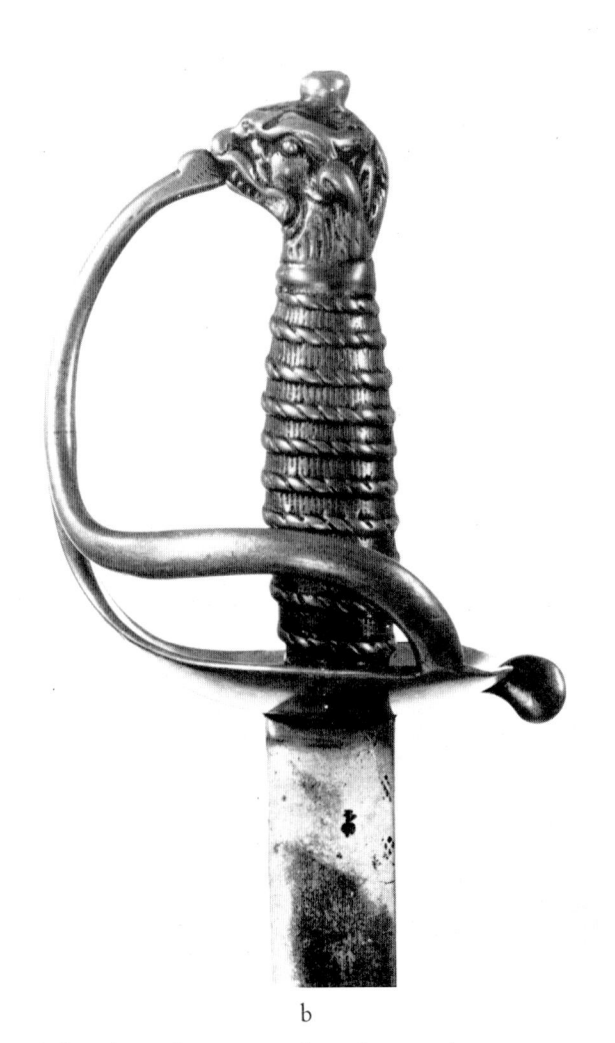

b
English military hangers, 17th–18th centuries.

c

PLATE 67

a

b

c

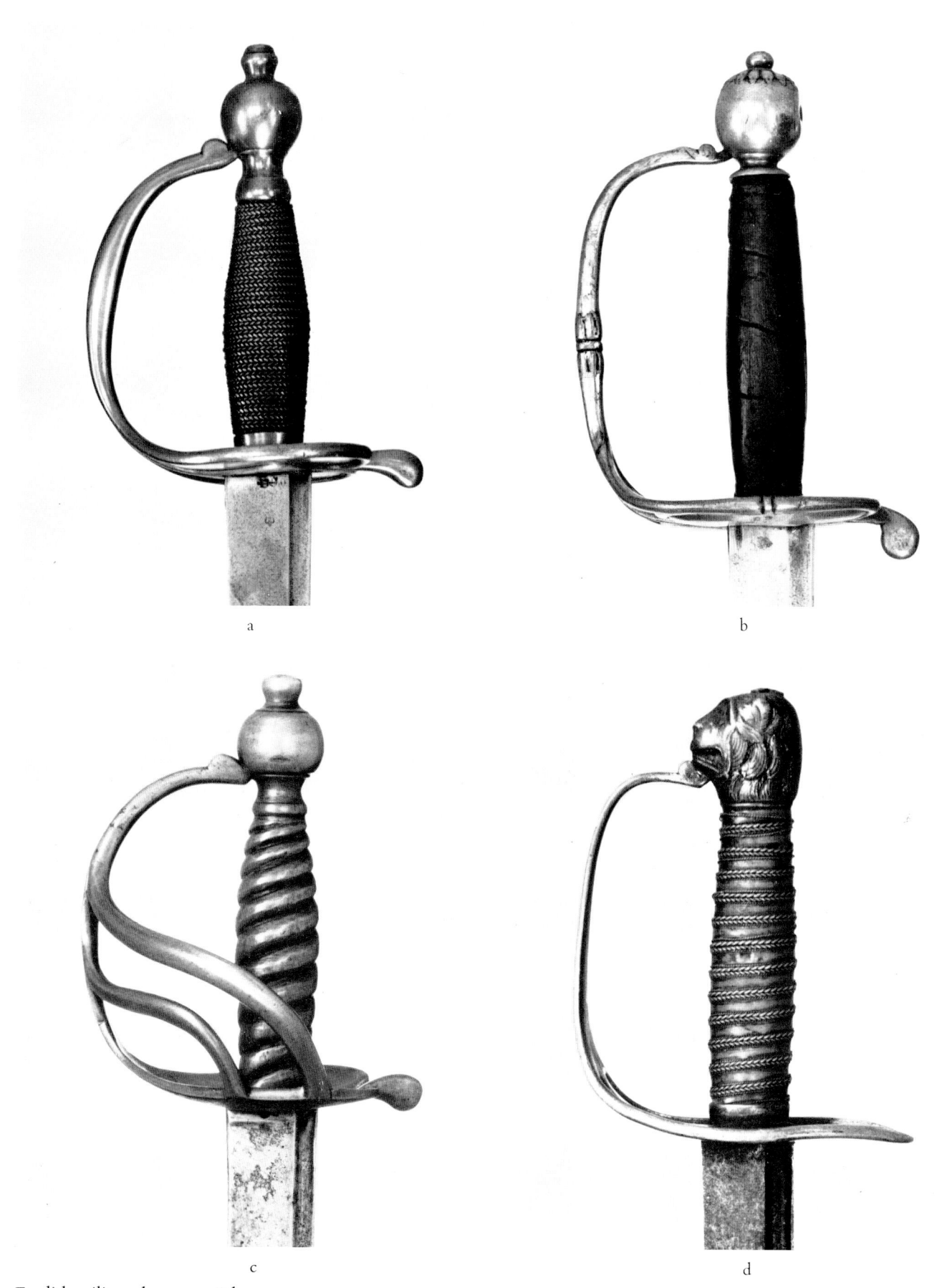

d

English military hangers, 18th century.

PLATE 68

a

b

c

d

English cavalry swords, 18th century.

PLATE 69

a

d

b

c

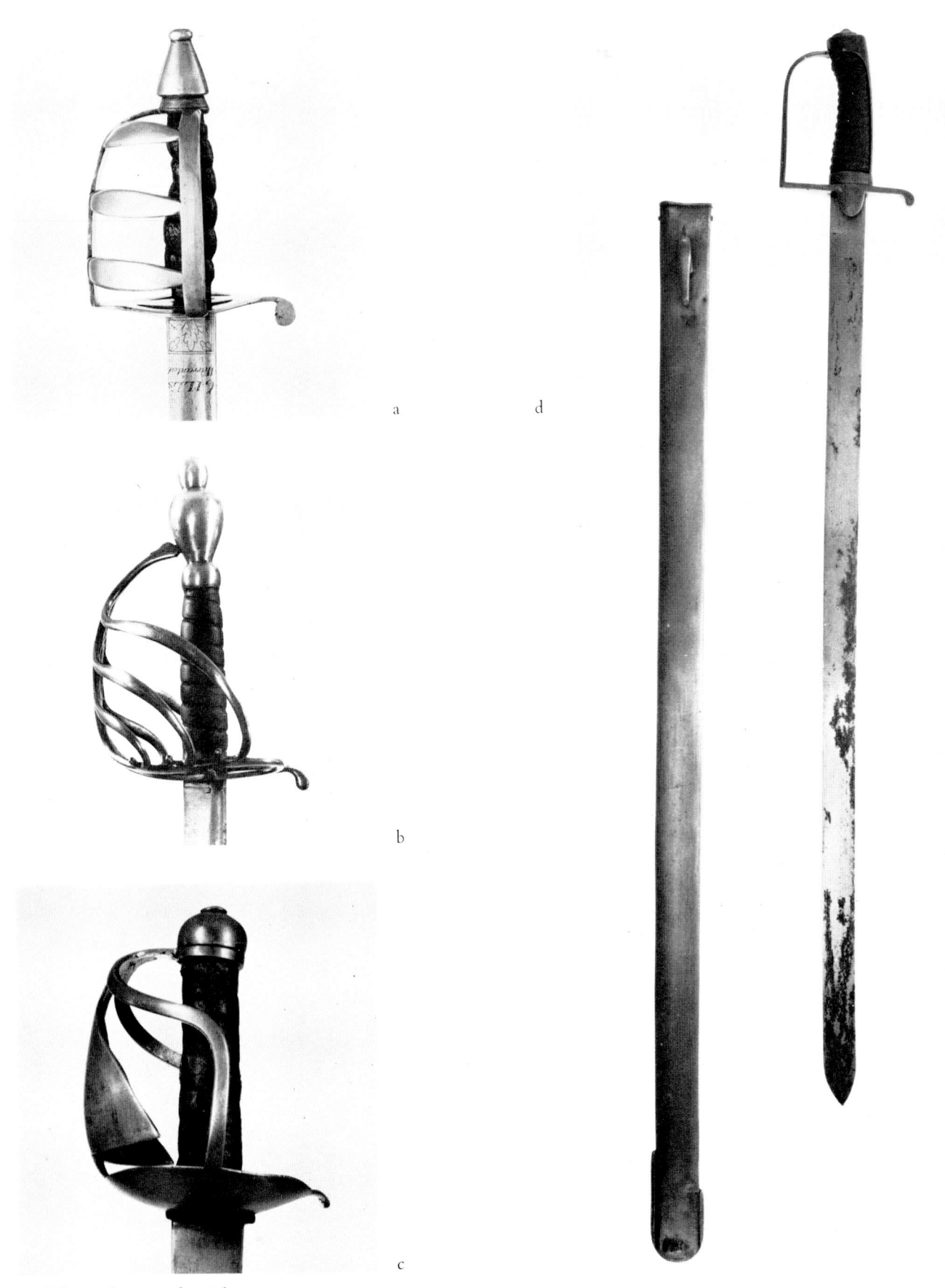

English cavalry swords, 18th century.

PLATE 70

a   b

c

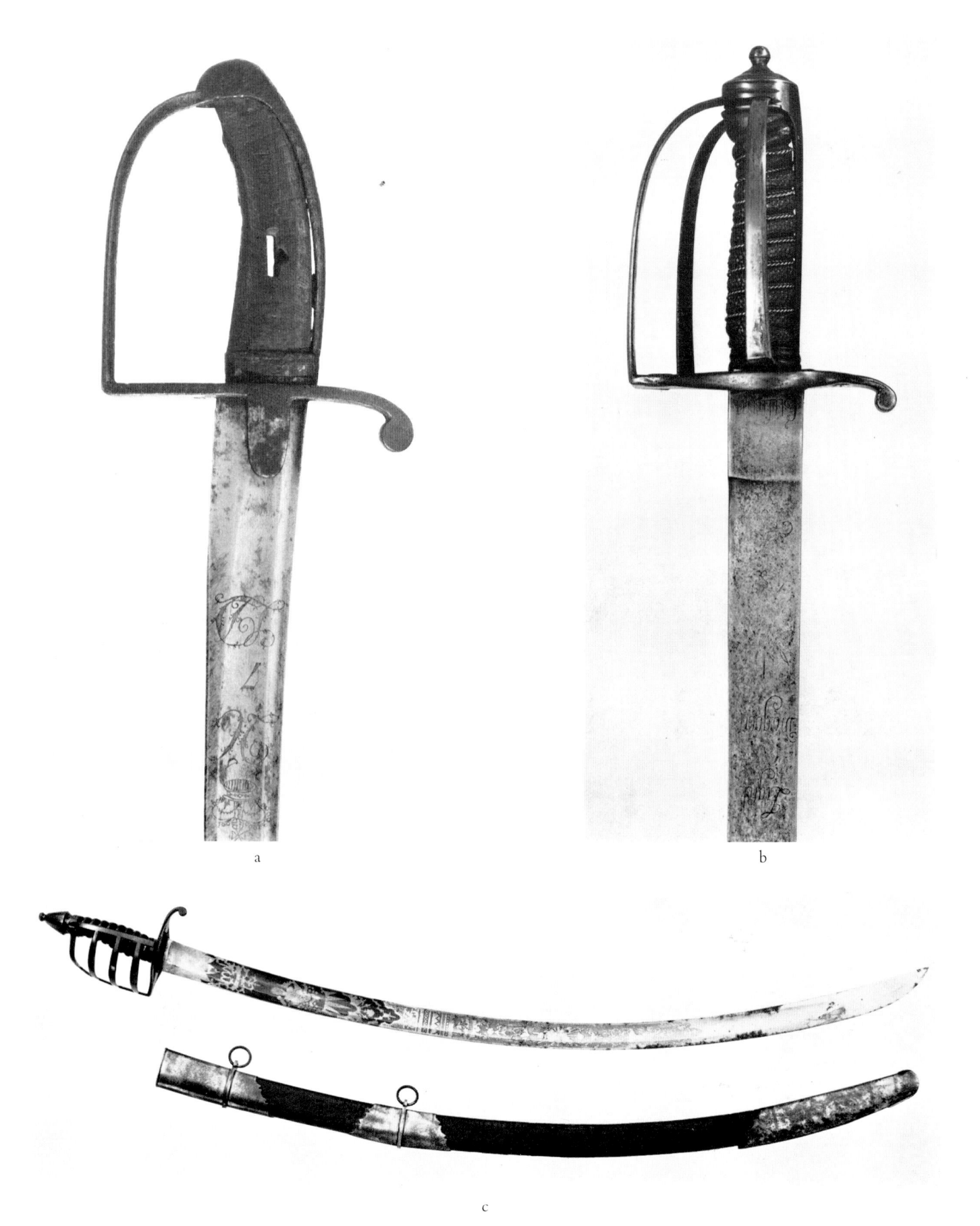

English and American cavalry swords, 18th century.

PLATE 71

a   b   c

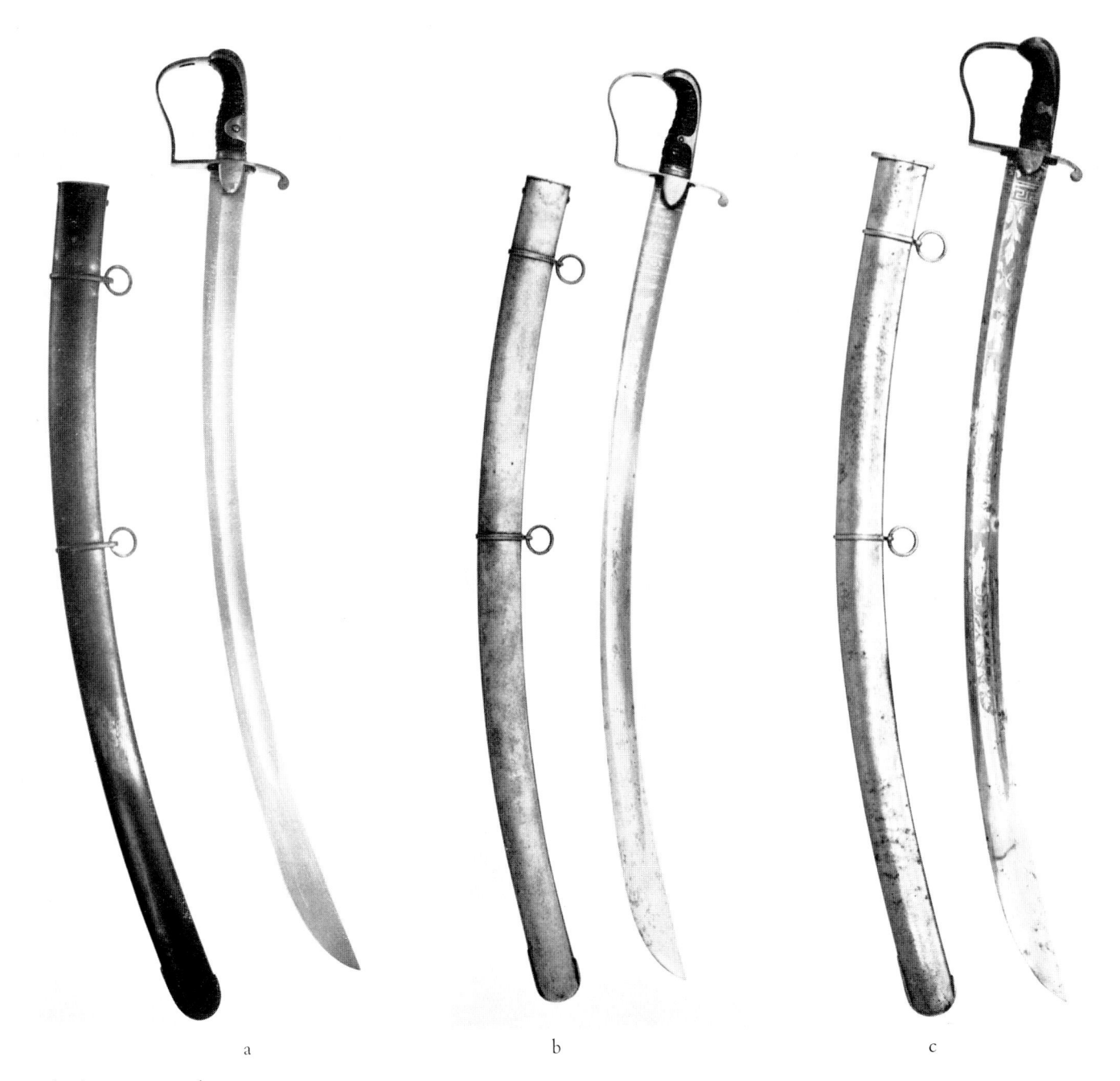

Light dragoon swords, 1796 pattern.

PLATE 72

a b c

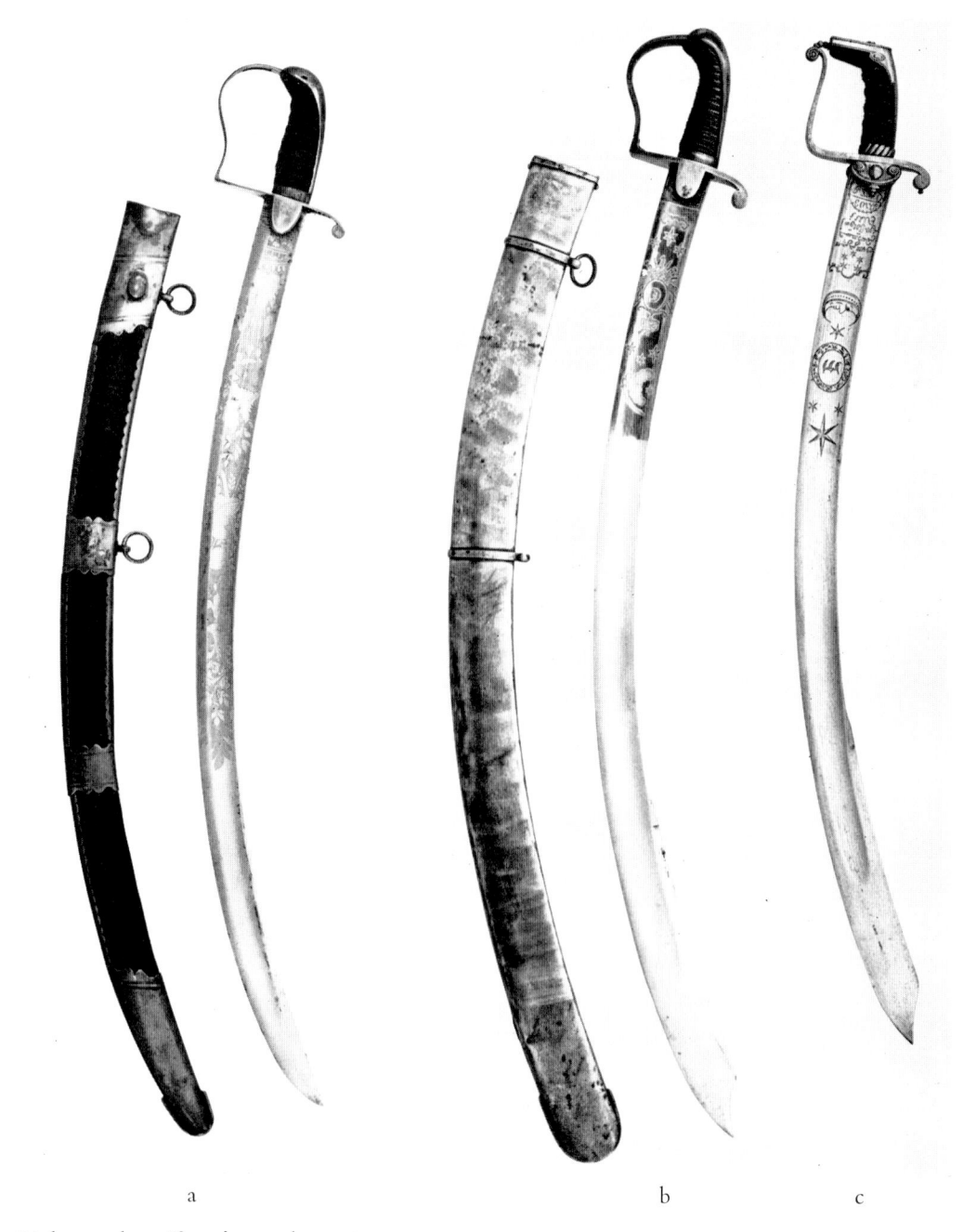

Light cavalry officers' swords, c. 1800.

PLATE 73

Watercolour commemorating a sword test at the Tower in 1804.

PLATE 74

a

British officers' swords, pattern of 1803.

b

c

PLATE 75

a b c

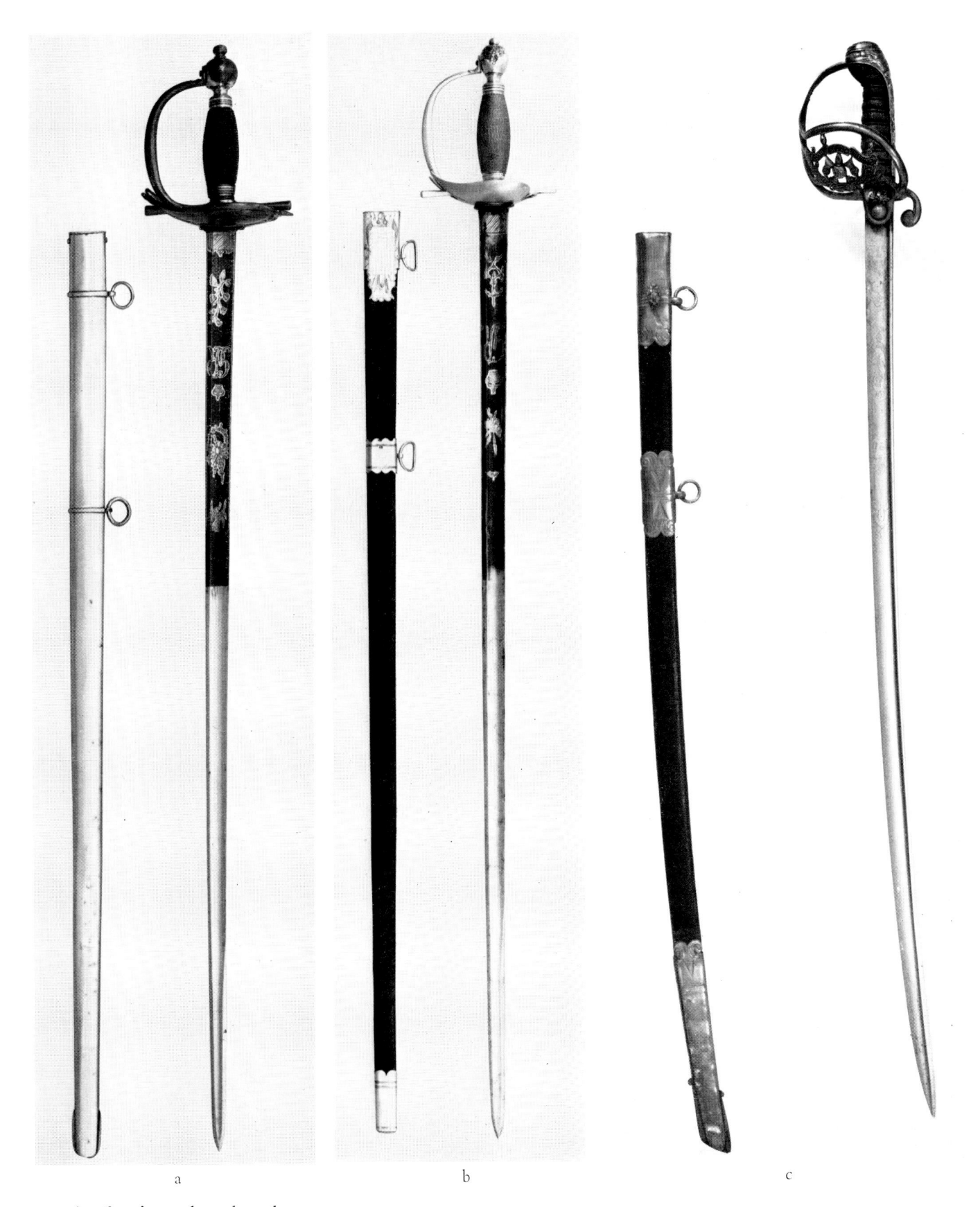

British officers' swords, early 19th century.

PLATE 76

a

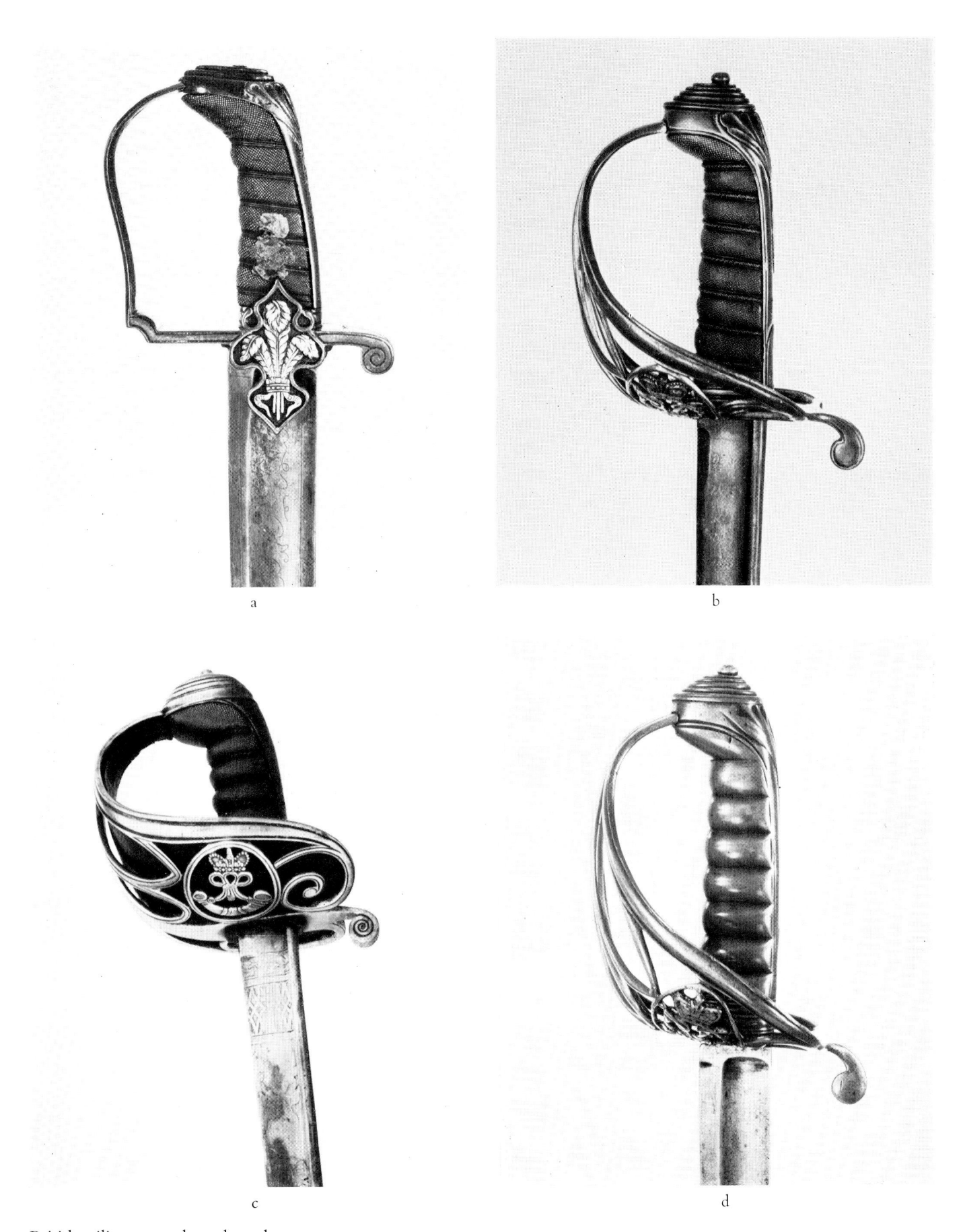

b

c

d

British military swords, early 19th century.

PLATE 77

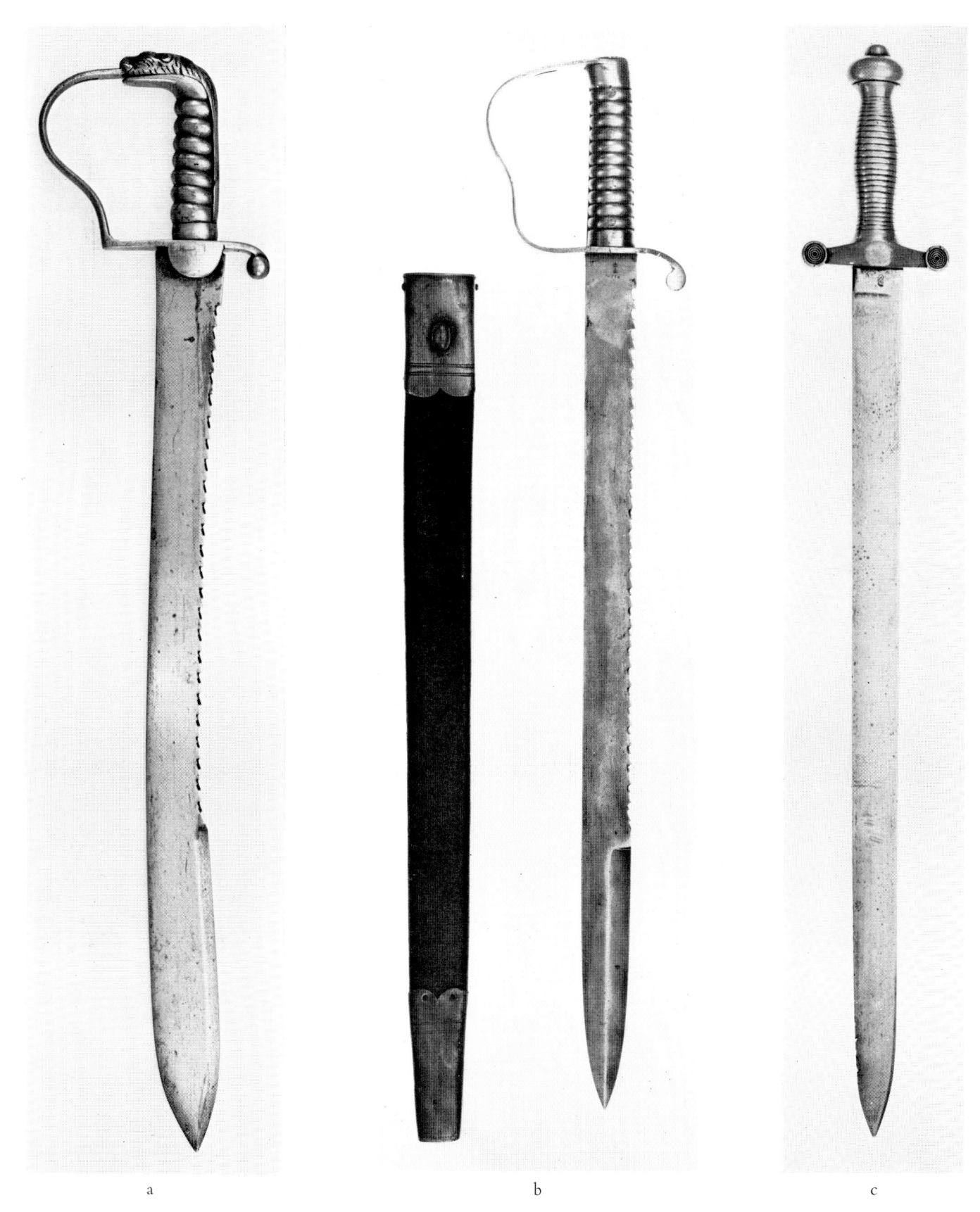

(a–b) British pioneers' swords; (c) Land Transport Company sword.

PLATE 78

a b c

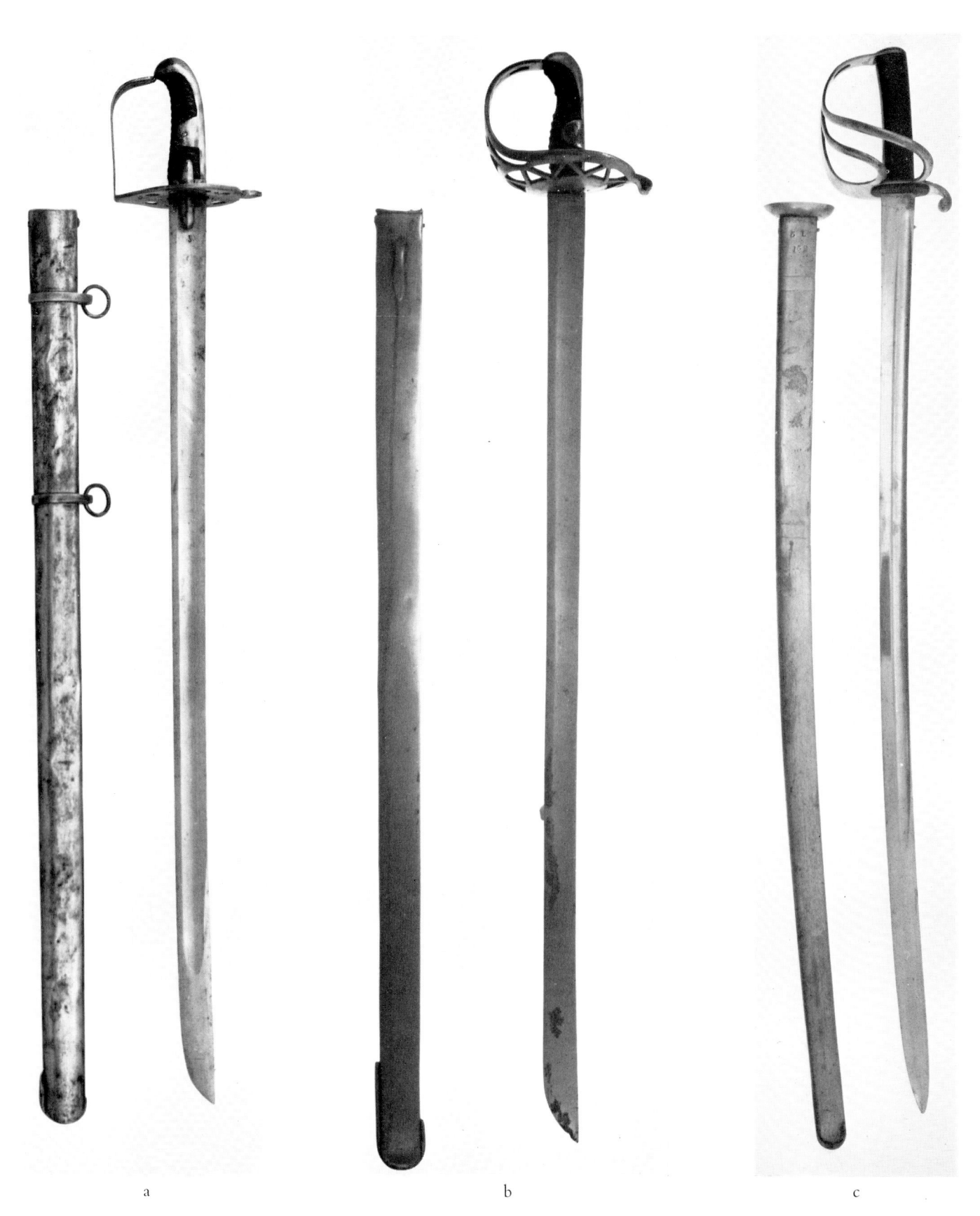

British cavalry troopers' swords.

PLATE 79

a b

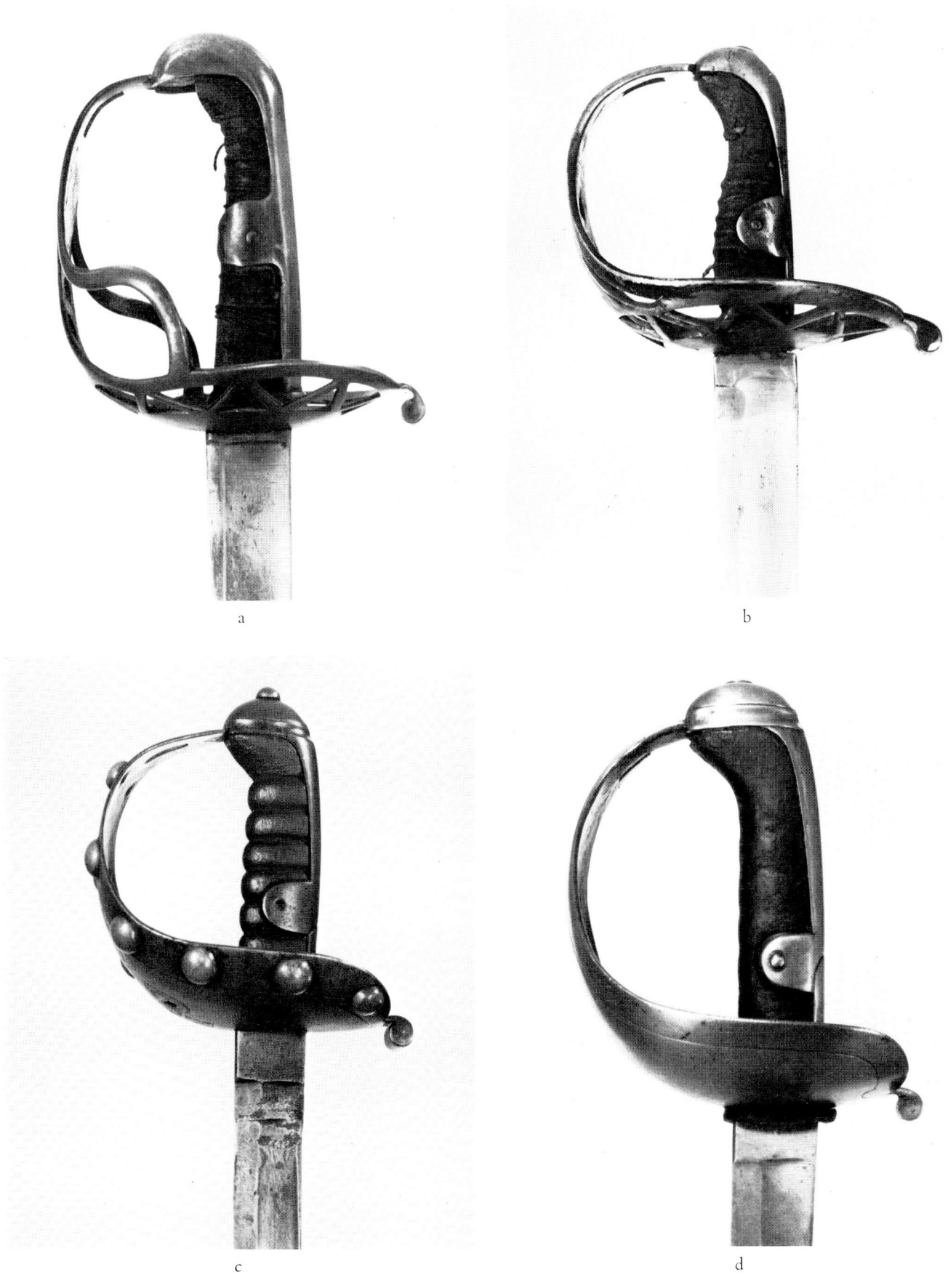

c d

Cavalry troopers' swords, 19th century.

PLATE 80

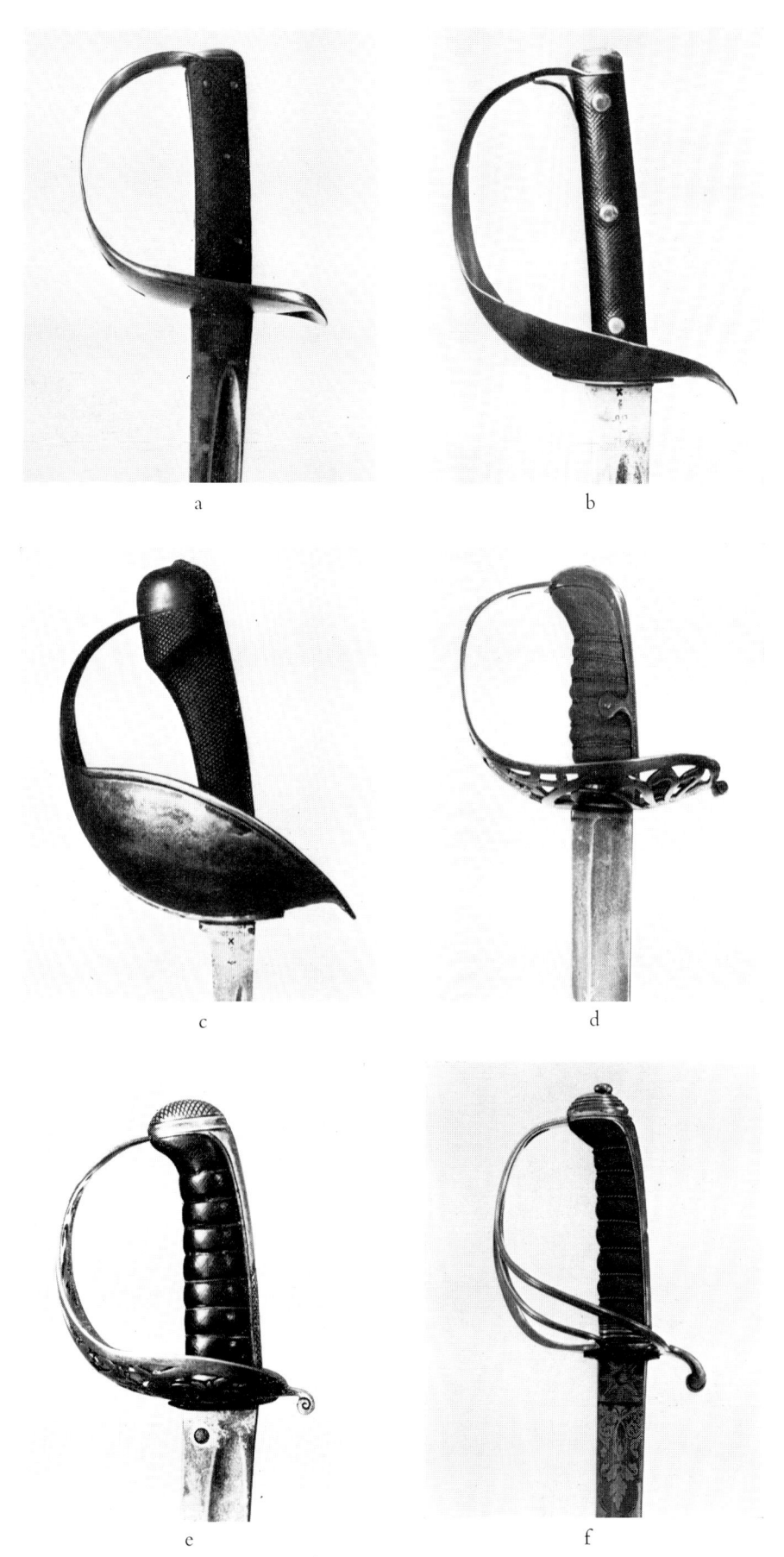

British military swords, 19th and 20th centuries.

PLATE 81

a b

c

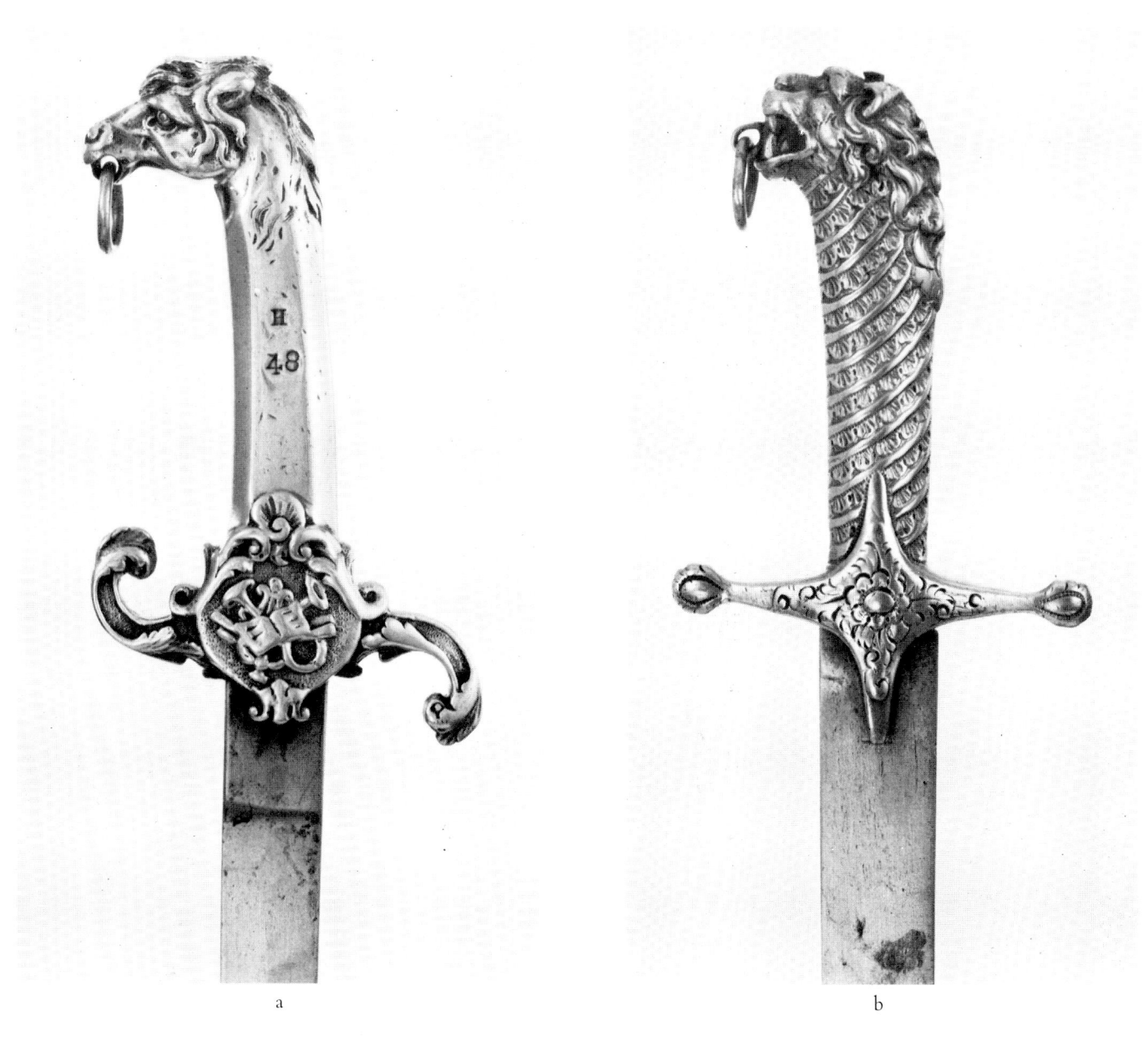

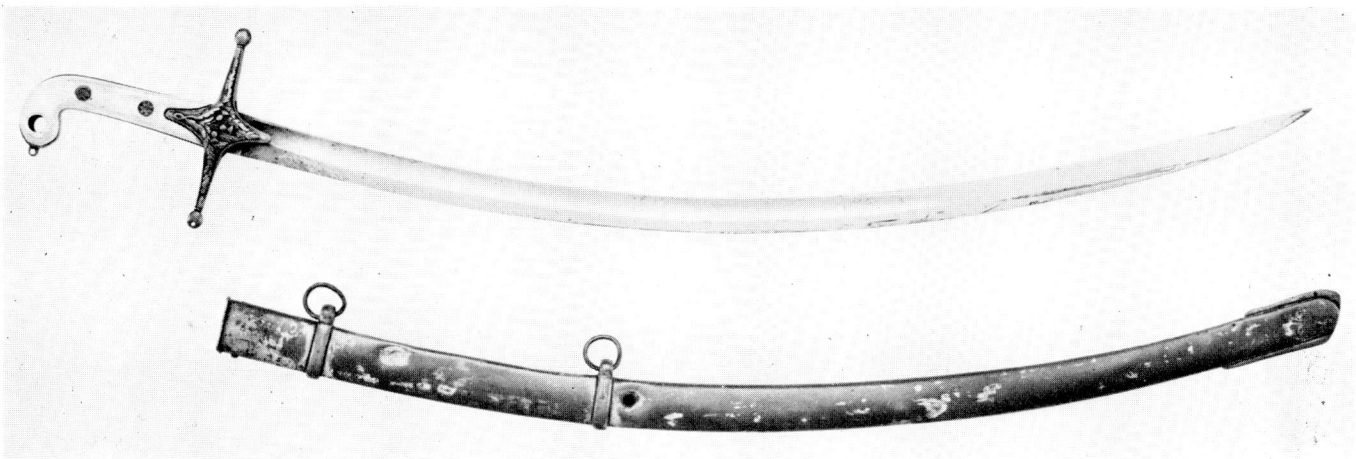

British band swords, 19th century.

PLATE 82

a b c d

British band swords, 19th century.

PLATE 83

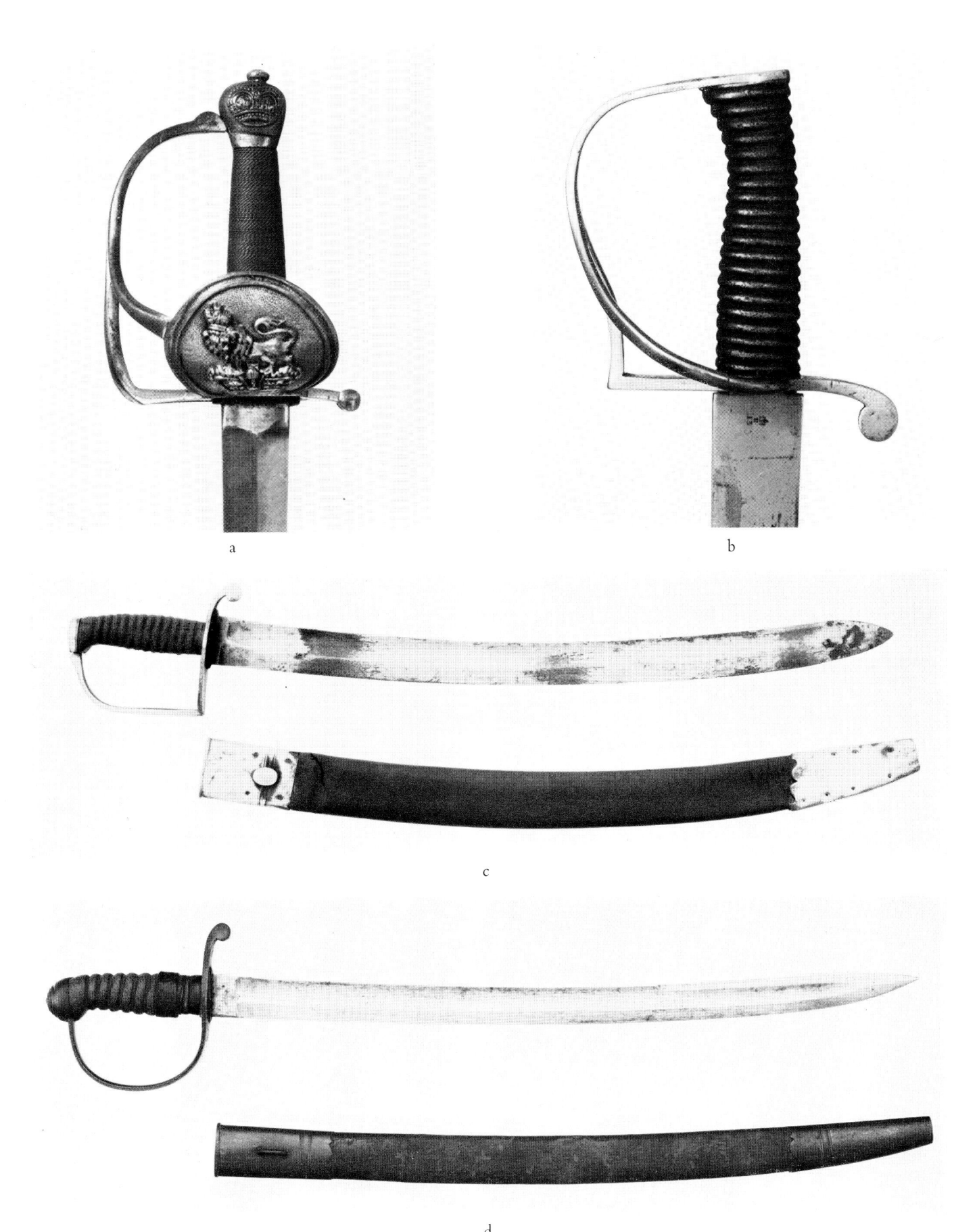

Service swords: (a) Yeoman of the Guard; (b) Coastguard; (c) Police; (d) Prison Officer.

PLATE 84

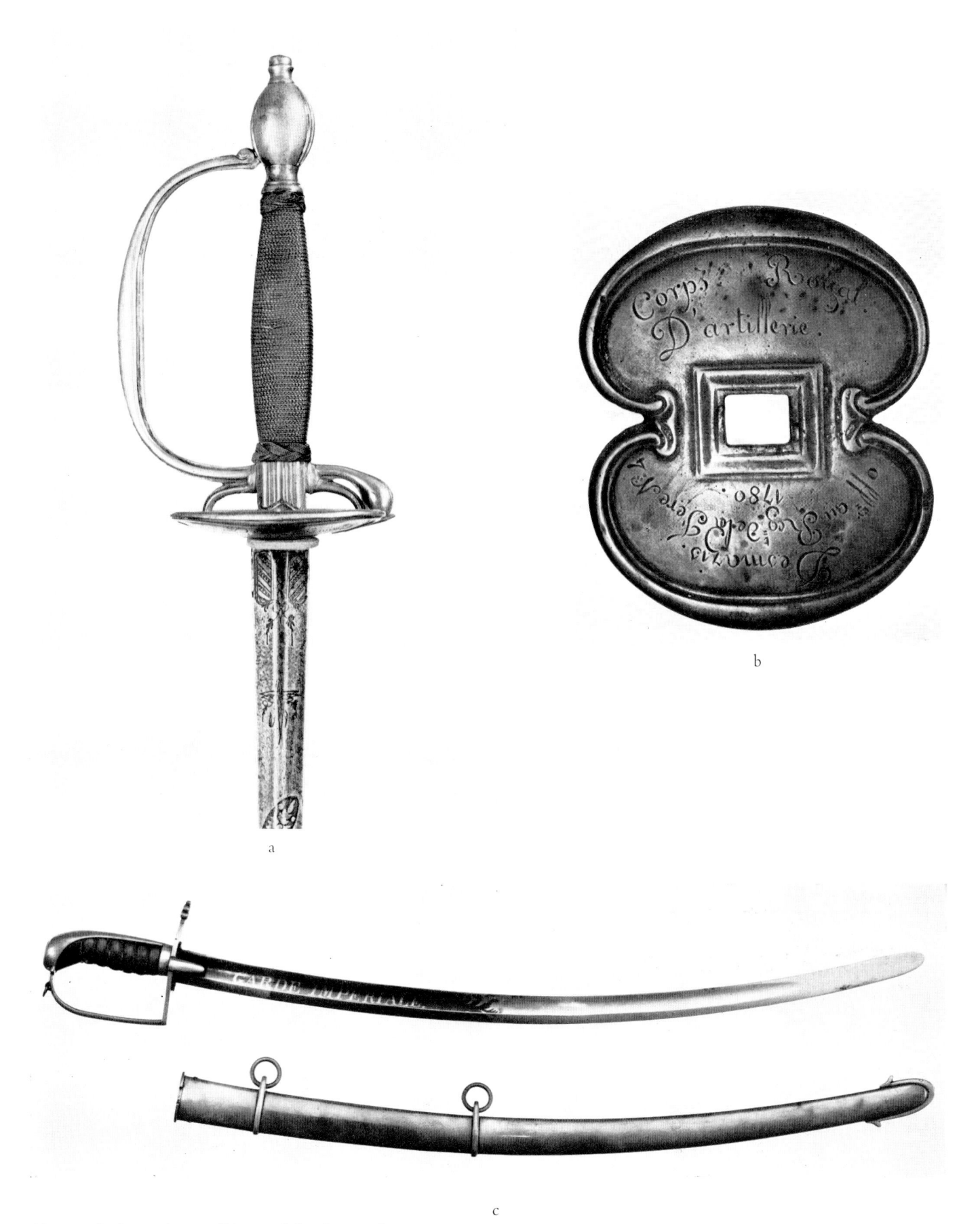

(a) Sword of Napoleon I; (b) French boy's sword.

PLATE 85

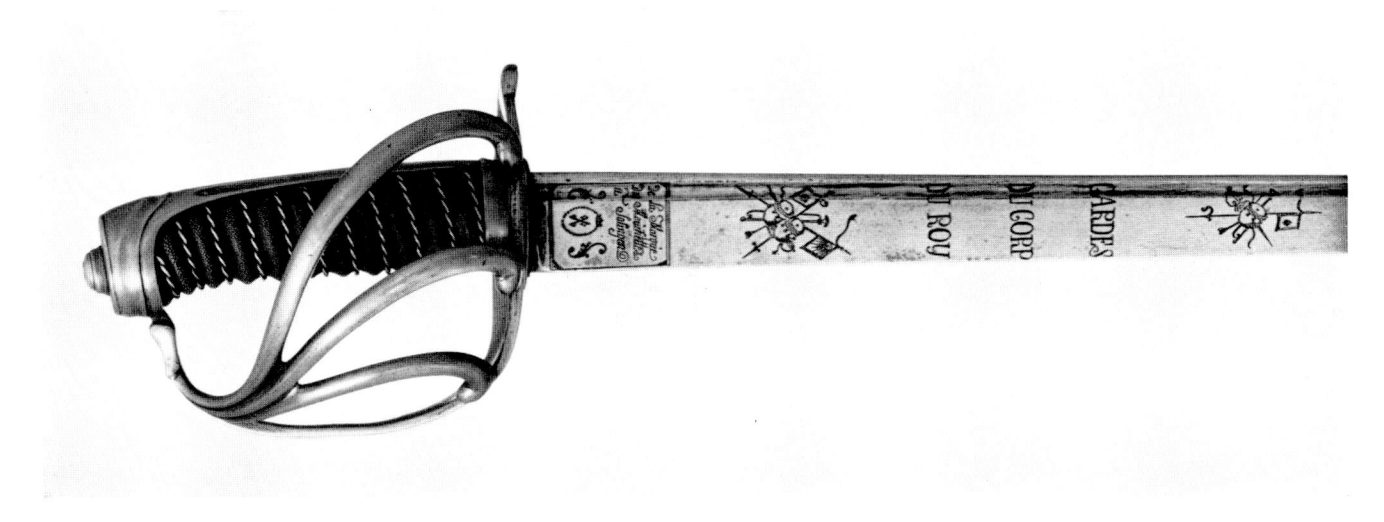

French cavalry swords, 18th century.

PLATE 86

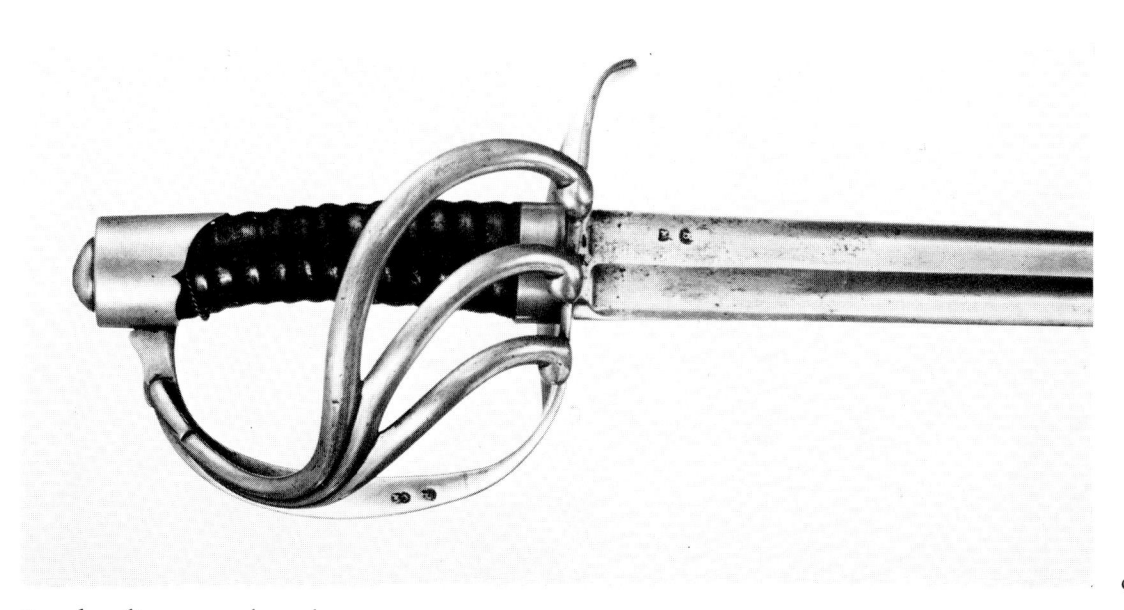

French military swords, 19th century.

PLATE 87

a b

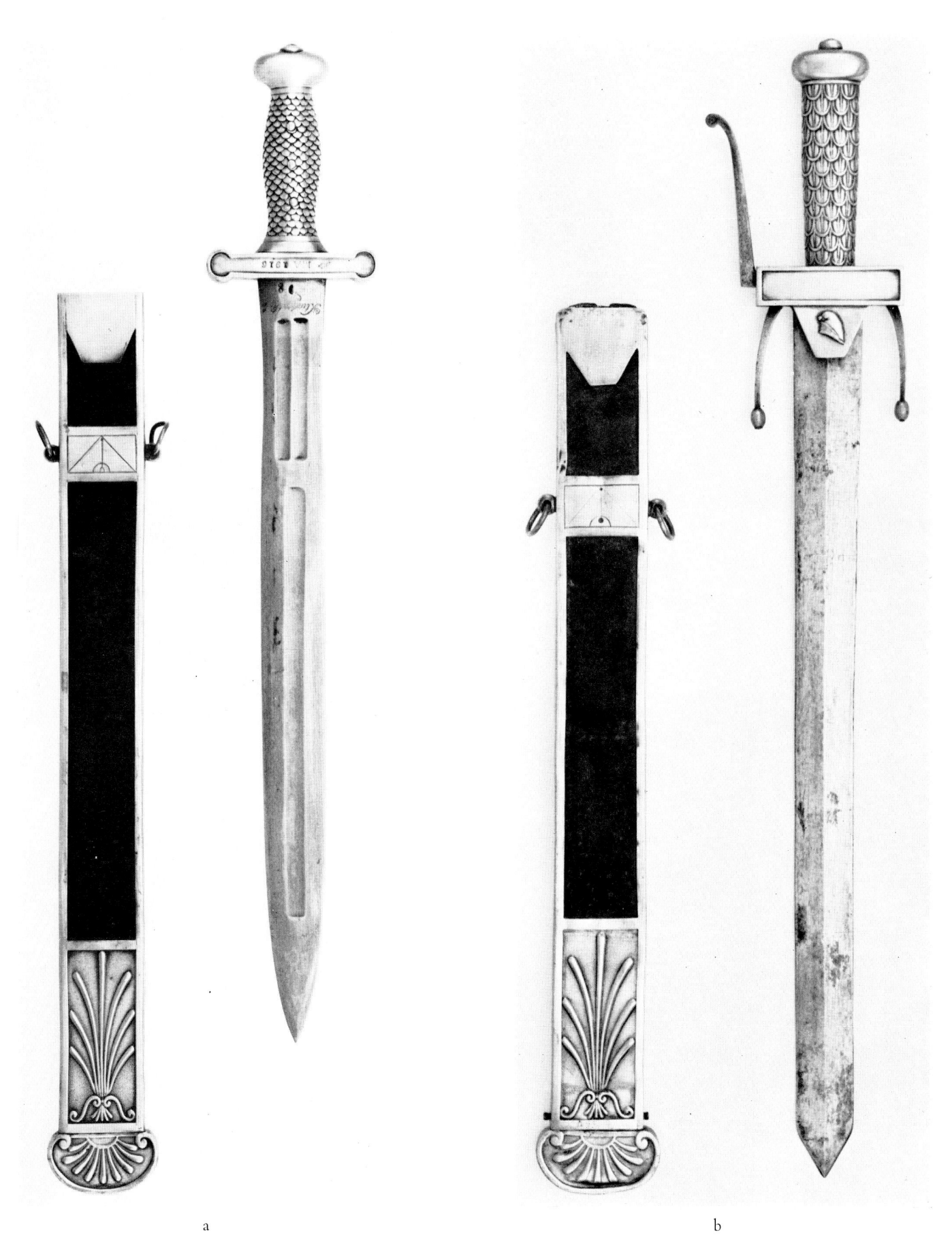

French cadet swords, *c.* 1790–5.

PLATE 88

a b c

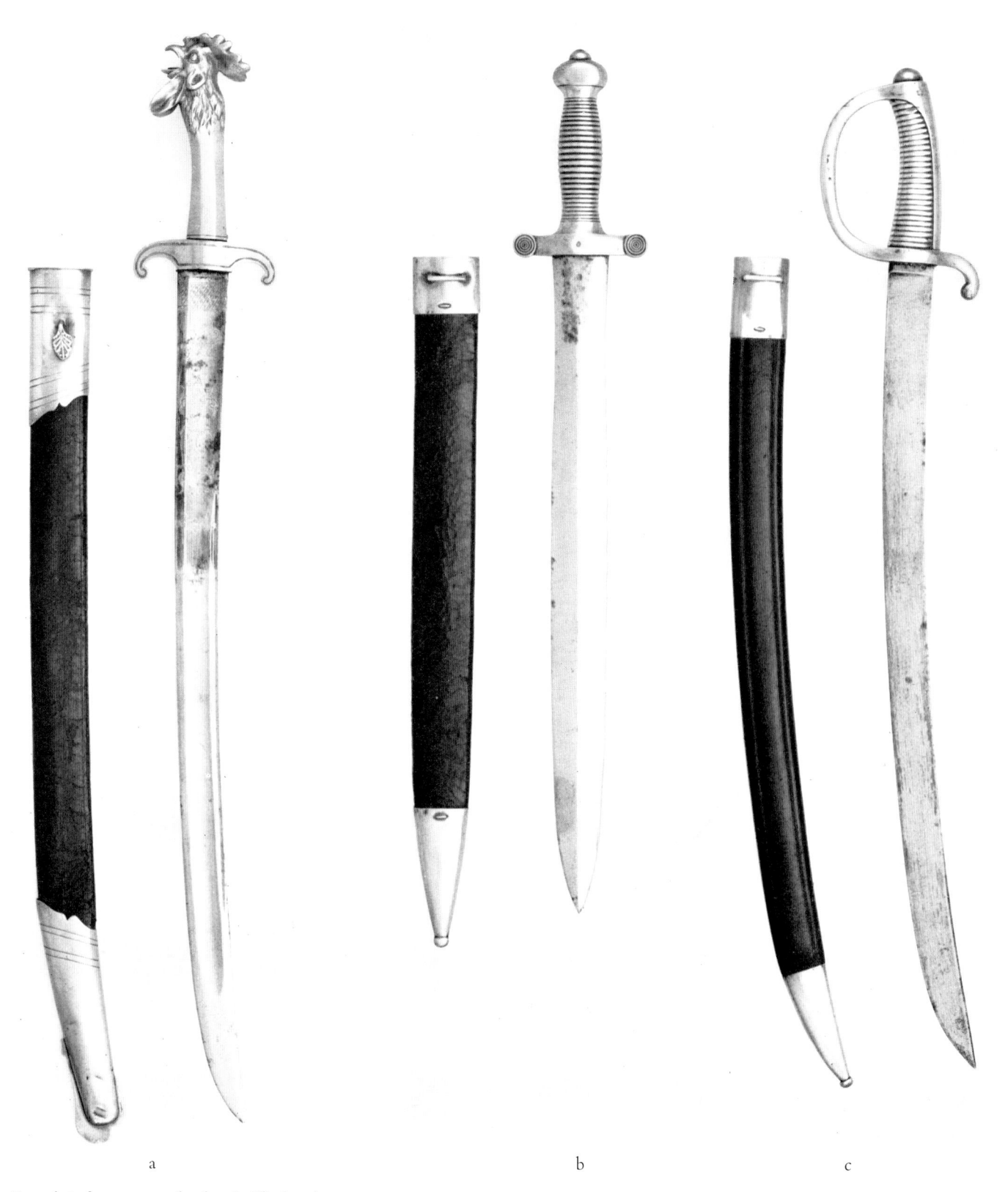

French infantry swords, first half of 19th century.

PLATE 89

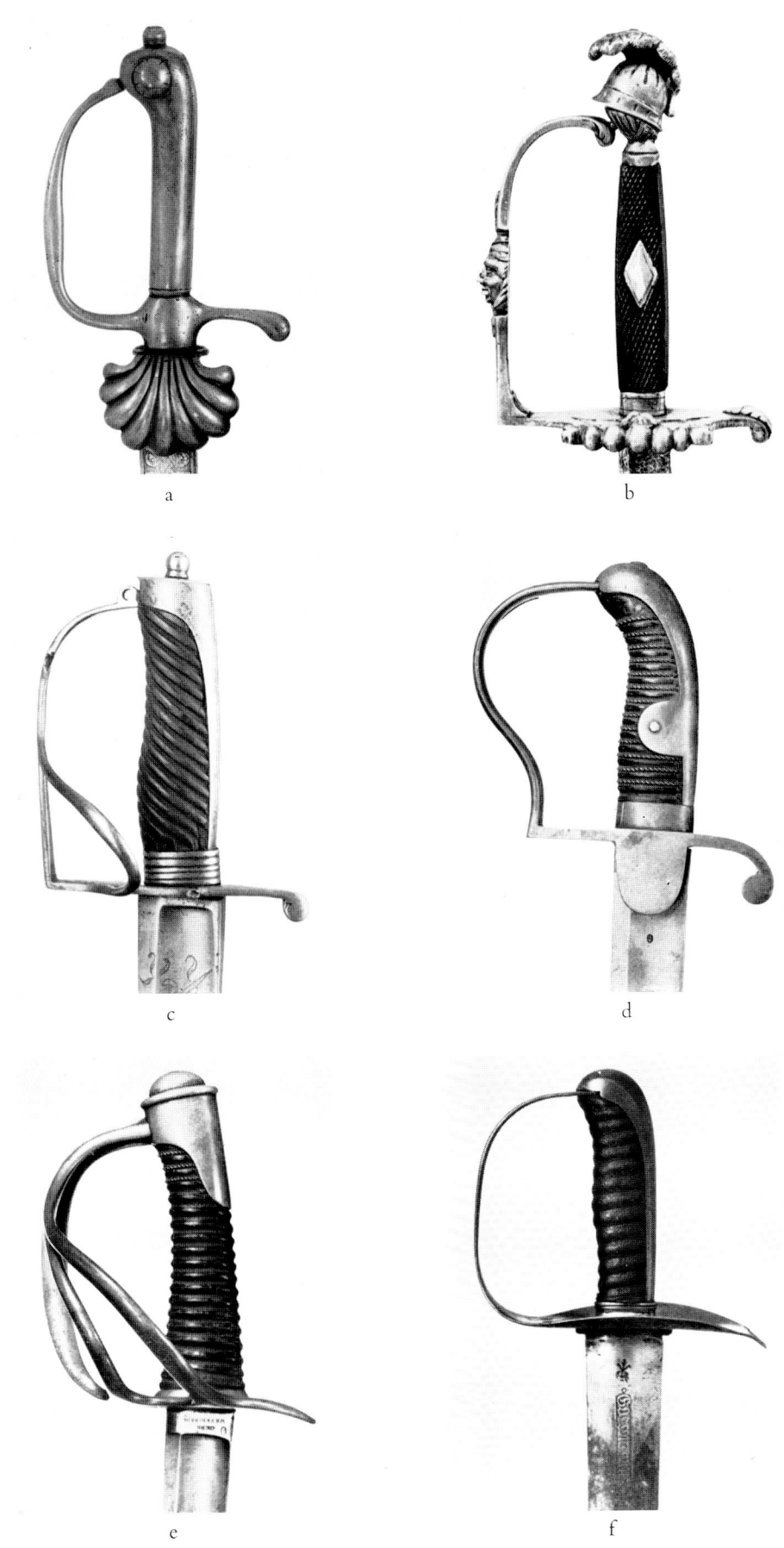

German and Austrian military swords.

PLATE 90

a b

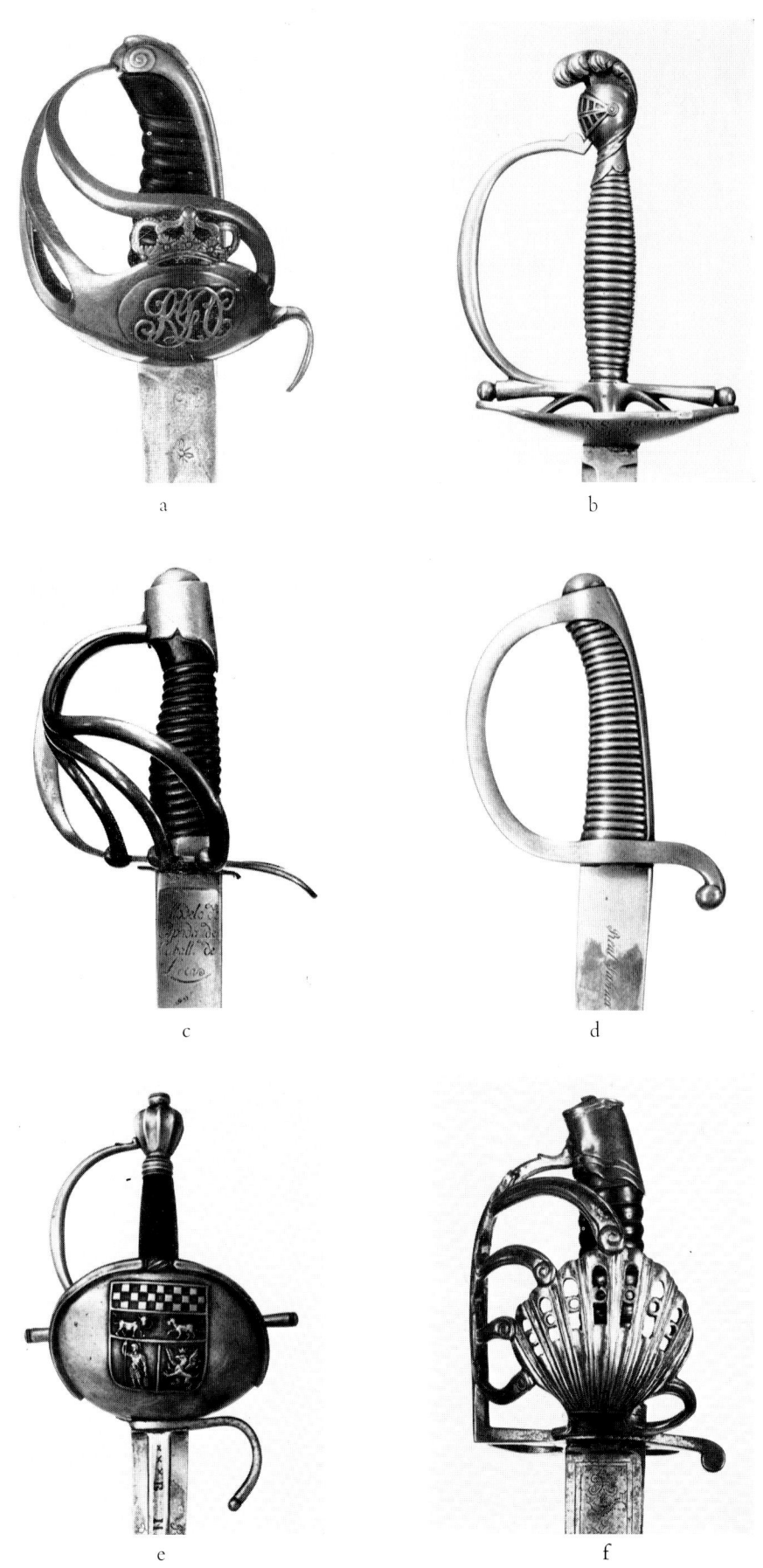

c d

e f

Spanish and Italian military swords.

PLATE 91

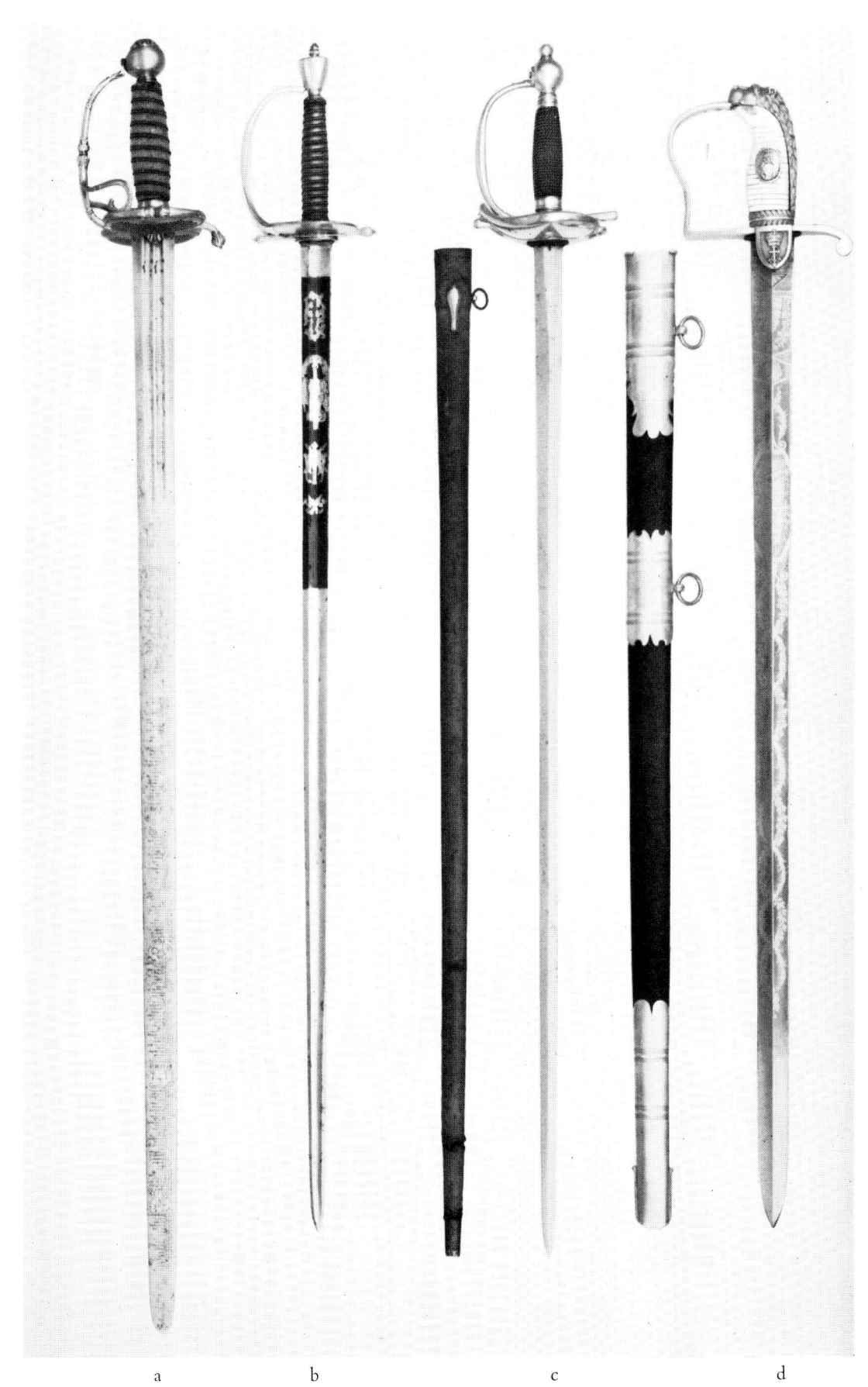

a b c d
Royal swords, George II to William IV.

PLATE 92

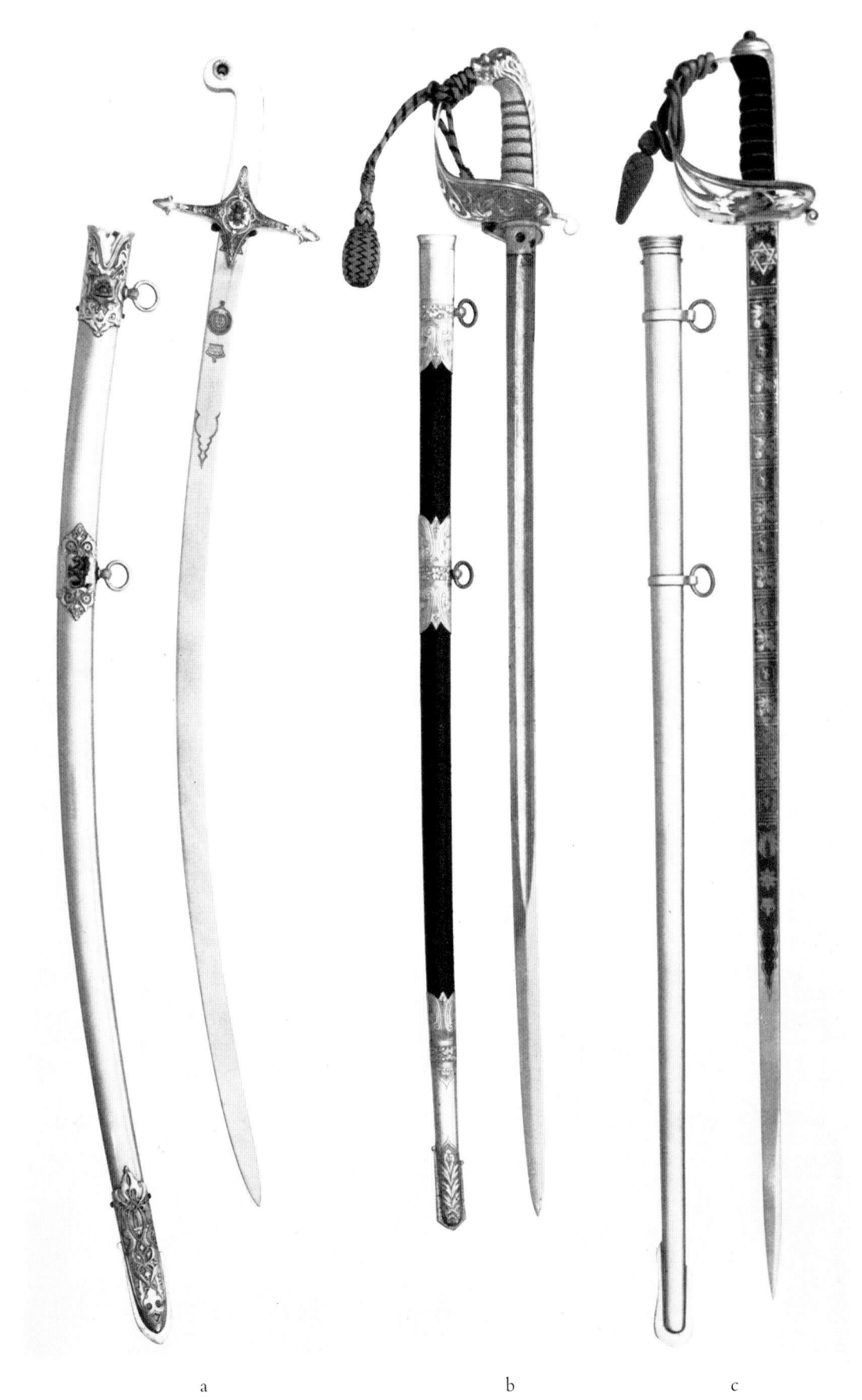

a b c
Royal swords, Edward VII to George VI.

PLATE 93

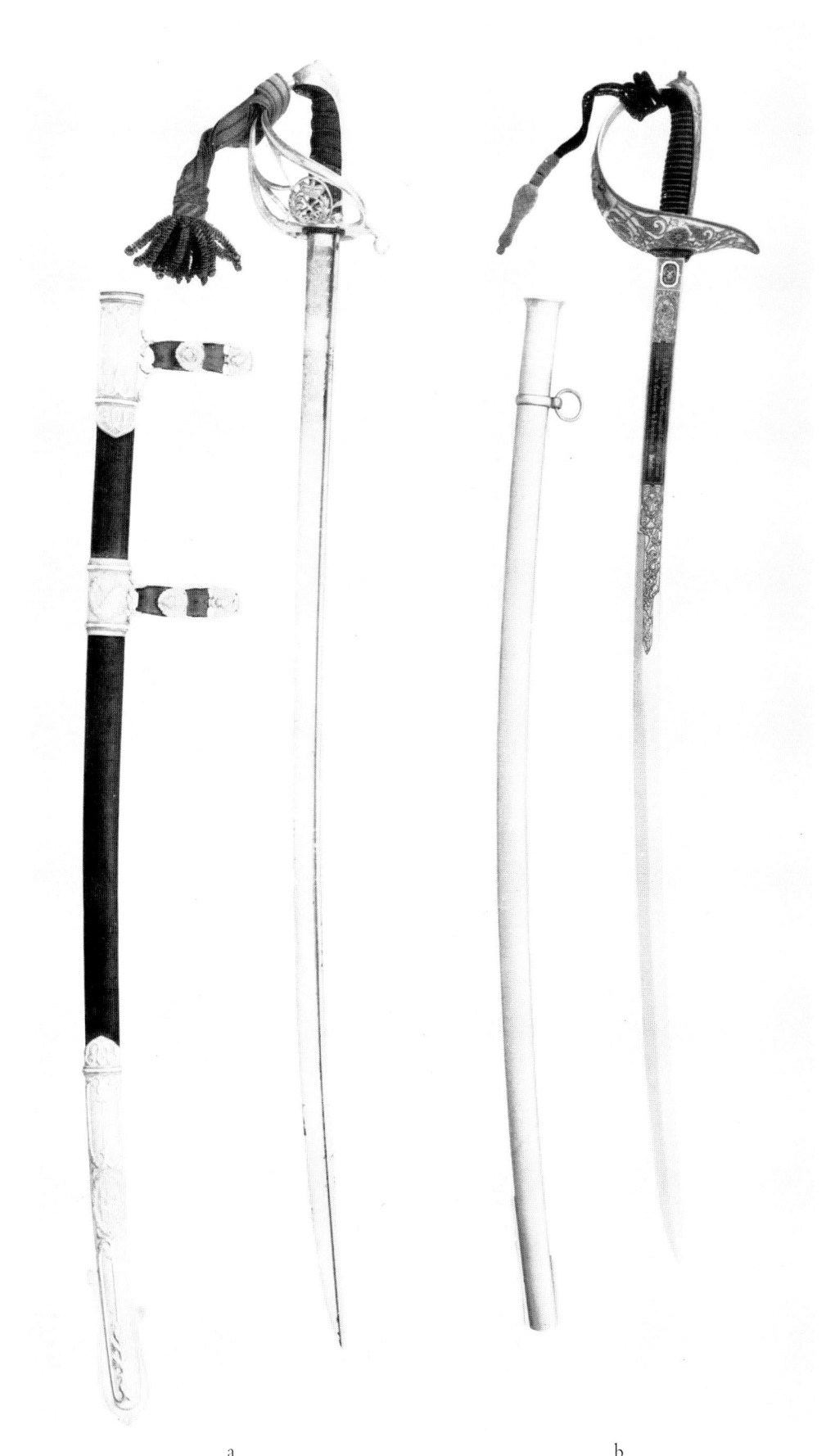

a   b
(a) Sword of the first Duke of York; (b) Sword of the Duke of Connaught.

PLATE 94

DAGGERS

a b c d

Daggers of the 15th century.

PLATE 95

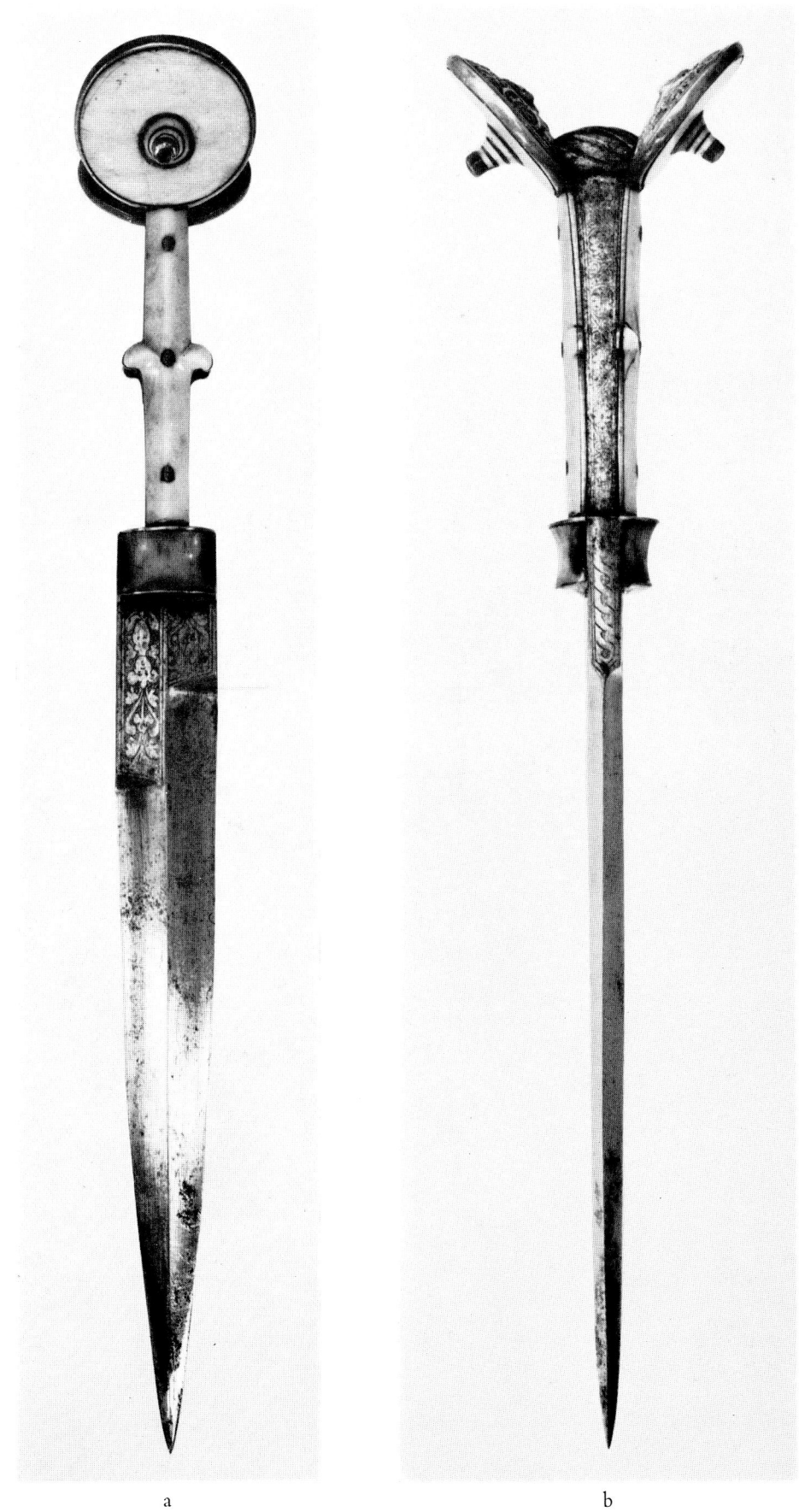

a   b
Italian 'ear' dagger, c. 1500.

PLATE 96

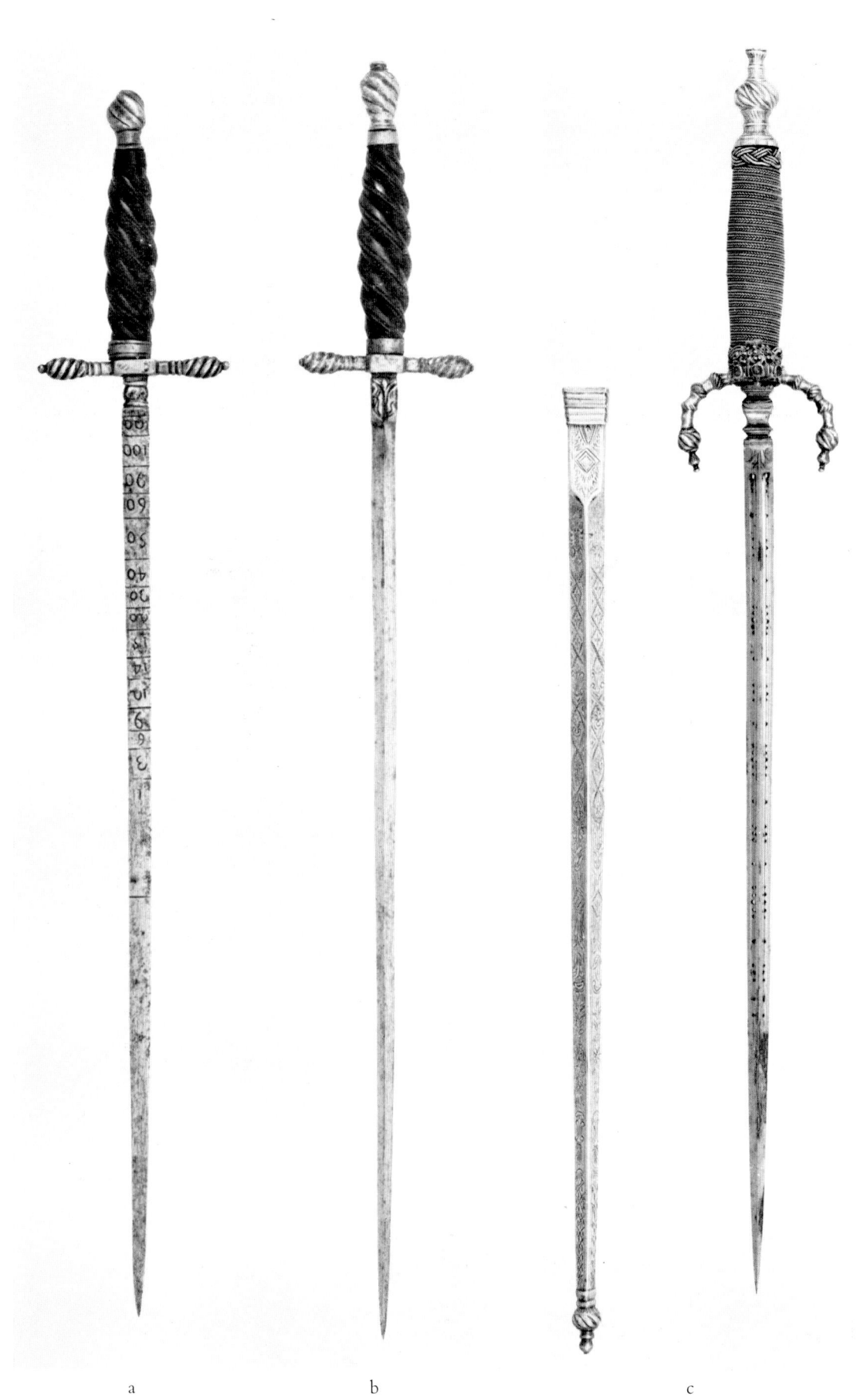

    a   b   c
(a–b) Gunners' stiletti, *c.* 1650; (c) Dalmatian dagger, late 18th century.

PLATE 97

f

e

d

c

b

a

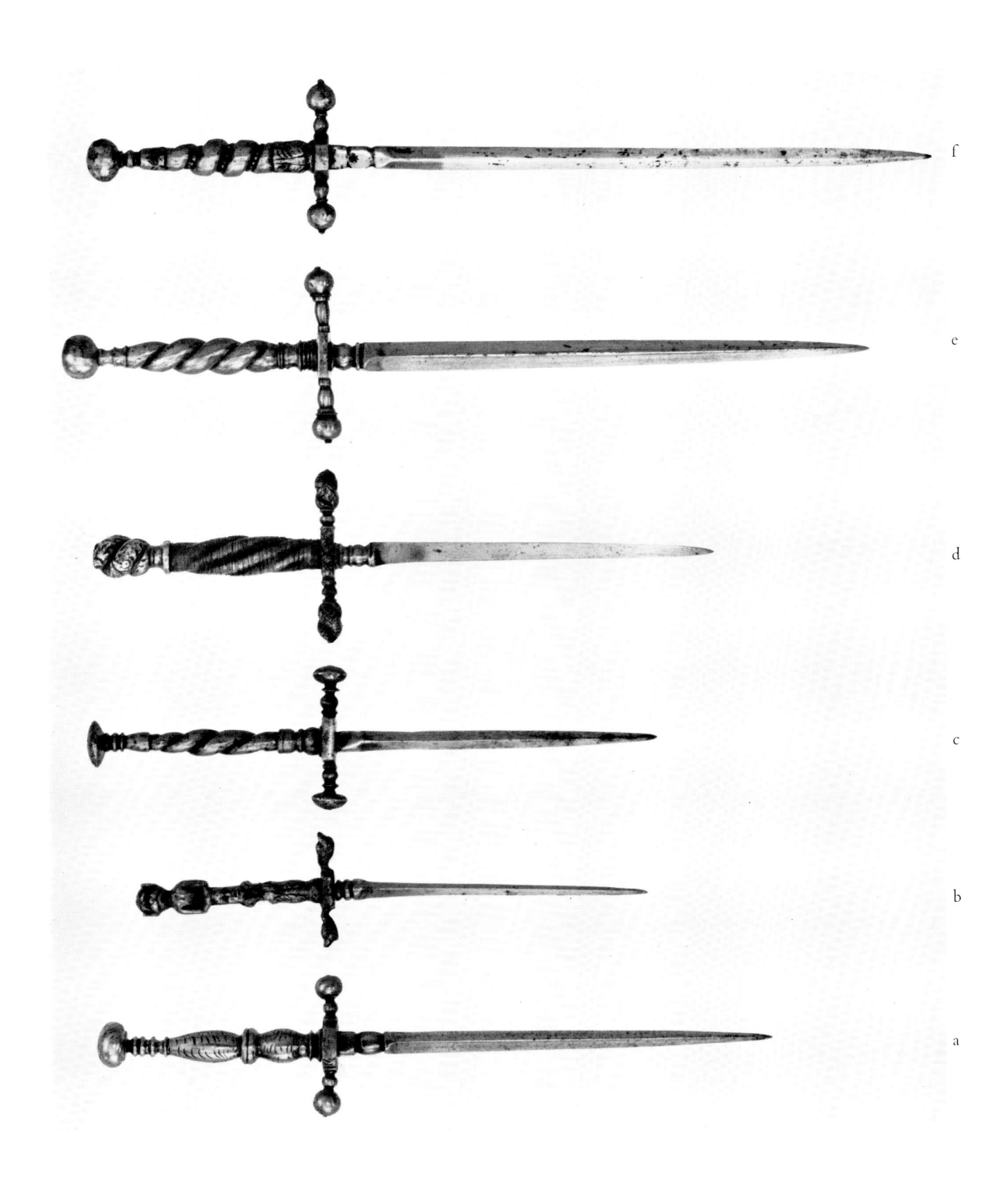

Italian stiletti, 16th century.

PLATE 98

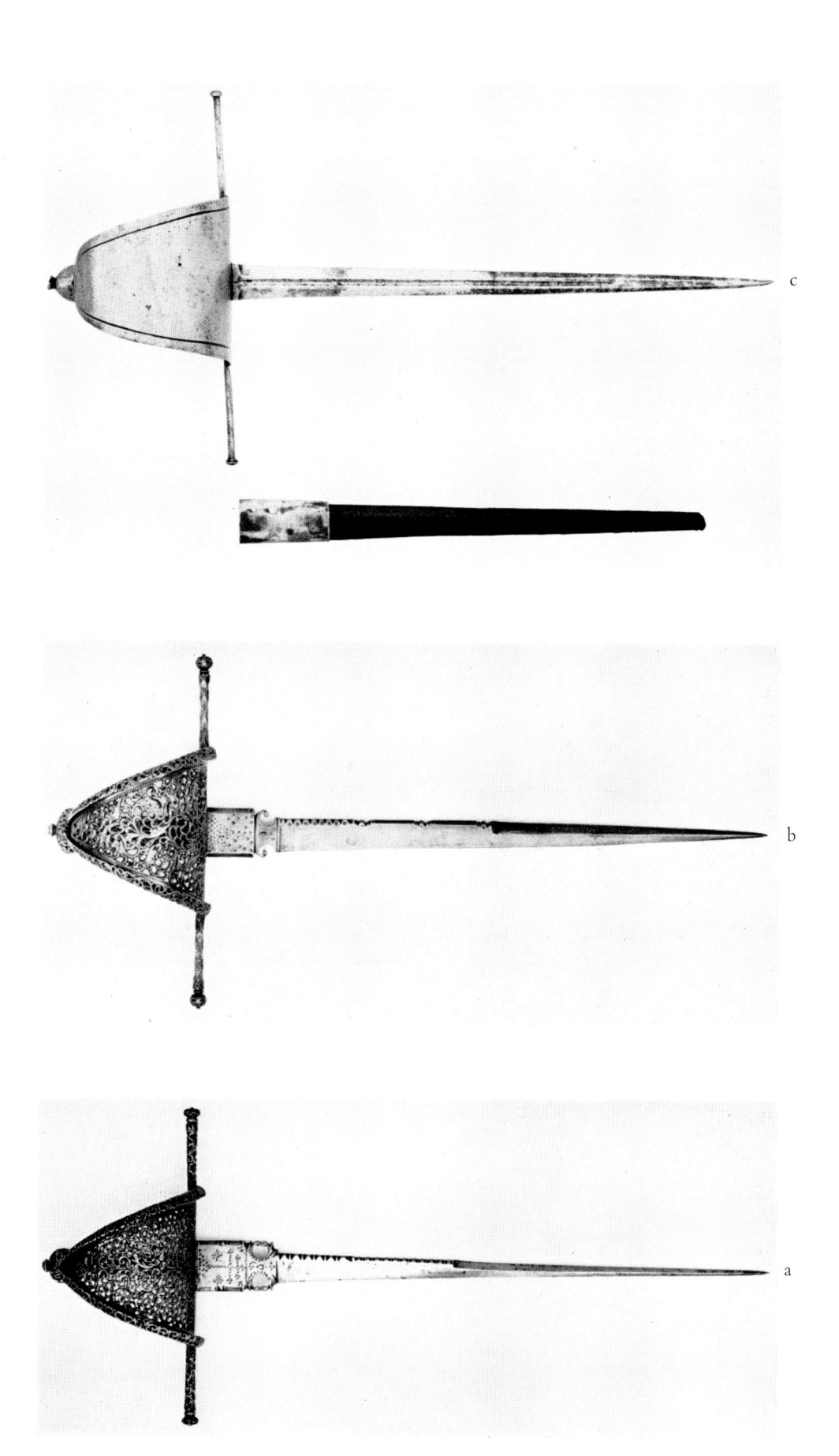

Spanish left-hand daggers, 17th–18th centuries.

PLATE 99

a   b

German left-hand daggers, *c.* 1610.

PLATE 100

a b c

Left-hand daggers, *c.* 1600.

PLATE 101

a
b
c

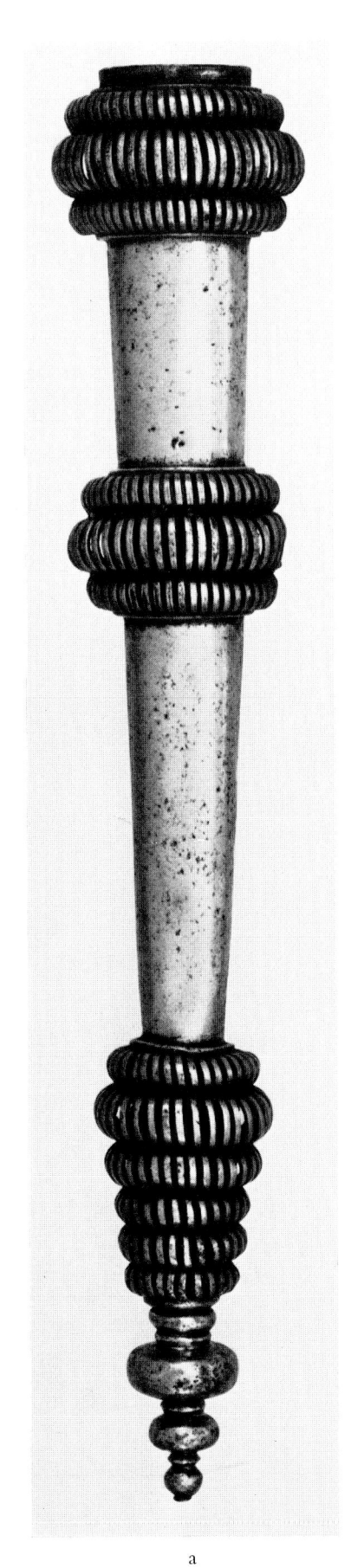

Sheaths, 16th and 17th centuries.

PLATE 102

a
Ballock daggers.
b
c

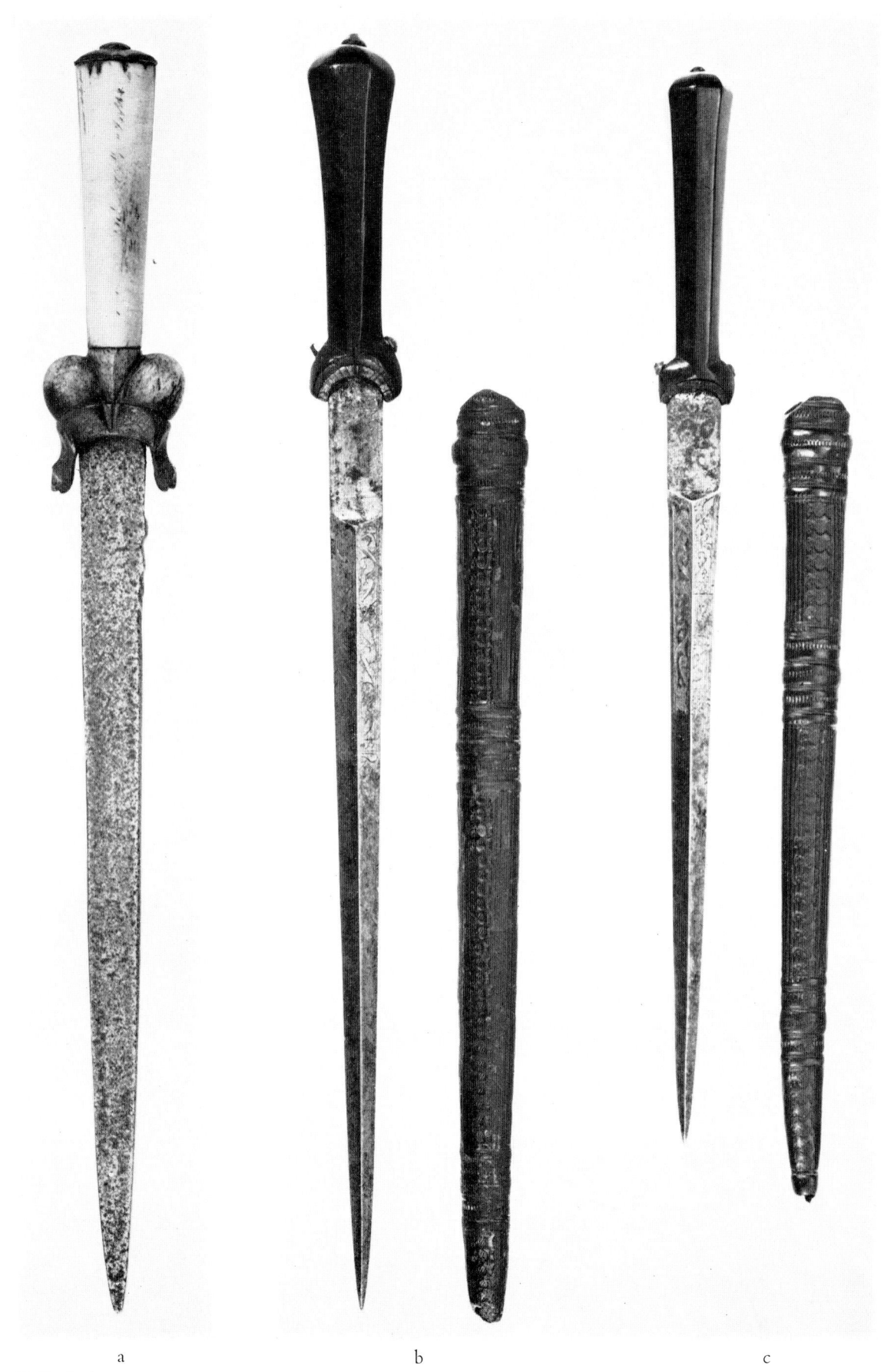

PLATE 103

a   b   c

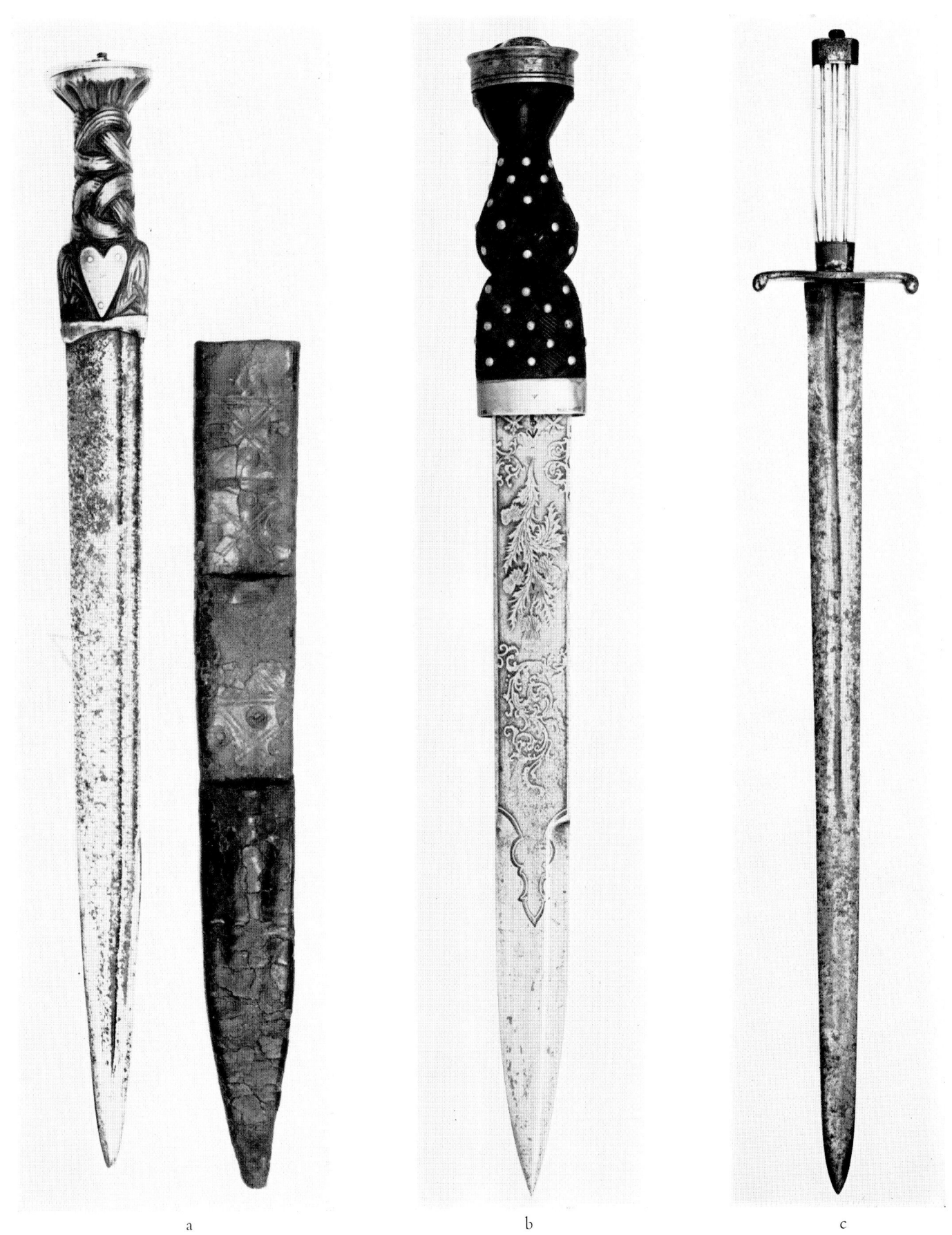

Military dirks, 18th–19th centuries.

PLATE 104

a

b

c

English daggers.

PLATE 105

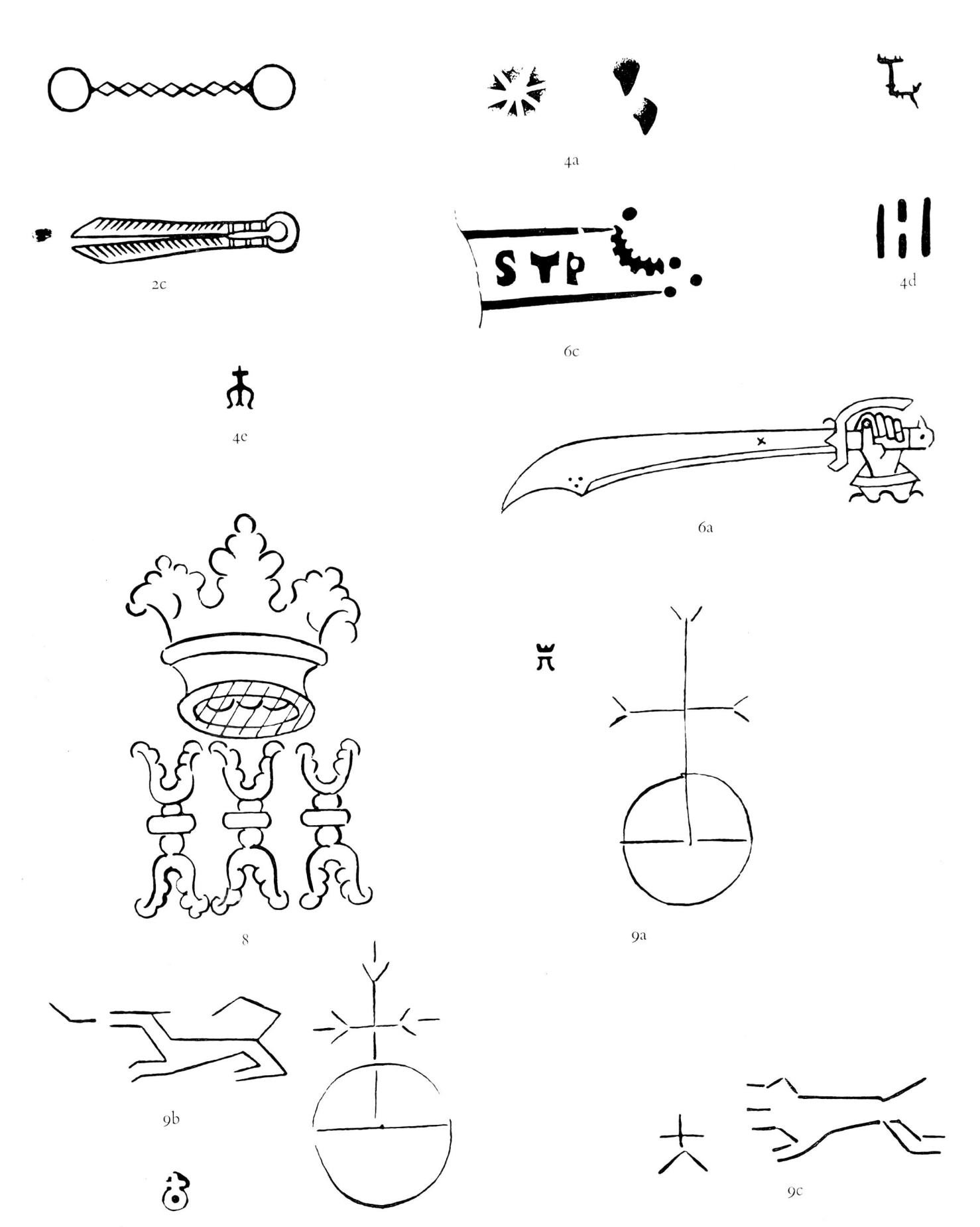

Makers' marks.

PLATE 106

Makers' marks.

PLATE 107

Makers' marks.

PLATE 108

Makers' marks.

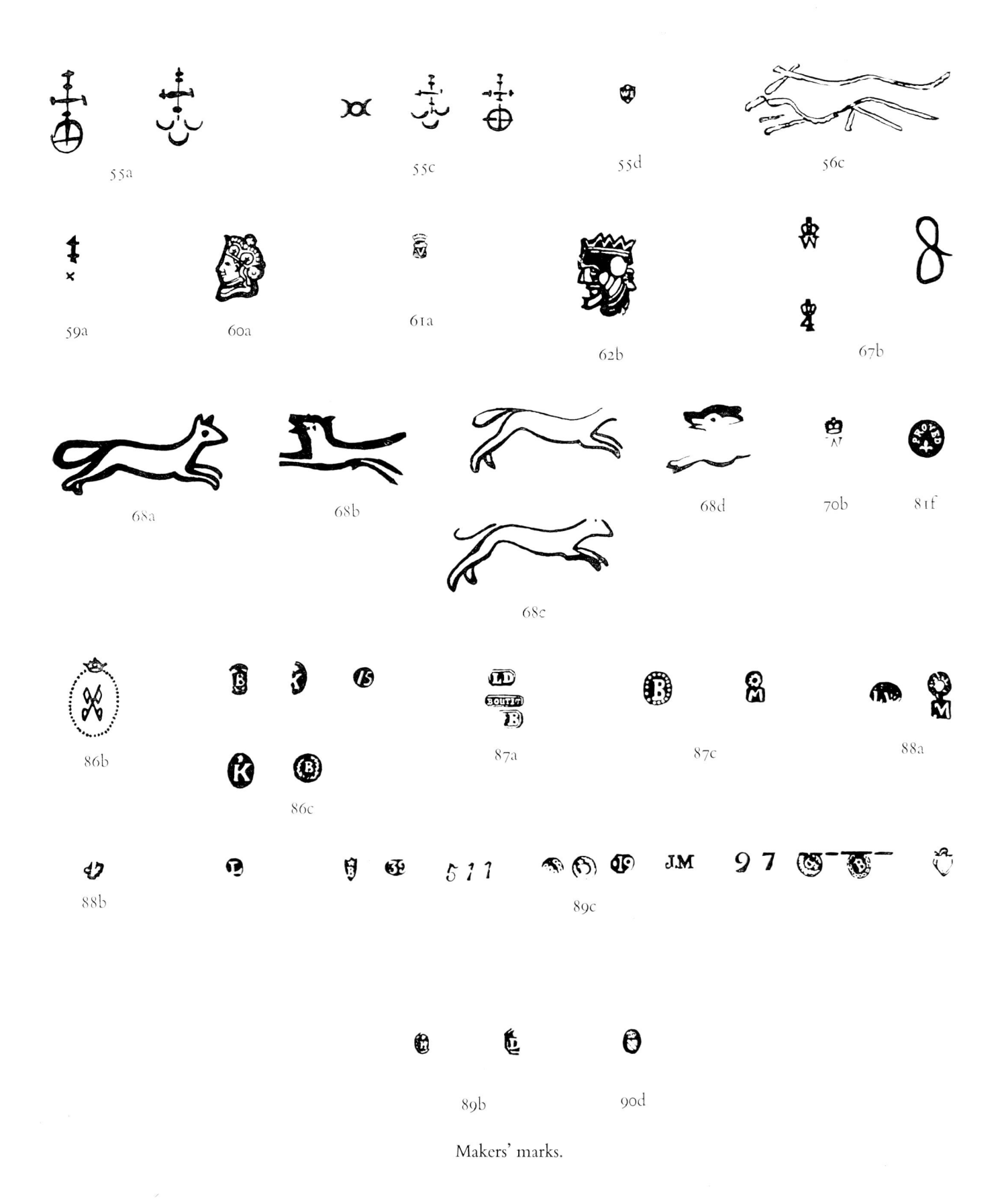

PLATE 109

TABLE OF TOWER INVENTORY NUMBERS AND LENGTHS OF SWORDS AND DAGGERS SHOWN IN THE PLATES

The length given represents the length of the sword or dagger over all. Swords catalogued as Mann are on loan to the Armouries from the Trustees of the late Sir James Mann.

Plate	Inventory Number	Length	Plate	Inventory Number	Length
1a	Mann	95 cms	16b	IX–984	92·7 cms
1b	IX–859	90·2 cms	17a	IX–898	109·9 cms
1c	IX–1081	96·5 cms	17b	IX–169	92·7 cms
2a	IX–12	99·1 cms	18a	IX–635	107·9 cms
2b	IX–1027	105·4 cms	18b–c	IX–1097	89·9 cms
2c	IX–1082	99·2 cms	18d	IX–1256	114·3 cms
2d	IX–1107	91·4 cms	19a	IX–155	92·7 cms
3a	IX–1083	101·6 cms	19b	IX–767	68·1 cms
3b	Mann	98 cms	19c	IX–146	70·8 cms
3c	IX–985	92·7 cms	20a	IX–767	68·1 cms
3d	IX–13	83·2 cms	20b	IX–146	70·8 cms
4a	IX–1084	107·9 cms	21a	IX–54	123·7 cms
4b	IX–1115	56·1 cms	21b	IX–1225	114·8 cms
4c	IX–14	128·4 cms	21c	IX–941	123·5 cms
4d	IX–915	122·3 cms	21d	IX–1029	98·6 cms
4e	IX–950	104·1 cms	22	IX–1225	114·8 cms
4f	IX–1106	112·4 cms	23a	IX–729 Mann	
5a	IX–16	119 cms		Mann	
5b	Mann	106·4 cms	23b	IX–880 –1261	
5c	IX–949	109·7 cms			
6a	IX–926	173·5 cms	24a	IX–55	135·2 cms
6b	IX–991	156·5 cms	24b	IX–56	137 cms
6c	IX–6	192·1 cms	24c	IX–113	126·5 cms
7a	IX–9	171·5 cms	24d	IX–57	124·7 cms
7b	IX–4	193·1 cms	24e	IX–62	128 cms
7c	IX–5	168·5 cms	25a	IX–900	121·5 cms
8a–b	IX–629	203·2 cms	25b–c	IX–861	121·5 cms
9a	IX–912	149·5 cms	26a	IX–878	119·4 cms
9b	IX–943	148·5 cms	26b	IX–893	125·2 cms
9c	IX–11	140 cms	26c	IX–123	106·7 cms
10a	IX–1024	231·1 cms	26d	IX–877	130·8 cms
10b	IX–628	190·5 cms	27a	IX–870	120·7 cms
11	IX–764	126·8 cms	27b	IX–869	126·2 cms
12a–c	IX–728	105·4 cms	27c	IX–99	116·8 cms
12d	IX–875	110·5 cms	27d	IX–879	119·4 cms
12e	IX–35	100·6 cms	28a	IX–940	105 cms
13a	IX–38	123·2 cms	28b	IX–899	115·4 cms
13b	IX–897	123·2 cms	28c	IX–970	113 cms
13c	IX–50	124 cms	28d	IX–833	118·1 cms
14a	IX–896	135·9 cms	29a	IX–982	105·4 cms
14b	IX–1033	130·4 cms	29b	IX–965	110 cms
14c	IX–763	111·3 cms	29c	IX–986	110·5 cms
15a	IX–144	80·4 cms	29d	IX–914	115·5 cms
15b	IX–1232	77·8 cms	30a	IX–1213	118·1 cms
15c	Mann	85·4 cms	30b	IX–952	120·8 cms
16a	Mann	84·2 cms			

Plate	Inventory Number	Length	Plate	Inventory Number	Length
31a	IX–797	97 cms	51b	IX–223	98 cms
31b	IX–125	104·8 cms	51c	IX–222	96·5 cms
31c	IX–795	109·2 cms	51d	IX–226	99·1 cms
31d	IX–796	102·9 cms	52a	IX–1287	100·4 cms
32a	IX–97	113·3 cms	52b–c	IX–1015	78 cms
32b	IX–885	112·6 cms	53a	IX–227	101·6 cms
32c	IX–884	114·4 cms	53b	IX–1080	100·1 cms
32d	IX–1101	110·8 cms	53c	IX–830	101·8 cms
33a	IX–885	112·6 cms	53d	IX–236	98 cms
33b	IX–887	127 cms	54a	IX–873	101·3 cms
33c	IX–1103	132·5 cms	54b	IX–999	99·4 cms
34a	IX–87	91·9 cms	54c	IX–958	104·1 cms
34b	IX–85	131·3 cms	55a	IX–942	74·4 cms
34c	IX–793	118·9 cms	55b	IX–755	73·2 cms
34d	IX–888	119·4 cms	55c	IX–157	74·4 cms
35a	IX–634	121·9 cms	55d	IX–918	66·8 cms
35b	IX–156	125·8 cms	56a	IX–1223	98·6 cms
35c	IX–907	106·3 cms	56b	On loan from the Dean and Chapter of Brecon Cathedral	55·6 cms
35d	IX–159	93·9 cms			
36a	IX–158	83·8 cms			
36b	IX–160	86·1 cms	56c	IX–1211	61·7 cms
36c	IX–161	77·7 cms	57a	IX–1218	89·5 cms
36d	IX–1013	101·8 cms	57b	IX–1219	46·3 cms
37	IX–745, 742, 750 732, 734, 737, 740, 739, 881, 731, 733, 741.		58a	IX–852	91·9 cms
			58b	IX–854	72·4 cms
			58c	IX–758	72·4 cms
			58d	IX–757	71·1 cms
38	IX–52	107·9 cms	59a	IX–858	68·6 cms
39a	IX–1217	95·4 cms	59b	IX–1034	83·4 cms
39b	IX–1248	100·3 cms	59c	IX–1249	75·8 cms
39c	IX–995	98 cms	60a	IX–960	70 cms
40a–b	IX–972	111·7 cms	60b	IX–978	73·7 cms
40c–d	IX–1004	101·6 cms	61a	IX–849	71·4 cms
41a	IX–180	108·2 cms	61b	IX–977	56·1 cms
41b	IX–184	90·2 cms	62a	IX–139	65·5 cms
41c	IX–48	98·7 cms	62b–c	IX–979	103·6 cms
41d	IX–165	92 cms	63a	IX–997	104·1 cms
42a	IX–69	107·1 cms	63b	IX–1002	98·5 cms
42b	IX–37	90·2 cms	63c	IX–894	97·1 cms
42c	IX–178	101·6 cms	63d	IX–935	99·1 cms
42d	IX–170	106·8 cms	64a	IX–892	100·3 cms
43a	IX–1200	98 cms	64b	IX–891	95·2 cms
43b	IX–641	102·9 cms	64c	IX–693	96·5 cms
43c	IX–194	99·3 cms	64d	IX–936	100·3 cms
43d	IX–953	96·5 cms	65	IX–909	101·6 cms
44	IX–198	106·2 cms	66a	IX–798	98·5 cms
45a	IX–934	99·3 cms	66b	IX–138	99·3 cms
45b	IX–917	106·7 cms	66c	IX–801	97·7 cms
46	IX–1096	97 cms	67a	IX–863	83 cms
47a	Mann	91·1 cms	67b	IX–435	82·1 cms
47b	IX–1214	98·1 cms	67c	IX–762	80 cms
47c	Mann	101·9 cms	68a	IX–374	86·8 cms
47d	IX–957	108·7 cms	68b	IX–375	91·5 cms
48a	IX–1086	97·4 cms	68c	IX–605	78·3 cms
48b	IX–1245	105·4 cms	68d	IX–791	85·6 cms
49a	IX–206	100·3 cms	69a	IX–1121	110·5 cms
49b	IX–1010	109·2 cms	69b	IX–1204	101·2 cms
49c	IX–1089	91 cms	69c	IX–233	102 cms
50a	Mann	98·6 cms	69d	IX–606	111·8 cms
50b	IX–1046	105·4 cms	70a	IX–320	106·9 cms
50c	IX–944	104·9 cms	70b	IX–253	101·6 cms
51a	IX–1114	99·1 cms	70c	IX–235	105·7 cms

Plate	Inventory Number	Length	Plate	Inventory Number	Length
70d	IX–327	103·7 cms	90c	IX–471	97 cms
71a	IX–378	103·8 cms	90d	IX–358	94·8 cms
71b	IX–331	105·4 cms	90e	IX–486	107 cms
71c	IX–955	123·2 cms	90f	IX–653	107·3 cms
72a	IX–245	95·3 cms	91a	IX–444	98·2 cms
72b	IX–835	95·3 cms	91b	IX–458	95 cms
72c	IX–922	96 cms	91c	IX–448	109·7 cms
73a	IX–1005	81·2 cms	91d	IX–467	73·9 cms
73b	IX–1056	104·6 cms	91e	IX–1019	118 cms
73c	IX–913	94 cms	91f	IX–231	105·6 cms
74	I–63		92a	IX–1243	104·6 cms
75a–b	IX–243	90·7 cms	92b	IX–1244	97 cms
75c	IX–620	95·8 cms	92c	IX–1239	98·6 cms
76a	IX–901	100 cms	92d	IX–1242	94·5 cms
76b	IX–1091	97 cms	93a	IX–1240	89·1 cms
76c	IX–381	96 cms	93b	IX–1241	90·4 cms
77a	IX–387	95·2 cms	93c	IX–1238	97·8 cms
77b	IX–394	96 cms	94a	IX–1237	89·4 cms
77c	IX–382	95·2 cms	94b	IX–1102	94·5 cms
77d	IX–393	94·8 cms			
78a	IX–411	67·7 cms			
78b	IX–413	70·2 cms			
78c	IX–414	71·1 cms			
79a	IX–968	102·9 cms			
79b	IX–256	102·4 cms		DAGGERS	
79c	IX–339	104·6 cms	Plate	Inventory Number	Length
80a	IX–255	106·4 cms			
80b	IX–256	102·5 cms			
80c	IX–317	109·2 cms	95a	X–297	49 cms
80d	IX–342	105·7 cms	95b	X–270	30·5 cms
81a	IX–343	101·6 cms	95c	X–1	33·5 cms
81b	IX–699	101·8 cms	95d	X–2	50·3 cms
81c	IX–700	108·5 cms	96	X–258	31·8 cms
81d	IX–334	101·1 cms	97a	X–249	56·9 cms
81e	IX–704	101·6 cms	97b	X–250	59·7 cms
81f	IX–344	101·6 cms	97c	X–232	54·2 cms
82a	IX–430	97·6 cms	98a	X–30	33·9 cms
82b	IX–421	83·4 cms	98b	X–31	32·8 cms
82c	IX–713	81·3 cms	98c	X–33	25·2 cms
83a	IX–538	46·5 cms	98d	X–34	23 cms
83b	IX–539	62·2 cms	98e	X–35	20·8 cms
83c	IX–540	47 cms	98f	X–32	27·3 cms
83d	IX–541	62·2 cms	99a	X–256	59·5 cms
84a	IX–443	92·7 cms	99b	X–367	55·9 cms
84b	IX–536	79·6 cms	99c	X–239	42·5 cms
84c	IX–469	68·5 cms	100a	X–254	41·9 cms
84d	IX–1090	66·1 cms	100b	X–255	46·2 cms
85a–b	IX–908	99·7 cms	101a	X–17	47·5 cms
85c	IX–1095	59·7 cms	101b	X–260	40·6 cms
86a	IX–638	118·1 cms	101c	X–252	39·5 cms
86b	IX–643	109·2 cms	102a	X–234	28·5 cms
86c	IX–644	114·3 cms	102b	X–61	20·6 cms
87a	IX–475	79·6 cms	102c	X–63	27·5 cms
87b	IX–619	105·4 cms	103a	X–283	38·6 cms
87c	IX–477	102·3 cms	103b	X–214a	39·1 cms
88a	IX–647	63·5 cms	103c	X–214b	30·7 cms
88b	IX–967	66·1 cms	104a	X–285	40·6 cms
89a	IX–969	91·5 cms	104b	X–217	43·4 cms
89b	IX–965	63·5 cms	104c	X–332	54·2 cms
89c	IX–966	74·2 cms	105a	X–267	31 cms
90a	IX–419	74·9 cms	105b	X–299	31·3 cms
90b	IX–931	97·8 cms	105c	X–374	40·2 cms

Printed in England for Her Majesty's Stationery Office by Swindon Press, Swindon, Wilts.
Dd 503947 K24 3/74

INDEX

(References to the Notes Section are in italics and are by plate numbers).

ALEXANDRIA *4d*
ALLAN, John (Sr.) *53a*
  ,,   John (Jr.) *54c*
  ,,   Walter *53b,c*
ANTWERP, Archaeological Museum *2d*

BARCELONA *42b*
BATE, Thomas *72c*
BATTISTA, Giovanni *26c*
BAVARIA, Charles, Duke of *90c*
BERNE *43a*
BIRMINGHAM *70a, 71a, 79b, 83a*
BISCOTTO *15c, 16b*
BLOOD, Colonel 7, *103b*
BOTARELLO, Carlo *61b*
BOUTET, Nicolas-Noel *87a*
BRABENDER, Heinrich *26a*
BRACH, Johannes *92a*
BRESCIA 8, *31c,d, 61b,*
BRUNSWICK 11, *8*

CAINO *26d*
CARMAN, John *58b*
CARTER & Co. *93b*
CHARLES I of England *28d, 29c, 47, 48*
COLOGNE, Beer Brewers' Guild of 7, *6b*
COLLINGWOOD, Vice-Admiral Lord 11, *65*
CONNAUGHT, Duke of *94b*
CONSTANCE, Lake *4f*
COPENHAGEN, Battle of *104c*
COULAUX *87b*
CRAIG, Robert *54b*
CROMWELL, Oliver 7, *46*
CULLUM *71b*
CYPRUS *4c*

DAGGERS
  Dirks *104*
  Ear *96*
  Left-hand *25a, 99-101*
  Mediaeval *95*
  Stiletti *16a, 97, 98*
DAVIS, Capt. Delmé 11
DAWES *79b*
DESMAZIS, Alexandre *85a*
DRESDEN, Armoury of the Electors of Saxony *21c, 39a, 57*
DROGHEDA 7, *46*

EAST INDIA CO. *81e*
ECKSTEIN, Sir Bernard 11
EDWARD VII of England *93a*
EDWARD, the Black Prince *52b*
EHINGER, Adam *62a*
ENFIELD *53d, 80d*
ERNANDEZ, Sebastian *91e*

FERDINAND IV of Sicily *91f*
FERRARA, Andrea 8, *31a, 39b, 47c, 49b, 51a, 53b, 54a,b*
FRANKFURT-AM-MAIN *59a*
FREDERICK V of Bohemia *62b*

GARDEN & SON. *81e*
GEORGE II of England *92a*
GEORGE III of England 7. *76b, 92b*
GEORGE IV of England *92c*
GEORGE V of England *93b*
GEORGE VI of England 11, *93c*
GIHAMI, Vincencio *28d*
GILL, Thomas *70a, 72b*
GLASGOW *54a,b*
GODFREY, Sir Edmund Berry *105b*
GOUBAUD, Le Sieur *85c*
GRUSON *67c*
GUSTAVUS ADOLPHUS of Sweden *38*

HAMBURGER ROGERS & Co. *81f*
HARPER, Thomas *65*
HENRY VI of England *9*
HENRY VIII of England *9*
HERBERT & Co. *82b,c*
HERMESTHORPE, John de *6*
HERNANTEZ, Sebastian *63b*
HEWITT, John 11
HOLLIER, Thomas *67a*
HORTUNO DE AGUIRE *32b*
HORTUNO, Maria de *32a*
HOUNSLOW *28c, 29a*
HUDSON'S BAY CO. *59b*

KEISSER, Hermann *30b*
KEULLER, Clemens *12c*
KING, William *59c*
KINNDT, Johannes *28c, 29a*
KIRSCHBAUM, Carl *78c*
KLINGENTHAL *86c, 87, 89a*
KNEGT, Jean *73c*
KNUBLEY, John *73b*

LE COURT *66b*
LONDON
  Bankside House, Southwark *3c*
  City Train Band *49b*
  Cutlers, Co. of 10, *58b, 59b, 74*
  Houses of Parliament *3d*
  London Bridge *5a*
  Tottenham Association *68c*
  Wallace Collection *33c*
  Wormwood Scrubs Prison *84d*
LOXHAM, Edward *59b*
LOXHAM, William *58b*
LUCCA *16b*

155

MADRID, Royal Armoury *32b*
MALTA *11*
MANBERGER, Phillip *59a*
MANSFELD, Ernst, Count of *62b*
MARTI, Joseph *42b*
MEYRICK, Dr. Samuel *18c*
MOLE, Robert *83a, 104b*
MONTE, Pedro del *64a*
MOUM, Hans *29b*
MUNICH *6a, 11, 35b*
MUNICH, Peter *40*

NAPOLEON I of France *11, 85*
NASSAU, Princes of *62b*
NERO, Coin of *19b*
NEWBURY *2a*
NOSO *45b*

OATES, Titus *105b*
OLLICH, Hans *33c*
ORDNANCE, Board of *10, 67a*
OSBORN, Henry *74*
OSBORN & GRUNDY *72a 78a*

PAETER, Peter *52a*
PARIS *10, 11, 8, 66b, 88a*
PARKER, W. *84c*
PARKER FIELD & SONS *84d*
PATEY, Midshipman *104c*
PICHINIO, Antonio *64b*
POPISH PLOT *105b*
PORRETT, Robert *11*
PRINCE, Colonel *7, 76b*
PROSSER, John *94a*

REEVES, Charles *79c, 84b*
RUNKEL, John *74, 75c, 76a*
RUIS, Francisco *29c*

SAXONY, Armoury of the Electors of *21c, 39a, 57*
SCABBARDS & SHEATHS *8, 9, 11, 14c, 16a, 19b, 21c, 23b, 57, 58b, 59b,c, 65, 66b, 70d, 73a,b, 75a, 76b, 88b, 97c, 98c, 100, 103b.*
SHAW, John *79a*
SHOTLEY BRIDGE *68*
SIMPSON, John *54a*
SKINNER, Richard *10*
SMITH, Edward *93c*
SOLINGEN *12e, 26a, 29b, 30b, 32d, 33c, 34c, 39c, 40, 43a, 48a, 52a, 60a, 62b, 73c, 74, 75c, 78, 90e, 92a*
STADTAMHOF *62a*
STANTLER, Christof *6a, 11, 35b*
STIRLING *53, 54c*
STUART, James Edward (the Old Pretender) *10, 9c, 43c*
SWORDS
    Basket-hilted *10, 17b, 39a, 43a, 44, 45, 51-54, 69, 70*
    Bastard *13a*
    Bilbos *42a,b, 91e*
    Boy's swords *4b, 85c*
    Calendar-bladed *62, 92a*
    Cinquedeas *19, 20*
    Claymores *9, 9, 53d*
    Estocs *18a, 21a,c*
    Execution *7, 12*
    Falchion *36b*

SWORDS (*Contd.*)
    Hand-and-half *13, 14*
    Hangers *9, 10, 55, 56b,c, 59b,c, 67, 68*
    Landsknecht *6c, 16, 17, 18b*
    Mediaeval *1-5, 23a*
    Military (Austrian) *90f*
    „ (British) *67-83, 92, 93, 94a*
    „ (French) *85-89*
    „ (German) *80a, 90*
    „ (Italian) *91e, f,*
    „ (Spanish) *91, 94b*
    Mortuary *28d, 30a, 46-48*
    Processional *7, 10, 11*
    Rapiers *10, 21b,d, 23b, 24-34*
    Sabres *35-36, 73b, 73c*
    Schiavone *44, 45*
    Scottish *9, 10, 9, 52-54*
    Smallswords *63-66*
    Tucks *9, 10*
    Two-hand *7, 9, 11, 6-12*
    Viking *1*

SWORDSMITHS, CUTLERS, ETC.
    ALLAN, John (Sr.) *53a*
    ALLAN, John (Jr.) *54c*
    ALLAN, Walter *53b,c*
    BATE, Thomas *72c*
    BATTISTA, Giovanni *26c*
    BISCOTTO *15c, 16b*
    BOTARELLO, Carlo *61b*
    BOUTET, Nicolas-Noel *87a*
    BRABENDER, Heinrich *26a*
    BRACH, Johannes *92a*
    CAINO *26d*
    CARMAN, John *58b*
    CARTER & CO. *93b*
    COULAUX *87b*
    CRAIG, Robert *54b*
    CULLUM *71b*
    DAWES *79b*
    EHINGER, Adam *62a*
    ERNANDEZ, Sebastian *91e* (see also under HERNANTEZ)
    FERRARA, Andrea *8, 31a, 39b, 47c, 49b, 51a, 53b, 54a,b*
    GARDEN & SON. *81e*
    GIHAMI, Vincencio *28d*
    GILL, Thomas *70a, 72b*
    GRUSON *67c*
    HAMBURGER ROGERS & CO. *81f*
    HARPER, Thomas *65*
    HERBERT & CO. *82b,c*
    HERNANTEZ, Sebastian *63b* (see also under ERNANDEZ)
    HOLLIER, Thomas *67a*
    HORTUNO DE AGUIRE *32b*
    HORTUNO, Maria de *32a*
    KEISSER, Hermann *30b*
    KEULLER, Clemens *12c*
    KING, William *59c*
    KINNDT, Johannes *28c, 29a*
    KIRSCHBAUM, Carl *78c*
    KNEGT, Jean *73c*
    KNUBLEY, John *73b*
    LE COURT *66b*
    LOXHAM, Edward *59b*
    LOXHAM, William *58b*
    MANBERGER, Phillip *59a*

SWORDSMITHS, CUTLERS, ETC. (*Contd.*)
   MARTI, Joseph *42b*
   MOLE, Robert *83a, 104b*
   MONTE, Pedro del *64a*
   MOUM, Hans *29b*
   MUNICH, Peter *40*
   NOSO *45b*
   OLLICH, Hans *33c*
   OSBORN, Henry *74*
   OSBORN & GRUNDY *72a 78a*
   PAETER, Peter *52a*
   PARKER, W. *84c*
   PARKER FIELD & SONS *84d*
   PICHINIO, Antonio *64b*
   PROSSER, John *94a*
   REEVES, Charles *79c, 84b*
   RUNKEL, John *74, 75a, 76a*
   SIMPSON, John *54a*
   SMITH, Edward *93c*
   STANTLER, Christof *6a, 11, 35b*
   VELASQUEZ, Francesco *27a*
   VELMONTE, Pedro de *32c*
   WATTS *78b*
   WEILMS, Clemens *39c*
   WEYERSBERG *90e*
   WILKINSON *81c, 93a*
   WOOLEY & CO. *71a, 74*
   WUNDES, Johannes *60a, 62b*

TOLEDO 8, *29c, 32a, b, 32c, 45b, 53c, 64a, 92b,d,e, 94b, 99c*
TRAFALGAR, Battle of *65*
TRAJAN, Coin of *196*
TRIER *4c*
TURIN, Royal Armoury *61b*

VALENCE *85a*
VALENCIA *34b*
VELASQUEZ, Francesco *27a*
VELMONTE, Pedro de *32c*
VENICE 11, *14c, 44, 45*
VERSAILLES *87a*

WAKEFIELD, Battle of *15a*
WATTS *78b*
WEILMS, Clemens *39c*
WELLINGTON, Duke of *76a*
WEYERSBERG *90e*
WILKINSON *81c, 93a*
WILLIAM III of England *50a*
WILLIAM IV of England *92d*
WOOLEY & CO. *71a, 74*
WUNDES, Johannes *60a, 62b*

YORK, Duke of 11, *94a*

ZURICH, Swiss National Museum *14b*